OLD CANAAN IN A NEW WORLD

NORTH AMERICAN RELIGIONS

Series Editors: Tracy Fessenden (Religious Studies, Arizona State University), Laura Levitt (Religious Studies, Temple University), and David Harrington Watt (History, Haverford College)

In recent years a cadre of industrious, imaginative, and theoretically sophisticated scholars of religion have focused their attention on North America. As a result the field is far more subtle, expansive, and interdisciplinary than it was just two decades ago. The North American Religions series builds on this transformative momentum. Books in the series move among the discourses of ethnography, cultural analysis, and historical study to shed new light on a wide range of religious experiences, practices, and institutions. They explore topics such as lived religion, popular religious movements, religion and social power, religion and cultural reproduction, and the relationship between secular and religious institutions and practices. The series focuses primarily, but not exclusively, on religion in the United States in the twentieth and twenty-first centuries.

Books in the Series

Ava Chamberlain, *The Notorious Elizabeth Tuttle: Marriage, Murder, and Madness in the Family of Jonathan Edwards*

Terry Rey and Alex Stepick, *Crossing the Water and Keeping the Faith: Haitian Religion in Miami*

Jodi Eichler-Levine, *Suffer the Little Children: Uses of the Past in Jewish and African American Children's Literature*

Isaac Weiner, *Religion Out Loud: Religious Sound, Public Space, and American Pluralism*

Hillary Kaell, *Walking Where Jesus Walked: American Christians and Holy Land Pilgrimage*

Brett Hendrickson, *Border Medicine: A Transcultural History of Mexican American Curanderismo*

Annie Blazer, *Playing for God: Evangelical Women and the Unintended Consequences of Sports Ministry*

Elizabeth Pérez, *Religion in the Kitchen: Cooking, Talking, and the Making of Black Atlantic Traditions*

Kerry Mitchell, *Spirituality and the State: Managing Nature and Experience in America's National Parks*

Finbarr Curtis, *The Production of American Religious Freedom*

M. Cooper Harriss, *Ralph Ellison's Invisible Theology*

Shari Rabin, *Jews on the Frontier: Religion and Mobility in Nineteenth-Century America*

Ari Y. Kelman, *Shout to the Lord: Making Worship Music in Evangelical America*

Joshua Dubler and Isaac Weiner, *Religion, Law, USA*

Elizabeth Fenton, *Old Canaan in a New World: Native Americans and the Lost Tribes of Israel*

Old Canaan in a New World

Native Americans and the Lost Tribes of Israel

Elizabeth Fenton

NEW YORK UNIVERSITY PRESS

New York

NEW YORK UNIVERSITY PRESS
New York
www.nyupress.org

References to Internet websites (URLs) were accurate at the time of writing. Neither the author nor New York University Press is responsible for URLs that may have expired or changed since the manuscript was prepared.

Library of Congress Cataloging-in-Publication Data
Names: Fenton, Elizabeth A., 1978–   author.
Title: Old Canaan in a new world : Native Americans and the lost tribes of Israel / Elizabeth Fenton.
Other titles: North American religions.
Description: New York : New York University Press, [2020] | Series: North american religions | Includes bibliographical references and index.
Identifiers: LCCN 2019029669 | ISBN 9781479866366 (cloth) | ISBN 9781479891726 (ebook) | ISBN 9781479827534 (ebook)
Subjects: LCSH: Indians of North America—Origin. | Lost tribes of Israel. | Ethnology—North America.
Classification: LCC E61 .F46 2020 | DDC 970.004/97—dc23
LC record available at https://lccn.loc.gov/2019029669

New York University Press books are printed on acid-free paper, and their binding materials are chosen for strength and durability. We strive to use environmentally responsible suppliers and materials to the greatest extent possible in publishing our books.

Manufactured in the United States of America

10 9 8 7 6 5 4 3 2 1

Also available as an ebook

For Jen and Helen, my best friend family

CONTENTS

Introduction

In the Beginning: Lost Tribes, New Worlds, and the Perils of History

In May of 1803, Dr. Benjamin Rush, acting as medical advisor for the Lewis and Clark expedition, produced a list of questions for Meriwether Lewis to consider when encountering Native American populations in the western territories. The list appears in Rush's commonplace book, as well as in a more extensive list of questions prepared by William Clark in 1804. It is divided into three categories—physical history and medicine, morals, and religion—and it evinces a wide-ranging, proto-anthropological curiosity. Rush asks Lewis to record information about everything from illnesses to marital age to diet and the use of intoxicating substances among Native Americans. One of his most targeted questions, however, is reserved for religion. "What Affinity," Rush asks, exists "between [Native American] religious Ceremonies & those of the Jews?"[1] Although the question might jangle in the ear of a twenty-first-century reader, it probably struck Lewis as neither odd nor out of place. Indeed, Clark retained a version of the query a year later, in his master list of ethnographic questions: "What affinity is there," Clark writes, "between their religious ceremonies and those of the ancient Jews?"[2] Clark's addition of the word "ancient" is significant for two reasons. First, it suggests that he did not merely copy out Rush's questions, but revised them as he prepared his own guide for the expedition. Second, and more crucial for the purposes of this study, it reveals this question's investment in a longstanding discussion of the origins of indigenous American peoples. Specifically, Rush's inquiry and Clark's revision demonstrate an interest in what I will refer to in this book as the Hebraic Indian theory—the notion that indigenous Americans might be, in part or in whole, descendants of the lost tribes of Israel. When he asks Lewis to look for traces of "Jewish" practices across the American landscape,

Rush does not have contemporary Judaism or actual Jewish people in mind. As Clark recognizes, Rush's inquiry reaches instead for evidence of a past predating the development of the religion now called Judaism. Rush seeks the Kingdom of Israel, which disappeared around 722 BCE and which might, his question hopefully indicates, be on the verge of reappearance in the Americas.

In asking Lewis and Clark to determine whether Native American cultures demonstrated affinity with Judaism, Rush actually sought answers to two questions, one ancient, the other modern. These questions emerged in different historical periods, but over the course of the early modern era they became intertwined. The Puritan Edward Winslow summarizes the convergence of these questions in his 1649 work, *The Glorious Progress of the Gospel amongst the Indians in New England*. In perhaps the most concise summary of Christian investment in the Hebraic Indian theory, Winslow writes, "There are two great questions which have much troubled ancient and modern writers, and men of great depth and ability to resolve: the first, what became of the ten Tribes of Israel, that were carried into Captivity by the King of Siria, when their own Countrey and Cities were planted and filled with strangers? The second is, what Family, Tribe, Kindred, or people it was that first planted, and afterwards filled that vast and long unknown Countrey of America?"[3] Winslow's hope is that English colonial efforts have revealed a single answer to both questions. "It is not lesse probable that these Indians should come from the Stock of Abraham, then [*sic*] any other Nation this day known in the world," he writes, "Especially considering the juncture of time wherin God hath opened their hearts to entertain the Gospel."[4] Where are the lost tribes? In America. And who are the original Americans? The lost tribes. "The work of communicating and increasing the light of the Gospel," Winslow asserts, "is glorious in reference to Jews & Gentiles."[5] If the lost tribes are the indigenous peoples of America, then the arrival of English Protestants and their Bibles bears the promise of biblical prophecy. What better justification of settler colonialism could there be than the conversion of a lost biblical population to Christianity? As Rush would nearly two centuries later, Winslow hopes to demonstrate that imperial endeavors may have providential consequences.

This book is the study of an error that emerged during the colonial period in the Americas and that persists in some corners to this day. Beginning with the earliest English-language expositions of the Hebraic Indian theory and tracing its multiple iterations through the nineteenth century, this study examines writings that typically present incorrect information about indigenous Americans and Jewish people. To work with texts that are both old and unfamiliar often is to inhabit the space of anachronism. At its best, anachronism can produce moments of delight and revelation. At its worst, though, it prods longstanding cultural wounds, and hinders understanding. Thus I wish to say a few things about the use of certain terms in this book before moving into my analysis.

Many of the texts examined here contain what are in retrospect obvious historical inaccuracies, and they also deploy outdated terminology—much of which is baldly racist and anti-Jewish. It is not my aim simply to critique these works for their errors. I am concerned with how the authors examined here marshal history as they understand it to further their religious and political interests. But it would be inappropriate to pretend that some of the texts covered in this book are, by virtue of their age, inoffensive. Two important issues arise in reading these works, which I want to acknowledge from the outset. The first is that the texts explored in this book by and large configure the Hebraic Indian theory in terms of "Jewishness" and offer proof of the theory's veracity by comparing Native American cultural phenomena to "Jewish" practices. For this reason, the small body of existing scholarship on the theory has tended to refer to it as the "Jewish Indian" theory.[6] I have opted for the term "Hebraic" instead, for two reasons. The first is historical: Assyria conquered the Kingdom of Israel before the development of the religion we now call Judaism. The lost tribes, in short, were not Jewish. Thus I am attempting to skirt the anachronism that structures Rush's question about "the Jews" and most other expressions of the theory. I use the term "Hebraic" to refer to biblical peoples associated with the lineage of Eber, from whose line follow Abraham, Isaac, and Jacob. Although this book does explore one version of the theory that falls outside of this biblical lineage (found in *The Book of Mormon*), the term accurately describes the bulk of the theory's permutations. "Hebraic" is not a perfect description of the phenomenon assessed in this study, but it is more capacious, and, I think, more accurate than "Jewish."

The second reason I have opted not to use the word "Jewish" with respect to this theory is that most—though, importantly, not all—of the authors associated with it had very little interest in and even less knowledge of actual Judaism and Jewish people.[7] What passes for "Jewish" in most of these texts is little better than a caricature drawn from longstanding anti-Jewish stereotypes and dubious interpretations of Leviticus. The primary materials examined in this study often refer to cultural practices as "Jewish," but I avoid using the term when possible. This book is not about Judaism. It is, rather, about a distorted picture of Judaism that structures interpretations of Native American practices that are not Jewish.

Although I have altered the adjective most commonly found in this theory's title, I have retained its equally fraught noun—"Indian." This was not a choice I made lightly, as that word, too, carries within it an error. The word occupies a vexed position in studies of both the Americas broadly and US culture more specifically, because, as Scott Richard Lyons reminds us, it "is a misnomer having nothing to do with tribal peoples encountered by European explorers (nor for that matter with India) and everything to do with that great, world-historic navigational error of Columbus's."[8] The word emerged and operated only within the frame of colonialism, and part of its work was erasure. "Indian" can be deployed to elide cultural specificity, and it also can efface pre-Columbian American histories. And yet, as Lyons puts it, "We find both European and native fingerprints at the scene of the sign."[9] Noting that some indigenous peoples actively adopted the term for themselves and strove to define it beyond colonizing sensibilities, he argues for the importance of moving beyond facile notions of the word as merely European or inauthentically indigenous and treating "Indian" as a complex sign embedded in ongoing, globally significant negotiations of identity. The term is an important component of the label I have adopted for this theory, precisely because it evokes the complexity of European and American encounters and highlights the stakes involved in their negotiations.

European notions of indigenous ancestry and history were fraught with mistakes from the start. Retaining the word "Indian" in this context also highlights the lack of interest in specific Native nations that many European writers demonstrated in their pursuit of the theory. In the texts this study considers, the word "Indian" occludes myriad distinctions among cultures and histories. For these reasons, it is an appropriate descriptor for the theory, and I have retained it when it appears in the texts I cite. However, in my own analysis, apart from the name of the theory, I eschew the word "Indian" where possible, preferring to give specific tribal names or to use phrases such as "Native American" and "indigenous American" or simply "American" to describe actual Native populations.[10] I do this in part in the interest of distinguishing my perspective from those of the writers I examine. I also do this because I am aware of the longstanding and ongoing violence against indigenous peoples that this word has abetted, even as it has been appropriated and reconfigured by some Native American groups. And I am, finally, not blind to my own position as a white scholar analyzing (mainly) white writers' interpretations of Native American cultures. Just as this book is not about actual Judaism, neither is it about the real, lived histories of Native American people and nations. In tracing the Hebraic Indian theory from its origins in English literature through the nineteenth century, this book demonstrates how a fantasy of human origins infused the Western hemisphere and its colonial projects with urgent religious significance through three centuries.

Winslow's concern with the location of the lost tribes of Israel was nothing new in 1649. As Zvi Ben-Dor Benite has shown in his expansive history of this ancient question, the "lostness" of the lost tribes has made them an object of international interest for millennia. Many different groups have sought them, and many others have claimed to be them. "Over the course of 2,000 years," Benite writes, "Jews, Christians of various denominations, and, to a lesser extent, Muslims [have] used the tribes as a point of reference, tying historical developments to their exile and return."[11] The tribes' story begins, as many biblical stories do, with an argument over succession and an account of divine ire. The tribes are the descendants of Jacob's twelve sons, who for generations live in a unified kingdom ruled first by David and then by Solomon. They are named for those sons—Reuben, Simeon, Levi, Judah, Issachar, Zebulon, Dan, Naphtali, Gad, Asher, Joseph, and Benjamin. The math around the tribes always is a bit off, because the Levites are hereditary priests with no land of their own, and Joseph eventually splits into two tribes, Ephraim and Manasseh. Thus there are twelve landed tribes, plus the Levites who live among them. The narrative of the kingdom's division into the "ten" tribes that will be lost, on the one hand, and those who will become the world's Jewish population on the other, is found in the biblical books 1 and 2 Kings.[12] The only use of the phrase "ten tribes" in the Bible appears in 1 Kings, when the prophet Ahija tells the Ephraimite Jeroboam that God, out of anger at Solomon's transgressions, will divide the Kingdom of Israel. "Thus saith the Lord, the God of Israel," Ahija proclaims, "I will rend the kingdom out of the hand of Solomon, and will give ten tribes to thee" (1 Kings 11:31).[13] Following a period of mismanagement by Solomon's son, Rehoboam, Jeroboam fulfills the prophecy through a successful rebellion. The ten tribes secede, forming the Kingdom of Israel, while the tribes of Judah and Benjamin form the Kingdom of Judah, retaining control over Jerusalem.

Like Solomon and Rehoboam before him (and, really, like many biblical kings), upon achieving success through divine favor, Jeroboam begins a slide into iniquity and finds himself the subject of a new prophecy, also delivered by Ahija: "For the Lord shall smite Israel as a reed is shaken in the water," the prophet says, "and he shall root up Israel out of this good land" (1 Kings 14:15). In subsequent years, Israel turns on itself, rendering it vulnerable to conquest. The second prophecy is fulfilled after two centuries of decline, when the Assyrian empire conquers the Israelites and exiles them. The collapse of this once-great kingdom receives only brief mention in 2 Kings: "Then the king of Assyria came up throughout all the land, and went up to Samaria, and besieged it three years. In the ninth year of Hoshea the king of Assyria took Samaria, and carried Israel away into Assyria, and placed them in Halah and in Habor by the river of Gozan, and in the cities of the Medes" (2 Kings 17:5–6). Following this description of their exile, the tribes vanish from biblical and other historical records. The consensus among historians is that nations conquered by Assyria generally assimilated into the cultures among which they were exiled.[14] The "disappearance" of the tribes is therefore most likely a metaphor for gradual (though no less devastating) cultural change. Despite this fact, the status of the missing Kingdom of Israel became and has remained for some an important biblical mystery. This is the case because the tribes can be read into prophetic texts that announce a future gathering of Israel and its remnants. The books of Isaiah and Ezekiel, for example, promise the nation's someday readmission to its lost land: "For a small moment have I forsaken thee," reads Isaiah, "but with great mercies will I gather thee" (Isaiah 57:7). Ezekiel appears to concur: "Thus saith the Lord God; I will even gather you from the people, and assemble you out of the countries where ye have been scattered, and I will give you the land of Israel" (Ezekiel 11:17). If the historical record is silent on the location of the tribes, the prophetic record, from some readerly vantage points (though certainly not all), is explicit. The tribes have been scattered, but someday they will return, and thus they must be somewhere, hidden from view but waiting to reappear. They are lost, yes, but that means they could be found.

Though the story of Jeroboam's rebellion and its aftermath might seem a straightforward account of national disputes and shifting borders, the narratives of 1 and 2 Kings are not history in any modern sense. "At least the first part of the actual (as opposed to the prophetic) history of the ten tribes story (the first book of Kings, which tells the story of the united kingdom created by David and its split into two under his grandson)," Benite explains, "is considered by biblical scholars to be almost entirely fictional. The second part, found in 2 Kings . . . is thought to have been heavily edited and full of interpolations."[15] Like many religious and literary works, 1 and 2 Kings have undergone significant reevaluation by scholars over the past half-century. These books are products of both authorship and redaction, assembled over the course of many years from the writing and editing of source materials composed by several hands. In their introduction to a volume dedicated to the controversies and competing theories surrounding these texts, Klaus-Peter Adam and Mark Leuchter note that the "authors/redactors of the work regularly engage ideas both imported from foreign cultures and recycled from Israelite religious and social traditions, and the end result is a corpus that both creates a linear historical narrative and yields a complicated system of thought and political/theological meditation."[16] Within the field of biblical studies, debate over how best to understand Kings is ongoing, and scholars are particularly concerned with its relationship to other biblical books, such as Deuteronomy.

It is not the aim of this book to parse the historical accuracy of Kings, nor is it to stake out a position on its relationship to other biblical texts or the manner of its composition. Those questions are beyond the scope of my expertise, and they emerged after the texts examined here were written. The writers represented in this book took biblical texts seriously (often literally), read them closely, and debated their significance; but they were by and large unconcerned with the kinds of issues that have structured recent scholarship on sacred texts. I treat the story of the ten tribes as a significant mythology rather than documentary history, but it is important to keep in mind that the figures explored in this book believed—in different ways and for different reasons—that the narratives in 1 and 2 Kings and the prophecies that apparently referred to the tribes in other biblical books were true. The biblical account of the formation and conquest of the Kingdom of Israel may be a contentious puzzle to contemporary biblical scholars, but it operates more simply in the works assessed here: as a set of historical facts pointing to a sacred mystery with urgent bearing on the human present.

Scholars of the lost tribes phenomenon have outlined many of the features that have made it appealing for so many years to so many distinct groups with differing interests. In Benite's view, "The lostness represented by the ten tribes is, in Western historical consciousness, one of the most acute and oldest known instances of loss still 'alive' today."[17] Global searching for the tribes is and will be ongoing, he suggests, because their "lostness" is at once simple and profound. They are missing, and thus they should be sought. In a sociological assessment of the history of lost tribes theories, Stanford Lyman notes that a "quest for the descendants of the lost tribes has been begun many times, usually associated with the resolution of immediate, local, secular, or sacred issues that emerged in a particular era and at a particular place."[18] Though the story of the tribes themselves—their rebellion, ascendance, and fall from grace—is frozen in a few biblical passages, their as-yet-unnarrated future holds infinite possibility for the remedy of national and religious crises. The tribes form a lacuna in the sacred as well as profane record, holding open the possibility that human and divine history someday will converge in a single line. Lyman's survey of engagements with the tribes across two millennia demonstrates a paradox in lost tribes thinking: the tribes never emerge, and thus they always might emerge. The eternal deferral of their return makes them eternally available for narrative engagement. Tudor Parfitt makes a similar point about the malleability of lost tribes mythology providing it with a unique staying power. "From generation to generation and from place to place," he writes, "the way people believed the myth and precisely what it meant to them changed."[19] As Parfitt demonstrates in his own search for versions of the lost tribes myth, this is why the tribes have been "discovered" in every era and on every habitable continent since their disappearance. Because they are absent, the tribes always can be evoked as the solution to a crisis. This book will explore how one version of the lost tribes' story, the Hebraic Indian theory, emerged time and again as a means of addressing a variety of American crises.

Lost tribes mythology always has been linked to developments in geographic knowledge. For Europeans, as the boundaries of the known world expanded, the tribes' potential locations continuously moved to just beyond the edges of mapped territory. Thus, as Lyman notes, before the fifteenth century European postulations about the tribes generally situated them somewhere in central Asia, but "after 1492, the search for the Lost Tribes tended to shift, moving into the 'New World' of the Americas and toward the farther reaches of Africa, China, and India."[20] The line beyond which the tribes could be living kept just ahead of explorers encountering people who were new to them but who were not the Kingdom of Israel. The Americas never have been the sole focus of lost tribes theories, but they are the focus of this book, which will examine expressions of the theory concerned primarily with North America.

Although Columbus never admitted that he had not made port off the Asian coast, the reality of what his voyage revealed rapidly became apparent to other Europeans. Several scholars have noted that the publication and reprinting of Columbus's accounts of his voyages posed threatening challenges to longstanding assumptions about the composition of the earth and its human inhabitants.[21] Rather than returning with tales of "monstrous races," as David Livingstone notes many Europeans expected, Columbus "explicitly informed Luis de Santangel that he had encountered 'no human monstrosities, as many expected,' in the islands, though he did consider that there were in existence cannibals—Anthropophagi—as well as men with tails."[22] Columbus's simple description of the people he encountered as "well-formed" had world-altering implications. Europeans were accustomed to conceiving of the globe in three parts, each corresponding to the lineage of Noah's sons (Ham, Shem, and Japheth) following the flood described in Genesis.[23] As Livingstone notes, this model "was an altogether tidy arrangement integrating a threefold continental schema with a tripartite racial taxonomy."[24] Europeans who subscribed to this scheme claimed descent from Japheth, while assigning Asian populations to Shem and Africans to Ham. The tripartite globe had the added benefit of taking the shape of a cross, further suggesting a conceptual link between the Christian sacred record and the material reality of life on earth. The possibility that a "fourth" kind of human lived on an unknown continent threatened to upend a millennium of geographic and biblical certainty. When Columbus's voyages revealed not monsters but men, this model, with its neat biblical symmetry, became untenable. Thus the second question that would come to be embedded in Rush's list emerged: who were the people of the western hemisphere?

It rarely occurred to Europeans that they might take seriously indigenous American accounts of human history in the hemisphere, or that American peoples might have their own theories about the Europeans who landed in their territories. Indeed, Europeans may have responded to the revelations of Columbus's travels and later explorations with more surprise than did their "New World" counterparts. John Sutton Lutz notes that the western hemisphere had been a cultural contact zone for centuries prior to Columbus's voyage. "Five hundred years before Columbus, northern Europeans—Vikings—had built one and probably more settlements on the eastern shores of America. Possibly, other undocumented strangers had come from the east. Almost certainly, indigenous Americans had intermittent visitors from the west."[25] What is more, the people inhabiting the western hemisphere, like those inhabiting all the other populated continents, were accustomed to encounters with each other. When Hernan Cortes marched into Tenochtitlan in 1519, for example, the Aztecs only had occupied the city for two centuries, having arrived in the Valley of Mexico as a conquering force around 1300. To Cortes, the Aztecs were an indigenous nation; to the populations they had subjugated, the Aztecs were colonial invaders. This is a truism worth repeating: the history of human life in the western hemisphere before European arrival is not a singular history, and neither is the story of colonialism in the hemisphere simply one of European ascendance. Indigenous histories were readily available, but rather than drawing on Native knowledge, Europeans attempted to reconcile their own systems of thinking with the new information produced by settler colonialism. As Lutz notes about Columbus, "His encounter was the product of expectations conditioned by imaginary worlds conjured up long before his arrival."[26] For Columbus, indigenous peoples were Asians, and thus his accounts of them mirrored Orientalist notions of life in the "East." For those who could see the broader implications of his voyage, though, the question of lineage for American peoples was an epistemological entanglement that threatened to upend centuries of Christian thinking about the composition of the world.

Confronted with the realities of previously unknown continents teeming with previously unknown people, Europeans scrambled to either locate the western hemisphere in the biblical record or explain why it was not there. Many theories of life in what came to be called the Americas emerged among Europeans in the colonial era to explain the existence and histories of indigenous populations. These theories were as diverse as the aims of their theorists, and they occupied a broad spectrum of plausibility.[27] This book is concerned with how the story of the missing Kingdom of Israel emerged in the aftermath of Columbus's accidental stumbling into the "New World" to explain the existence of human life in the Americas. For its proponents, the Hebraic Indian theory possessed an elegance that others lacked, in that it simultaneously accounted for the presence of American peoples, explained their absence from biblical narratives, and solved a longstanding sacred mystery. If American people were the lost tribes of Israel, the hemisphere's absence from biblical accounts of creation would make sense, because it would have been—eternally and by design—the designated hiding place for the tribes. Drawing on a variety of different expressions of the Hebraic Indian theory—from religious tracts to memoirs to novels—this book shows that the theory allowed writers to establish an eschatological timeline in conjunction with colonial pursuits and situate their own national interests within it. Although proponents of the theory assigned it global and immutable significance, they differed wildly in their exposition of its particulars and potential consequences. The Hebraic Indian is not, despite its proponents' insistence, an unchanging figure. Rather, it serves as a flexible sign through which writers of several eras gather up the fraying strands of national time and tie them to a single cosmic destiny.

This book is comprised of six chapters and a coda. Its first three chapters explore the emergence and evolution of the Hebraic Indian theory from the colonial era to the early nineteenth century. Individually, these chapters chart the evolution of the theory from the earliest English encounters with American peoples through the era of Jacksonian Indian Removal. Together, they show how first European and then US writers struggled to align what they knew about Native Americans with the teachings of revealed religion. Although the idea of American Hebraism encountered skepticism from the moment it emerged, it persisted across centuries, evolving and reforming as historical circumstances changed. The book's second half explores critical responses to the Hebraic Indian theory in the nineteenth century, showing how US writers unconvinced by its claims used it to promote their own accounts of America's sacred history and national destiny. As a whole, this study demonstrates the malleability of the Hebraic Indian theory, a discourse that through several centuries buttressed and contradicted Christian millennialist claims, highlighted and papered over the fractures within American Protestantism, legitimized indigenous and Jewish claims to sovereignty in the Americas, and made space for entirely new religions. The book's coda jumps forward in time to examine twenty-first-century genetic studies conducted in the hopes of laying to rest debates over American origins. Though often "secular" in method, these scientific works are as fraught with religious stakes as the much earlier works I examine. By showing how the Hebraic Indian theory first allowed Christians to square emerging knowledge about the world with biblical history and then became a sticking point in discussions of US destiny, this book offers a new account of the intersections of religious belief and national interest. It also reveals the degree to which questions of human origins and migration patterns are enmeshed with beliefs about divine intent, providential history, and the biblical record.

In its focus on beliefs about the lost tribes of Israel, this study joins a growing body of scholarship concerned with American religious traditions. Moving away from traditional accounts of Puritanism as the exceptional origin point for US culture, in the past decade scholars have offered a more nuanced portrait of the nation's religious landscape and worked to better situate that landscape in a global frame. Such work has been deeply intertwined with scholarship addressing the parameters of

secularism and its complex relationship with (rather than simple opposition to) religion. It has explored the many divisions within American
Protestantism, the role of Catholicism and Judaism in the hemisphere,
the United States' complex and varied engagements with Islam, and the
fraught relationships between slavery and religion.[28] This book contributes to this field by showing how one biblical narrative shaped colonial
and nineteenth-century attitudes about issues as diverse as evangelism,
trade policies, national expansion, and scientific endeavor. It also departs from much previous scholarship (including my own) by focusing
on a single theological proposition—that the lost tribes of Israel remain
intact somewhere on the globe—rather than a specific religious tradition
or moment in American religious history. The Hebraic Indian theory
captivated writers across a broad theological spectrum, from the Calvinist settler colonists of Massachusetts to the English moderates they left
behind to the Methodist Pequot William Apess to the prophet Joseph
Smith. It varies widely in its appearances in the literature of the period,
as do the consequences different writers assign to it. Still, at the core of
every exposition of the Hebraic Indian theory lies a set of epistemological puzzles: How can secular evidence answer biblical questions? How
can biblical books respond to profane crises? And how should revealed
religion respond to changes in scientific understandings of the world?[29]
Charting two centuries of inquiry into the origins of American peoples,
it offers insight into the impossibility of separating ostensibly secular
accounts of the world from their religious counterparts and considers the longstanding consequences of one Bible story on the American
landscape.

Crucial to this book has been recent scholarly work uncovering how
first European and then US religious beliefs—particularly Christian
millennialism—simultaneously abetted the project of settler colonialism and were transformed by it. As Stephanie Kirk and Sarah Rivett's
work has shown, the western hemisphere operated as both a site of religious desire in the colonial era, as sects competed for dominance within
it, and as a space of religious change, as European colonists adapted to
meet the demands of a "New World." "The collision of European traditions with American environmental and cultural realities," they write,
"the reinstitution of religious hierarchy in colonial settings, and the challenge of indigenous cultures and new population configurations engen-

dered religious innovation."[30] European nations certainly viewed control of American territories as an avenue to greater wealth and power,[31] but religious considerations are inseparable from economic and nationalist ones in the history of American colonialism. From the earliest Spanish incursions into the region to later voyages by the English, European colonial efforts were couched in religious rhetoric and often configured as efforts to spread Christianity—Catholic or Protestant—to the furthest corners of the earth. In the English context, the survival of first Protestantism in the face of European Catholicism and then Puritanism in the face of English Anglicanism often was depicted as the engine driving settlers across the Atlantic, while the conversion of Native populations was offered up as the force that kept them in the Americas once they arrived. This rhetoric of religious imperative persisted even as settler colonists engaged in genocidal conflicts over land and introduced African slavery into the hemisphere. The notion that American settlement marked the fulfillment of a divine order, in other words, justified all manner of colonial horrors.

Of central importance to this study is the notion of providence, particularly its significance first within English colonial endeavors and then to the emergence of the United States as a settler state.[32] Nicholas Guyatt's study of the long history of providential thinking within English and American colonialism provides crucial context for this work. As Guyatt notes, "Two basic presumptions [about providence] enjoyed wide currency in Europe from the sixteenth to the nineteenth century: first, that God controlled everything that happened on earth; second, that God had a particular plan for human history."[33] Within the framework of providence, everything serves a divine design, and humans can read the signs of that design in both the workings of their own lives and the larger trajectory of history. The limits of human perception, however, prevent perfect knowledge of the workings of providence as well as of its ultimate end. The gap between intent and interpretation, Guyatt demonstrates, has produced a structure in which atrocities could be justified by recourse to providential history. This is especially clear in the context of Indian Removal and genocide, as well as New World slavery. Guyatt's work aptly shows how colonial and nationalist projects in the Americas often were preoccupied with the question, "What was the providential significance of the American Indians?"[34] Had Europeans been directed by a divine hand to the Americas to Christianize these populations? Or were Native peoples, as many Protestants asserted, divinely destined to "vanish" from the earth in the face of white Christianity? The Hebraic Indian theory sits at the crux of such questions, presenting its proponents with the possibility not only that contact between Europeans and Americans had set the stage for the providential fulfillment of biblical prophecies but also that indigenous vanishing would reach its apex when Native American populations remembered their history and transformed into the "Jews" they had been all along.

This book begins with an examination of the documents comprising the first sustained English engagements with the Hebraic Indian theory: Thomas Thorowgood's books, *Iewes in America* (1650) and *Jews in America* (1660). Though their titles are nearly identical, these works are distinct, complementary engagements with the theory and its potential consequences for English and Anglo-American readers. The first chapter demonstrates that Thorowgood's work employs an emergent notion of probability to make its case for American Hebraism. His works are religious treatises, certainly, but they anticipate a shift in the discourses of science and mathematics, drawing on a concept of "the probable" that would become increasingly operant as the century wore on. Both *Iewes in America* and, even more explicitly, *Jews in America* deploy the concept of probability to argue that absolute certainty of the Hebraic Indian theory is not required for that theory's general acceptance and to posit that in the absence of conclusive evidence of a religious postulation, belief is always a better bet than disbelief. Thorowgood's recourse to the probable, rather than the certain, situates him at the fore of evolving European attitudes regarding epistemology. It also allows him to incorporate evidence of the theory from a variety of sources, including the Puritan divines John Eliot and Roger Williams, who did not agree with his thesis but whose work nonetheless made it seem probable. In pushing the theory into the space of the possible, Thorowgood set the stage for its survival in English discussions of American origins.

That the Hebraic Indian theory did not die on the vine in the seventeenth century owes much to the publication of James Adair's *History of the American Indians* (1775), which significantly altered the discourse of indigenous origins by grounding it in what might be called an anthropological approach. The earliest expositions of the Hebraic Indian theory relied mainly on biblical exegesis for their claims, and many were written by those who never set foot in the Americas. Writing to contradict the theory of polygenesis—that is, the theory that indigenous Americans derived from a distinct, non-Adamic creation—Adair insisted that careful observations of Native cultural practices revealed incontrovertible proof that they derived from a biblical source. A self-proclaimed "Indian trader" who from about 1735 lived in what is now the southeastern United States, Adair offered readers detailed, personal accounts of several American cultures. His *History* thus asserted that American Hebraism was observable, tenable, and available to anyone who cared to look. Adair has been long ignored by literary critics and scholars of this period, so this book's second chapter aims in part to recover his important place within early discussions of indigenous history. More particularly, though, it shows that Adair's approach to the question of American origins, which privileged empirical observation, allowed his work to become the proof text for later versions of the Hebraic Indian theory. Adair refrained from drawing conclusions about the religious implications of his theory, and thus his *History* was of use to millennialist Christians such as the Reverend Ethan Smith and the Jewish utopian Mordecai Manuel Noah. His work also laid the groundwork for scholarly studies of indigenous peoples of the southeastern United States. Through analysis of Adair's methods and his work's legacy, this chapter explores the complex relationship between biblical inquiry and anthropological study in the United States.

This book's third chapter examines the most significant exposition of the Hebraic Indian theory produced in the nineteenth century, Elias Boudinot's 1816 treatise *A Star in the West*. Boudinot was a prominent Presbyterian and former president of the Continental Congress, and his reputation lent a degree of legitimacy to the Hebraic Indian theory. Beginning with an analysis of Boudinot's professed "accidental" reading of the apocryphal Book of Esdras, the chapter first explores how he uses the notion of the accident to construct a theory of providential history that culminates in the revelation of the Hebraic Indian. It then turns to William Apess's 1829 memoir, *A Son of the Forest*, which incorporates Boudinot's book as an appendix. A dedicated Methodist and self-described Pequot Indian, Apess might at first seem an unlikely proponent of the Hebraic Indian theory. The theory, however, allows him to situate his own Christianity outside of English and US colonial practices—to reach back to an earlier historical source for his religious identity. It also, this chapter contends, enables Apess to present his version of American history as running along a timeline distinct from that of white Christians and to disrupt the teleologies of both white ascendance and Native disappearance in the Americas. Apess's conversion of Boudinot's book into an appendix thus creates a temporal disruption in *A Son of the Forest* that enables the Pequot to lay claim to Christian sovereignty by assuming the mantle of a lost Israelite.

Having examined the most significant expressions of the Hebraic Indian theory produced into the nineteenth century, this book turns to revisions to, and rejections of, its claims. Chapter 4 explores a significant but often misunderstood revision of the Hebraic Indian theory: *The Book of Mormon*. *The Book of Mormon* posits a Hebraic origin for indigenous Americans, but it explicitly rejects the lost tribes theory. Its indigenous Americans derive from previously unknown biblical disappearances. Although they are absent from its narrative, though, the lost tribes of Israel operate at *The Book of Mormon*'s margins. Analyzing the book's simultaneous evocation and deferral of lost tribes mythology, this chapter argues that *The Book of Mormon* formally presents sacred time as iterate and proliferating rather than linear and singular. *The Book of Mormon* thus forces readers to confront the continued "lostness" of the tribes and the theological consequences of their absence. In its closing section, the chapter turns to later writings that combine *The Book of Mormon*'s claims with contemporary scientific (and pseudo-scientific) theories about the earth to explain the continuing absence of the lost tribes. For over a century, writers affiliated with the Church of Jesus Christ of Latter-day Saints have posited a variety of locations for the tribes: from outer space to the earth's core. This chapter shows how *The Book of Mormon*'s relegation of the tribes to still unknown parts of the universe creates a paradox within its theology, by coupling an insistence upon imminent millennium with the endless deferral of one of that millennium's main prerequisites.

Chapter 5 explores the waning influence of the Hebraic Indian theory in the aftermath of the era of US Indian Removal, taking as a case study James Fennimore Cooper's most explicit engagement with the theory, *The Bee-Hunter; or, The Oak Openings*. Published in 1848 but set during the War of 1812, *The Bee-Hunter* is emblematic of midcentury rejections of the Hebraic Indian theory, which tended to present it as the irrational fantasy of overly enthusiastic millennialists. In *The Bee-Hunter*, Cooper establishes an orderly colonial geometry that depends simultaneously upon the practice of honey gathering and the disappearance of indigenous peoples. A threat to this frontier order arrives in the figure of Parson Amen, an itinerant Methodist who has traveled to the nation's western edge to convince Native Americans that they are latent "Jews." Amen's theological geometry operates in opposition to that of the bee hunter, and thus the parson's message must be neutralized within the novel. In Cooper's work, then, it becomes apparent that the Hebraic Indian theory presents a problem not only for Protestant eschatology but also for the project of Indian Removal. Ultimately, in *The Bee-Hunter*, the vanishing that becomes most important to white nationalism is that of the Christian sympathetic to the cause of indigenous sovereignty. The death of the parson and the conversion to Christianity of the novel's most radical Native American figure foreclose the possibility of the alternate American history offered by the Hebraic Indian theory. The future Parson Amen predicts is replaced by the steady progress of white Christianity, and in declaring himself "no Jew," the Native American becomes a vanishing Indian.

Building on the fourth chapter's discussion of early Latter-day Saint interest in hollow earth theories, chapter 6 recovers and analyzes De Witt Clinton Chipman's long-forgotten 1895 novel, *Beyond the Verge: Home of the Ten Lost Tribes of Israel*. A fanciful account of an indigenous American man who encounters the lost tribes and travels with them into the earth's core, Chipman's novel distinguishes between indigenous Americans and Hebraic peoples but nonetheless posits an American journey for the tribes. This chapter first situates *Beyond the Verge* within the long history of American "mound-builder" literature, a collection of texts concerned with the possibility that white people might literally excavate American history from the earthen mounds that dotted the hemisphere. Writers from Thomas Jefferson to William Cullen Bryant describe the possibilities and disappointments involved in digging into American soil to uncover its past. In Chipman's novel, the mound builders reject the lost tribes and have no bearing on the earth's millennial future. For him, the truly important discovery within the earth will be the hidden city at its center. The chapter shows how Chipman's novel operates within a larger, scientific discussion about the possibility of a habitable hollow earth. Edmund Halley had endorsed the notion as early as 1692, and the hollow earth theory gained popularity through the nineteenth century. In shifting the lost tribes into earth's core, *Beyond the Verge* suggests that America's destiny lies not beneath its own soil, where only the bones of dead and forgotten peoples lie. In Chipman's rendering, the Americas are not the site of millennial glory but rather a waystation for the tribes as they march into the earth's core to await a better and more universal destiny.

Although the Hebraic Indian theory might itself seem a strange relic of the past, its echo can be heard in contemporary discussions of the origins of human life. As knowledge of the earth's habitable spaces has expanded, and the territory available to the lost tribes has disappeared, a new space of possibility has opened in discussions of the tribes: DNA. This book concludes with a brief coda discussing the mutual impact that the Hebraic Indian theory and the popular discourse of human genomics have had upon each other. As this book's chapters demonstrate, the Hebraic Indian theory often inhabits the space of epistemological change. Developments in probability theory, ethnography, geography, astronomy, and geology all have served as sites for the theory to manifest and evolve. This is no less true, it turns out, of advances in genetics. Exploring both general studies of human genomic sequencing and works specifically interested in the question of whether traces of Hebraic origins might be found in "Native American DNA," this conclusion suggests that a notion of the sacred is as operant in the search for human origins today as it was three centuries ago. Just as earlier efforts to uncover the American past bore religious weight for those who engaged in them, popular discussions of human genetics often are couched in the language of creation, teleology, and salvation. The search for American ancestry, however secular its method, always is infused with the sacred.

1

Proof Positive

Hebraic Indians and the Emergence of Probability Theory

In 1660, the English Presbyterian minister Thomas Thorowgood published *Jews in America; or, Probabilities, that those Indians are Judaical, made more probable by some Additionals to the former Conjectures.* As the subtitle suggests, with its promise of "more probable Additionals," this book defends the claims made in Thorowgood's earlier work on the same subject, *Iewes in America; or, Probabilities That the Americans are of that Race* (first published in 1650 and reissued as *Digitus Dei: New Discoveries* in 1652). Thorowgood had sent a copy of *Iewes in America* to the Anglican controversialist Hamon L'Estrange, who responded, to Thorowgood's chagrin, by publishing *Americans No Iewes; or, Improbabilities that Americans are of That Race* (1651). The 1660 *Jews in America* is thus a response to L'Estrange's critique and a supplement to Thorowgood's initial publication. Despite their nearly identical titles, the books differ substantially in content. They are, however, mutually concerned with proving a "Jewish"[1] origin for Native Americans. Specifically, both books contend that indigenous American peoples—in both the northern and the southern parts of the hemisphere—are the ten lost tribes of Israel.

Thorowgood was not the first European to speculate about the origins of human life in the Americas. Theories regarding the continents' human history among Europeans were as old as their arrival in the hemisphere, and debates over this question were very much in play in the seventeenth century.[2] The 1650 *Iewes in America*, however, marks the first known English publication to offer a sustained inquiry into the Hebraic Indian theory—a hypothesis holding that Native Americans shared a lineage with Jewish peoples. Deploying both biblical exegesis to track the tribes' movements following the Assyrian conquest and proto-ethnographic evidence to highlight ostensible similarities between Native American and "Jewish" cultural practices, *Iewes in America* and *Jews in America* presented readers with the tantalizing possibility that European colonialism had solved one of the Bible's greatest historical mysteries and effected a merging of sacred and secular timelines.

Iewes in America and *Jews in America* are difficult books to assess, for several reasons. First, although Thorowgood is identified as the author of both works, they are composite texts containing substantial writings by figures with varying, and sometimes competing, relationships to the Hebraic Indian theory. Richard Cogley has conducted the most extensive inquiry into the histories of Thorowgood's books and the men who contributed to them, and I do not wish to replicate his work here. Still, some background information is essential both for a general understanding of how these books came into being and for the kind of analysis I will pursue in this chapter.

As Cogley has demonstrated, the writers packaged together in these works inhabited a wide spectrum of belief about the Hebraic Indian theory and its potential consequences.[3] Thorowgood himself was a former Anglican priest who embraced Presbyterianism during England's tumultuous 1640s. He was a reformist, but neither his political nor his theological outlook was particularly radical, and, as Cogley notes, Thorowgood "was almost certainly not a millenarian, or a person who believed in the future establishment of a millennial or messianic kingdom on earth."[4] Despite his relatively moderate views, Thorowgood corresponded enthusiastically with men who believed not only that indigenous peoples could be the lost tribes of Israel but also that their "discovery" by English Protestants heralded an impending millennium. He included writings by these prominent millennialists in both *Iewes in America* and *Jews in America*. In the former, his personal assessment of the Hebraic Indian theory is bookended by an "Epistolicall Discourse" by John Dury, whom Richard Popkin calls "perhaps the most active millenarian theoretician in the Puritan Revolution,"[5] as well as an account by the Dutch rabbi Manasseh ben Israel, who (being Jewish) did not personally subscribe to Christian millenarianism but did deploy it for political use.[6] *Jews in America* similarly features a lengthy letter Thorowgood received from the Puritan missionary John Eliot, whose religious views did not fully align with Thorowgood's but who was willing to entertain the question of American Hebraism. In addition to incorporating writing by others directly engaged with the theory, within both books Thorowgood offers extensive citations of everything from biblical texts to Spanish accounts of the Americas to classical works of history and philosophy. Thus neither *Iewes in America* nor *Jews in America* offers a singular argument regarding the Hebraic Indian theory, and the arguments these books contain at times run counter to each other.

A second challenge to the assessment of Thorowgood's books is the question of time, specifically of time lag. Thorowgood produced *Iewes in America* during the English civil wars and *Jews in America* at the end of the Interregnum. England's political instability during this period not only caused publication delays but also had an impact on the texts themselves. Thorowgood began investigating the Hebraic Indian theory sometime in the 1630s—when he wrote to the Puritan minister Roger Williams to ask his opinion of it—and composed his first book in the mid-1640s. *Iewes in America* was approved for publication in 1648, but it was held up at the press because of Pride's Purge and the arrest of King Charles I. The delay was in some respects fortuitous, because the book's original dedication was to Charles, whose trial and 1649 execution rendered such laurels not only unnecessary but also dangerous. Cogley's work on the publication history of *Iewes in America* shows that Thorowgood did not shelve the book during the two years that lapsed before it appeared in print but instead took advantage of its postponement by augmenting it in the meantime. Beyond changing the dedication—now to the knights and gentlemen of Norfolk—"he added materials from [Edward] Winslow's *Glorious Progress of the Gospel,* which was published in mid-1649, and also from the charter of the New England Company, the missionary corporation created by parliament in July 1649."[7]

The incorporation of material from the Puritan Winslow's book is intriguing, because that text includes an appendix in which Dury argues that the lost tribes of Israel are in the Americas. By Dury's own account, though, his interest in the Hebraic Indian theory owed entirely to his reading of the unpublished *Iewes in America.* His "Epistolicall Discourse" to Thorowgood, written in 1649 and included in Thorowgood's first book, explains, "Before I had read your discourse and seriously weighed matters, when I thought upon your theme, that the Americans should be of the seed of Israell, it seemed to me somewhat strange and unlikely to have any truth in it."[8] *Iewes in America* changed Dury's mind, which made it possible for him to write Winslow's appendix. By a twist of political fate, Winslow's book, written second but published first, becomes a proof text for Thorowgood. In citing *Glorious Progress*, in other words, Thorowgood essentially is citing himself. A product of both collaboration and delay, *Iewes in America* is an odd artifact, drawing on numerous sources that in turn draw from it. With its nearly identical title and reworked dedication to the king—now the newly restored Charles II— the 1660 *Jews in America* occupies an equally fraught temporal space. It at once reaches back to the original *Iewes in America*—replicating its argument, first dedication, and title—and, with its incorporation of new materials by Eliot and its Restoration vantage point, looks forcefully toward a prophetic future for England and its colonies.

In this chapter, I am concerned with what I see as Thorowgood's main intellectual contribution to the perpetuation of the Hebraic Indian theory: namely, his insistence on considering it in terms of "probability" rather than certainty. This chapter's first section situates *Iewes in America* within the context of evolving notions of probability and the probable in the early modern era. Thorowgood, this context reveals, develops a model of probability that mitigates the need for absolute proof within a hypothetical frame. During the period in which Thorowgood was writing, ideas about probability shifted dramatically in Europe, as the concept transitioned from a philosophical sense of plausibility to a mathematical concept of predictive certainty. In the decade that lapsed between the publication of *Iewes in America* and that of *Jews in America*, Blaise Pascal and Pierre de Fermat began their now-famous correspondence regarding the calculations of odds in gambling, and the Dutch mathematician Christiaan Huygens published the first tract on what is now sometimes termed "stochastic probability"—the mathematical prediction of possible outcomes in a field of random variables.

This nascent work in what would become a branch of mathematics was primarily concerned with games of chance, but it reflects a broader commitment in the era to the development of clearer methods for establishing degrees of certainty and predicting results in a variety of situations. In pushing against demands for absolute or even overwhelming proof in the presentation of a hypothesis, Thorowgood's books construct an epistemological space in which uncertainty is not sufficient grounds for the rejection of a theory. I am not contending here that Thorowgood was familiar with developments in the field of mathematics and consciously adopting them—that would be an improbable claim—but I am suggesting that his books make a case for belief in the face of incomplete evidence that anticipates later developments in probabilistic thinking. Through analysis of his deployment of the notion of probability, this chapter demonstrates how Thorowgood simultaneously acknowledges the limits of his work and suggests that those limits need not form the basis for incredulity. This is precisely the epistemological position required for entertaining the Hebraic Indian theory.

If probability is a feature of *Iewes in America*, it is the explicit framework for the 1660 *Jews in America*. The second section of this chapter will explore how this later book strategically deploys evolving conceptions of probability to refute arguments made by critics of the first book. If *Iewes in America* lays out evidence for the plausibility of the Hebraic Indian theory, then *Jews in America* makes the case that uncertainty itself can be grounds for acceptance of a hypothesis. It is precisely this recourse to probability that allows Thorowgood to incorporate so many competing Hebraic Indian theories into his work.

This chapter's final section assesses Thorowgood's engagement with writings by Eliot and his fellow Anglo-American reformer, Roger Williams, to show that Thorowgood deploys a notion of the probable to work around the challenges these men's writings pose to his exposition of the theory. Although Williams was open to the idea of American Hebraism when he first corresponded with Thorowgood, he ultimately abandoned the theory. Eliot more thoroughly entertained the notion that Native Americans were of Hebraic origin, but the letter he sent to Thorowgood (which was printed in *Jews in America*) significantly revises Thorowgood's version of the theory. Nonetheless, writings by both men operate in Thorowgood's work as partial, and thus probable, proof-texts for his claim. My contention is that this is the case because Thorowgood presents belief in the theory as a wager similar to one later developed by Pascal around religious belief. As I will explain in more detail, Thorowgood frames the Hebraic Indian theory as a bet that holds no risk for the loser yet offers the possibility of gaining everything to the winner. Offered to readers thusly, Thorowgood's Hebraic Indian theory operates as the bet every Christian should hedge, and its probability becomes more than enough grounds for its acceptance.

Probable: *Iewes in America* and the Assessment of Evidence

From its outset, the 1650 *Iewes in America* evinces an interest in the epistemological potential of the probable. Dury's "Epistollical Discourse," which introduces Thorowgood's argument, begins with an expression of gratitude explicitly linked to the book's framing of its subject around the question of probability. "I am bound to thank you for the communication of your booke," Dury writes, "which I have read with a great deale of delight and satisfaction; for the rarity of the subject, and the variety of your observations thereupon, which you have deduced with as much probability to make out your theme, as History can afford matter."[9] As I noted above, Dury claims to have been skeptical of the Hebraic Indian theory before reading *Iewes in America*. He acknowledges as much in his "Discourse," noting, too, that it is not unreasonable for others to share his former doubts. "At first blush," he explains, "the thing which you offer to be believed, will seeme to most men incredible, and extravigant."[10] For Dury, though, all that is required to overcome disbelief in the theory is a careful consideration of Thorowgood's evidence. "When all things are laid rationally and without prejudice together," he writes, "there will be nothing of improbability found therein, which will not be swallowed up with the appearance of contrary likelyhoods, of things possible and lately attested by some to be truths."[11] Though the syntax is a bit murky, Dury's recourse to the probable is clear. *Iewes in America* has real knowledge value, he suggests, because it moves the Hebraic Indian theory out of the realm of the "incredible" and into the world of the possible.

Dury was not simply an early and enthusiastic reader for Thorowgood; he also introduced Thorowgood to the work of Manasseh ben Israel, the most influential Jewish thinker to entertain the Hebraic Indian theory. Indeed, while the publication of *Iewes in America* initially was delayed for political reasons, Dury was probably responsible for further extending the time between the book's approval and publication because he was hoping to receive information from Manasseh that would strengthen Thorowgood's claims. As Cogley explains, "When he read the draft of *Iewes in America* in late 1648, Dury recalled an astonishing story that he had heard in Holland in 1644 . . . about a Marrano who claimed that he had encountered the lost Israelites in South America."[12] Dury wrote to Manasseh seeking confirmation of the story, and he held onto Thorowgood's book while he waited for a reply. Manasseh responded in November of 1649, sharing with Dury a French translation of the Marrano's account (the man's name was Antonio de Montezinos) along with an affidavit from Manasseh himself attesting to its authenticity. Dury translated Manasseh's materials into English and had them printed at the end of *Iewes in America*. He frames his inclusion of these materials as operating in the service of probability. "[W]hereof to confirme your probable conjectures," Dury writes in his "Discourse," "I shall give you that information which is come to my hands . . . which to the probability of your conjectures adde so much light, that if the things which I shall relate be not meere fictions (which I assure you are none of mine, for you shall have them without any addition, as I have received them) none can make any further scruple of the truth of your assertion."[13] Here, the already probable is made more probable through the addition of the equally probable. Dury is not laying out a case for absolute certainty, even as he embraces Thorowgood's thesis. Rather, through the accumulation of source materials and logical deductions, Dury argues for the likelihood of the Hebraic Indian theory.

Dury's sense that "probable conjectures" bore epistemological weight may have grown out of his reading of *Iewes in America*, a text that itself is invested in the relationship among evidence, probability, and certainty. Thorowgood introduces the text proper of *Iewes in America* by stating that he at first took an interest in the Americas because he was curious about "what Genius devoted our Country-men so willingly to forsake their Friends, and Nation, exposing themselves to voyages long and perilous."[14] A Presbyterian who opted to remain in England through the civil wars, Thorowgood was perhaps understandably curious about those reformers who departed for what he viewed as even less friendly shores. Noting that "some were hastened by their dislike of Church Government" and that "other perhaps were in hope to enrich themselves," Thorowgood contends that the most significant development in English colonization of North America is the potential for the conversion of Native American peoples (1). "Or else those pious soules by a divine instinct, might happily bee stirred up to despise all hazards," he writes, "that the Natives for their temporall accommodations might bee spiritually enriched by the English" (2).

Having concluded that, whatever their initial motivations, the colonists' true errand is to bring Christianity to the western hemisphere, Thorowgood arrives at the heart of his project. The "next desire," he explains, "was, if possible, to learne the Originall of the Americans, and by observations from Printed Books, and written Letters, and by Discourse with some that had travelled to, and abode in those parts severall years, the probability of that opinion as yet praeponderates, that the Westerne Indians be of Jewish race" (2). Here Thorowgood lays out his methodology as well as his purpose. His goal is to determine "the probability" of a Hebraic origin for the Americas; in the service of that goal, he will collect data by reading books about the Americas and corresponding with those who have lived there. Though in our own moment this may seem a relatively neutral approach to the resolution of an open question, with its emphasis on probability and its recourse to testimonial proof, *Iewes in America* participates in an epistemological shift sweeping Europe in the early modern era and even anticipates some philosophical arguments regarding evidentiary proof that would be published in its wake.

To understand Thorowgood's deployment of probability as the basis of his belief in the Hebraic Indian theory, it is necessary to consider the transformation that the notion of probability underwent in Europe in the seventeenth century. As Anders Hald writes in his history of early probability and statistics, the "concept of probability is an ambiguous one. It has gradually changed in content, and at present it has many meanings, particularly in the philosophical literature."[15] Part of the confusion surrounding the concept, he explains, stems from the fact that the term "probability" is deployed in both qualitative and quantitative disciplines, where it denotes several different kinds of knowledge. On the one hand, he writes, "Aleatory probabilities are used for describing properties of random mechanisms or experiments," while "epistemic probabilities are used for measuring the degree of belief in a proposition warranted by evidence."[16] The division of probability into these two categories began in the middle of the seventeenth century. Although scholars continue to debate the precise history and contours of probabilistic thought in this period, intellectual historians broadly agree that around 1650 the significance of "probability" as a source of knowledge began to shift.[17] During the period when Thorowgood composed his work on the Hebraic Indian theory, the idea that rational belief or action could be based on the probable rather than the certain began to undergird everything from religion to history to science. This shift, I would suggest, authorizes Thorowgood's project and allows him to amass a frankly inconclusive data set in the service of his hypothesis.

The shifting role of probability in European thought occurred on several axes simultaneously during the mid-seventeenth century. This is, for example, when the concept made its first entry into the field of mathematics. Before this period, the word had no numerical connotation, and there was essentially no quantitative element to probability. Perhaps unsurprisingly, the concept enters mathematics primarily through discussions of gambling. Humans had been playing games of chance for centuries, and there are a few early works that address topics such as the odds of rolling different combinations of dice, but it was not until the 1650s that anyone in Europe made a serious attempt at systematic aleatory calculation.[18]

The first significant effort to quantify probability was undertaken, famously, in a series of letters exchanged by Blaise Pascal and Pierre de Fermat in 1654. The correspondence was inaugurated by Antoine Gombaud, Chevalier de Méré, who asked the mathematicians to solve the age-old "problem of points," which is sometimes referred to as the "division of stakes." The problem unfolds thusly:

1. Two players agree to play a set number of rounds of a game of chance.
2. They agree that the winner of the majority of rounds (two out of three, three out of five, etc.) will be declared the winner of the entire game.
3. They are interrupted before they can complete all the agreed upon rounds, but at the moment of interruption they are not locked in a tie.
4. How should they divide the pot?

This deceptively simple problem laid the foundation for modern mathematical probability theory, as Pascal used it to develop equations capable of calculating the odds of potential outcomes within a random field.[19]

Thorowgood could not have known about this correspondence, even when he wrote the 1660 *Jews in America*, as it would not be published until after his own books appeared in print. Still, Pascal and Fermat's correspondence took place within a broader framework of epistemological change in Europe. As Lorraine Daston puts it, "Mathematical probability theory was to be the codification of a new brand of rationality that emerged at approximately the same time as the theory itself . . . in contrast to the traditional rationality of demonstrative certainty."[20] As mathematicians grappled with the calculation of possibility, so too did scientists and philosophers entertain the notion that certainty might not be the necessary standard for rational belief—and, indeed, that certainty itself might be an improbable achievement.

Although the calculation of odds for gambling was perhaps the most obvious application of probability theory, the prediction of possibilities and the assessment of levels of plausibility became standard practice in several disciplines in this period. Hald notes that while Pascal and Fermat took up their hypothetical gambling problem, the demographer (and haberdasher) John Graunt undertook a statistical analysis of mortality rates in England in order to assess and predict the effects of a plague on the population.[21] His book, *Natural and Political Observations Made on the Bills of Mortality* (1662), not only tabulated data from mortality bills but also proposed that the systematic analysis of that data could allow officials to prepare for future epidemics. This notion that aleatory odds could be calculated from data about past occurrences and thereby lay groundwork for future actions was new in this era, and it had a broad impact on European cultural practices. Ian Hacking, author of the first major assessment of probability's emergence as an accepted epistemological standard, has suggested, somewhat controversially, that the shift in thinking around probability took place rapidly around 1650. While some historians of probability theory highlight its ties to older modes of thinking and suggest that the change in its meaning took place more gradually, Hacking's suggestion that "before 1650 or so, there was virtually none of our present web of probability ideas" is compelling, as is his contention that several new practices emerged almost all at once across Europe to alter the epistemological landscape.[22] Among those new practices, he notes, "Nations began to raise income by selling annuities, which demanded, but did not always receive, actuarial competence. . . . People of power and influence attended to the statistics of births and deaths . . . [and the] reliability of testimony was calculated."[23] Produced just as these cultural changes begin to take shape, Thorowgood's work evinces an investment in the idea that the calculation of odds could allow a thoughtful person to derive a conclusion from incomplete evidence and extrapolate a reasonable prediction out of historical data.

In addition to forming a new foundation for mathematical calculation in fields such as mathematics and demography, probability underwent alteration within qualitative fields during this period. It is this shift that seems to have had the greatest impact on Thorowgood's thinking about the Hebraic Indian theory. In her extensive study of seventeenth-century English approaches to probability, Barbara Shapiro demonstrates that "in the ancient world, probability had been associated with opinion and rhetoric and had . . . little philosophical significance."[24] In the long, Western philosophical tradition of categorizing and ranking forms of knowledge, probability rested close to the epistemological floor, below both the absolute certainty of divine knowledge and the lesser, human category of "moral certainty" (assurance beyond reasonable doubt). Until the mid-seventeenth century, the aim of most disciplines was to achieve moral certainty. Several factors converged to erode this impossibly high standard. Hacking suggests that probability gained traction in the natural sciences, as fields such as medicine and astrology came more and more to depend upon "observable signs" and empirical data. Where sensory information formerly had been deemed unreliable because potentially faulty, it emerged as one of the few sources of knowledge useful for medical diagnoses, and it formed the basis of astrological predictions.[25]

Questions surrounding what constituted appropriate evidence in support of a conclusion made their way into other areas as well. Shapiro notes that this era saw the emergence of several philosophers—Hugo Grotius being perhaps the most significant—who made an "attempt to find a rational basis for the truths of religion without making claims to the kind of religious certitude that dogmatic theologians were making."[26] Her work also demonstrates how in the mid-seventeenth century, "English historical thought first reached its modern state of methodological ambivalence," as historians grappled with the obscurity of the past.[27] In a similar vein, Daston argues that probability was most significantly transformed through its entry into legal discourse, noting that it was within the law that probability's emerging mathematical properties collided with its more subjective features, as jurists encountered aleatory contracts on the one hand and, on the other, situations in which conflict hinged on competing perspectives. "The hierarchy of proofs within Roman and canon law," she explains, "led mathematicians to conceive of degrees of probability as degrees of certainty along a graduated spectrum of belief."[28] As Europeans refashioned their knowledge systems with the limits of human understanding in mind, probability emerged as a new standard of reasonable belief in the absence of total certainty.

The notion that probability could form the backbone of a spectrum of certainty was in its infancy when Thorowgood composed *Iewes in America*, and yet that book explicitly constructs its argument in terms of the probable. Thorowgood's own text primarily is comprised of "conjectures" purporting to demonstrate cultural similarity between Native Americans and the Bible's missing Israelites. It bears repeating that Thorowgood's descriptions of both groups tend toward caricature. He possessed no first-hand knowledge of Native American nations, which he treats as a singular culture, and he appears to have been equally ignorant of the history and practice of Judaism (a religion that did not exist as Thorowgood understands it in 722 BCE, the purported year of the Kingdom of Israel's exile). Nonetheless, cultural comparison forms the basis of Thorowgood's argument, operating as an "observable sign" of his theory. His first conjecture, for example, asserts that "the Indians doe themselves relate things of their Ancestors, suteable to what we read of the Iewes in the Bible" (3). Native history, Thorowgood contends, is biblical and Israelite. "They boast their Pedigree from men preserved in the Sea by God himself," he writes, "that God made one man, and one woman . . . and how in a Famine hee rained bread for them from Heaven, who in a time of drought also gave them Water out of a Rock: many other things, themselves say were done for them, such as the Scriptures relate concerning the Israelites at their comming out of Aegypt" (4).

Thorowgood's primary source for this account of American history is José de Acosta's *Natural and Moral History of the Indies*, which was published in Spanish in 1590 and translated into English in 1604. It is likely, though, that Thorowgood encountered Acosta's work through his reading of Thomas de Malvenda's Latin text *De Antichristo* (1604), a treatise on the antichrist that is not primarily concerned with the Americas but refers to Acosta's work. *Iewes in America* cites both texts, and although the evidence presented primarily is Acosta's, Thorowgood concludes this exposition of Mexican historical accounts thusly: "Who seeth not[,] saith Malvenda[,] much probability that the Mexicans are Iewes, how could they else report the manner of their comming into the promised Land?" (4). Ostensible similarities between Mexican and biblical accounts of creation and migration add up, in Thorowgood's calculus, to a probable, if not absolute, conclusion.

The evidence Thorowgood presents in service of the Hebraic Indian theory would not satisfy a twenty-first-century reader, and for good reason, but *Iewes in America* laid important groundwork for future engagements with the theory, and thus an accounting of some of its proofs is in order. Thorowgood presents a set of practices ostensibly shared between Native American and "Jewish" peoples. His imagining of the culture of the lost tribes is essentially a catalogue of Jewish stereotypes, while his sense of Native American cultures is gleaned from an array of first- and second-hand colonial texts. This section of *Iewes in America* includes such arguments as the following:

> The Indians weare garments fashioned as the Jewes, a single coate, a square little cloake. . . . They constantly annoint their heads, as did the Jewes . . . They delight exceedingly in dancing . . . [T]hey eate no swines flesh tis hateful to them, as it was among the Jewes . . . The Indian women are easily delivered of their children, without Midwives, as those in Exod. 1.19. . . . Dowries for wives are given . . . [and] They nurse their owne children, even the Queenes in *Peru*, and so did the mothers in Israel. (6–8)

The text goes on like this at length, as Thorowgood covers perceived similarities between American and Jewish religious rites and suggests that indigenous American peoples speak a degraded form of Hebrew. Individually, his proofs might be unconvincing. The cumulative effect of these arguments, though, allows Thorowgood to slide the Hebraic Indian theory into the realm of the probable. The main stumbling block that Thorowgood and other advocates of the theory faced was that there was not a single piece of conclusive evidence to support it. There was, however, a collection of signs that could be interpreted as pointing to his claim. In the absence of certain proof, Thorowgood offers an almost overwhelming list of minor possibilities that he hopes add up to a clear conclusion.

Thorowgood frames two of his evidentiary claims specifically in terms of probability. In the first, he evokes the probable to stave off a potential argument against his theory. His sixth chapter begins, "This which followeth next, at first sight, will appeare a Paradox rather than a Probability." The sticking point in question is what he terms "the Man-devouring that is in America" (17). Thorowgood's main source of information regarding cannibalism in the Americas is Peter Martyr d'Anghiera's *De Orbe Novo*, a set of reports detailing Spanish explorations of Central and South America, first translated into English in 1555. Martyr's work offers several accounts by Spanish conquistadors of American cannibalism, including a description of "people called Caniblaes, or caribes, which were accusto[m]ed to eate mans flesh (& called of the olde writer, Anthropophagi)."[29] Thorowgood borrows Martyr's phrasing when he asks, "What an inference may this seem to bee; there bee Carybes, Caniballs, and Man-eaters among them, therefore they be Jewish?" (17).

The question of whether, and under what circumstances, cannibalism occurred in the precolonial Americas is highly charged and has generated a great deal of scholarly debate. As the anthropologist Barry Isaac notes in his study of accounts of cannibalism in Mesoamerica, "Aztec cannibalism is a controversial topic because we cannot yet answer the question: do the early Colonial-period reports of it reflect actual behavior or merely a post-Conquest reinterpretation of tradition?"[30] There is no such thing as an unmediated account of cannibalism in the Americas, and Europeans often conjured the practice to prove the "savagery" of indigenous peoples. Despite the many references to "man-eating" in Martyr's work, and its near ubiquity in popular representations of pre-Columbian Mesoamerica, Isaac reminds us that "no eyewitness accounts of Aztec cannibalism exist."[31]

The accuracy of Thorowgood's source material matters less here than the fact that he deemed accounts of cannibalism a problem for *Iewes in America* to solve. Perhaps unsurprisingly, this ostensible proof of difference becomes in his rendering simply another indication of similarity. In this case, though, it is not cultural comparison that proves an Israelite origin for Native Americans; rather, it is biblical prophecy. "But let it be considered," Thorowgood writes, "Among the Curses threatned to Israel upon their disobedience, wee read Levit. 26. 29. Yee shall eate the flesh of your Sonnes and of your Daughters" (17). Although the Israelites do not consume human flesh in the biblical narrative, Thorowgood contends that they are predicted to fall into the practice. "The Prophet Ezekiel," he writes, "speakes in the future tense of some new, and till then unheard of calamity, but such as should bee common afterward; I will doe in thee that I never did before, for in the midst of thee the Fathers shall eat their Sons, and the Sons their Fathers" (17). Reports of American cannibalism thus do not contradict the Hebraic Indian theory. On the contrary, they suggest the fulfillment of prophecy and stand as proof of the theory's relevance.

The idea that the lives of indigenous Americans should be understood within the frame of biblical prophecy also structures the second explicitly probabilistic evidentiary point in *Iewes in America*. In a chapter assessing the suffering of indigenous peoples, Thorowgood explains that they "have endured the extremities of most unspeakable miseries" (27). Those "miseries," Thorowgood admits, primarily have followed on the heels of European arrival in the hemisphere. Nonetheless, he asserts, American suffering is proof of both a divine plan and a Hebraic origin for the sufferers. "The Americans calamities are suitable to those plagues threatned unto the Jewes," he writes, citing the twenty-eighth chapter of Deuteronomy, which includes the verse, "The Lord shall cause thee to be smitten before thine enemies" (Deuteronomy 28:20). Just as cannibalism marks the fulfillment of prophecy, so, too, do the horrors of European colonialism. "Such a comment upon that terrible Scripture is not any where to be found, as among the Indians," Thorowgood argues, and "by this also it will appear probable that they be Jews" (26). "The Jews were a sinful people," he explains. "The Indians were and are transcendent sufferers" (26).

The tautology is both cruel and convenient. Native peoples suffer, because they were always already meant to suffer, because they are the Israelites, who were always already meant to suffer. Like the Assyrians before them, European colonists merely act in the service of a divine order, carrying out in the present the predicted decimation of a long-gone people. Within the parameters of *Iewes in America*, the proper conclusion to draw from the pain of Native Americans merely is that it is "probable that they be Jews." Although Thorowgood does assert that he offers this specific proof hoping to "provoke the readers every way to compassionate such transcendent sufferers," his sense that the Hebraic Indian is destined to endure divine punishment overshadows other considerations, and the "unspeakable miseries" of colonialism seem, in the end, to be merely more proof for his thesis.

At the end of his conjectures, Thorowgood admits that accumulation is his argumentative strategy. "And now if all these parallels will not amount to a probability," he writes, "one thing more shall be added" (33). There is no clear certainty in this model, only the stacking of possibilities. The final piece of Thorowgood's tower of small proofs is the mere fact that Native Americans reside in the Americas. That "one more thing," Thorowgood explains, is "the dispersion of the Jewes," of which, he writes, "'tis said, The Lord shall scatter thee among all people, from one end of the earth, even to the other, &c. Deut. 28. 64. The whole remnant of thee I will scatter into all winds, Ezek. 5. 10, 12, 14. & Zach. 2. 6. I have spread you as the foure winds of heaven" (33–34). If evidence of cultural overlap does not convince a reader of Thorowgood's claim, the very existence of the western hemisphere—unknown to Europeans until the fifteenth century—should carry enough epistemological weight to do so. "Now if it be considered how punctual and faithfull God is in performing his promises and threats mentioned in the Scripture of truth," Thorowgood explains, "we shall have cause to looke for the Jewes in America" (34). Confronted with both the specter of an unwavering deity and the ongoing absence of the lost tribes, the reader must admit the probability of American Hebraism.

Thorowgood concludes the conjectural portion of his book (after which follows a plea for funds on behalf of Protestant missionaries in North America) by asserting that the paucity of evidence for his thesis stands itself as a kind of proof. "If it be therefore well considered of what dark & darkened condition the Israelites were in these times, how many yeeres have passed since . . . it will not seem so strange if they [Native Americans] be wholly barbarous, seeing also the vengeance of God lies hard and heavy upon them for their injustice done to his Sonne" (53). This passage, it perhaps goes without saying, contains both error and anachronism. But it also is an apt summary of Thorowgood's reasoning throughout *Iewes in America*. The unlikeliness of his thesis, like the "barbarous" state he imagines indigenous Americans to inhabit, "will not seem so strange" if readers simply consider the breadth of divine reach and admit that within its scope, nothing is improbable.

More Probable: *Jews in America* and the Defense of Uncertainty

The idea that probability could form a rational foundation for belief is implicit throughout the 1650 *Iewes in America*, but it becomes an explicit, central concern for Thorowgood in 1660. *Jews in America* not only promises "Probabilities, that those Indians are Judaical," but it further announces that those probabilities have been "made more probable by some Additionals to the former Conjectures." This is not merely a hilarious seventeenth-century subtitle (although it is that). In asserting that "probabilities" can be made "more probable," Thorowgood is making a serious epistemological case for his evidence. As I noted above, he assembled *Jews in America* partly in response to Hamon L'Estrange's rather cruelly titled 1651 work, *Americans No Iewes; or, Improbabilities that the Americans are of that Race*. As L'Estrange explains, Thorowgood sent him a copy of *Iewes in America*, which he read "with more diligence and delight for the Authors sake, but . . . fell upon many Sands and Rocks of reluctance."[32] L'Estrange critiques *Iewes in America* from several angles, suggesting both that the original peopling of the Americas predates the Assyrian conquest and that the similarities Thorowgood identifies between "Jewish" and American peoples are insufficient to convince a reasonable person of the Hebraic Indian theory's veracity.

Although L'Estrange's conclusion—that Native Americans are not Jewish—is correct, it is important to note, in fairness to Thorowgood, that the reasoning L'Estrange follows in *Americans No Iewes* is not substantially different from that of *Jews in America*. In contending that the Americas were settled "forthwith after the Confusion of tongues" described in the Genesis story of the Tower of Babel, for example, L'Estrange offers proofs that historians today would deem lacking. Aware that readers even in his own time might balk at the idea of ancient people undertaking a perilous transoceanic voyage, L'Estrange defends his Tower of Babel migration scenario by suggesting that "at the time of the said Captivity of the ten Tribes, and long before, ships and shipping were well known and in use; for Iason about Anno mundi 2740 . . . sayled out of Greece and performed his expedition for the Golden Fleece."[33] L'Estrange also evokes the story of Ulysses as evidence for the prowess of ancient mariners. To compare *Iewes in America* to *Americans No Iewes* is thus not to compare a less accurate text with a more accurate one. Rather, it is to see that those refuting the Hebraic Indian theory in this period often accept the same kinds of epistemological premises as the theory's proponents. For L'Estrange as well as for Thorowgood, the question is not whether America's human origins can be determined for certain; the question is merely what is or is not possible.

L'Estrange's odd historical positing aside, *Americans No Iewes* attempts to debunk Thorowgood's specific "conjectures," particularly his claims regarding cultural overlap. In addition to devoting six entire pages to refuting Thorowgood's claim that Native people "constantly annoint their heads, as did the Jewes," L'Estrange declares Thorowgood's other ethnographic proofs invalid. To the latter's claim that Native American garments resemble those of Jewish people, for example, the former writes that such clothing "is no more peculiar to the Iewes or Americans than to any other Nation."[34] Similarly, to Thorowgood's assertion that both groups "delight exceedingly in dancing," L'Estrange replies, "This is so cheap and prostitute a custome all the World over (and must needs be most among naked people). . . . It is a ravishment of the Intellectuals."[35]

This kind of reasoning forms the basis for much of his rejection of *Iewes in America*; the cultural specificity Thorowgood wishes to assign to these practices disintegrates upon close examination. What Thorowgood presents as evidence in the service of probability, L'Estrange contends, points instead to the improbability of his claim. "I conceive he expected to prevaile most by the power of his paralleles, and coherence of Customes," L'Estrange concludes, "so when upon examination I found so great diversity, disparity, contrariety and discord betwixt the ancient Iewish rights, and the Customes of America, I resolved . . . chiefly to bend my self to confute the wrong Petigree of the Americans, and to oppose and withstand a blind obedience and consent to weak, incertain, and fallacious conjectures."[36] The accumulation of probabilities does not, in L'Estrange's review of *Iewes in America*, add up to certainty. Despite its effort to convince reasonable readers that an unprovable thesis is nonetheless possible, *Iewes in America*, L'Estrange insists, offers only an uncertainty at best weakly articulated and at worst dangerously false.

Although *Americans No Iewes* primarily attacks *Iewes in America*'s evidentiary points, Thorowgood mounts a defense of his work that grounds itself in his deployment of "probabilities" in the service of his thesis. The 1660 *Jews in America* contains, in addition to the 1650 book's omitted dedication to Charles I—reworked as a dedication to the newly restored Charles II—and a reprinting of the dedication to the nobility of Norfolk, a new epistle to the "Impartial and Soul-loving Reader," which attempts to account for the perceived failures of Thorowgood's first book. "When I was directed, as hourse diverted from other studies, to look into the Books that write of the New World," he explains, "I had no thought, at first, to observe among them any semblance of Judaicall rites . . . but by some instinct, or providence upon further reading, and consideration, such cogitations increased in me."[37] Even as he claims that his investment in American Hebraism might trace to a divine origin, though, Thorowgood asserts that he never intended for *Iewes in America* to stand as a comprehensive proof of his theory. Describing that first book, he writes, "I was not at all in love with it . . . [I]t was neglected by me, as an unlikely fancy" (25). Interest in the book, his own and others', was awakened, however, by the political upheaval in England. "After the beginning of the long parliament," he explains, "there was againe serious speech and preparation toward the conversion of the Natives in America . . . [T]hose papers also were awakened, that had a long time slept in the dust, and, by a like providence they came to the view of some, that were not only curious, but, judicious" (26). If a providential hand pushed Thorowgood in the direction of the Hebraic Indian theory, it also pushed his version of the theory into the hands of others who would believe it. Nonetheless, Thorowgood contends, his first book's "countenance was modest, and bashfull, offered at no more than verisimilitude and probabilities" (26).

Where *Iewes in America* presented probability as an avenue to belief, *Jews in America* adopts a different posture, configuring itself around its author's own uncertainty and laying its emergence at the feet of historical contingency. Far from serving as a retraction, though, this position allows Thorowgood's text to absorb criticism while restating the claims of the earlier book. If readers are unconvinced by his evidence alone, which he admits is "no more than . . . probability," then they must take seriously the fact that he felt compelled to bring forth his text in a moment of political upheaval. "I say," this preface concludes, "be pleased to vouchsafe some share likewise to the Collector of those, and these Probabilities" (33). Acknowledging his and his evidence's vulnerability to critique, Thorowgood demands only thoughtful consideration and recognition that his claim, if not convincing, is at least possible.

In addition to foregrounding probability in this new preface, Thorowgood devotes an entire chapter of *Jews in America* to "The Notion or Meaning of the word Probabilitie," clarifying the standard of proof on which he has built his theory. After noting that philosophers of earlier periods treated probability as a function of rhetoric, tethered only tenuously to truth, Thorowgood lays out his own sense of the term. "The genuine meaning of the word Probabilities, the subject of this Chapter," he contends,

> is discernable by natural Logick and reason, without the help of that which is in Schools, and artificial; in plain English, therefore a Theme, Sentence, or Probleme is said to be Probable, when it cannot certainlie be affirmed, or denied, but the assent of the Reader, or Hearer is left to the weight of those arguments or examples which are laid before him, and are most prevalent with his right reason, which in some cases had need to be serious, and well informed, because there be some false things, which at first blush seem more probable, than those that be true. (10)

This definition contains two striking features, both of which point to the shifting nature of probability in this period. First, probability operates as an interpretive act in this treatise, rather than an ontological fact. The "Reader or Hearer" must apply reason to a proposition to ascertain its probability. More than a mere function of rhetoric, but less than an absolute proof, probability resides in the space of rational assessment. Within this epistemological frame, what once seemed impossible may become believable.

The second compelling feature of Thorowgood's definition is that it raises the possibility that truth does not always appear more probable than falsehood. A false premise, as he puts it, might "at first blush seem more probable" than a true one. Thus Thorowgood presents his readers with a conundrum: although the assertion that Native Americans are "no Jews" might seem more probable than the assertion that they are, the appearance of probability does not guarantee veracity. This introduces something of a paradox into his argument. Thorowgood offers readers a set of evidentiary points designed to convince them that his thesis is probable, yet he defends his work by asserting that the appearance of probability does not mean a premise is true.

Although this may seem a simple case of faulty reasoning (or perhaps poor writing), I would suggest that Thorowgood's stumbling around the issue of probability and its relationship to truth reflects a deliberate grappling with the evolving parameters of knowledge in this period. The Hebraic Indian theory operates simultaneously in *Jews in America* as the premise Thorowgood would like to prove and as proof in itself that certainty in religious matters is, despite arguments to the contrary, impossible. If the most reasonable position readers can take is that what at first seems improbable may in fact be true, how can rational individuals ever arrive at a satisfactory conclusion? Despite the confidence he displayed in the 1650 *Iewes in America*, by the time he writes the 1660 *Jews in America*, Thorowgood seems inclined to suggest that they cannot. "If therefore these dim and dark conjectures be not manifest, certain, and demonstrative," he asserts, "that was never intended, nor so much as pretended" (4a).[38] Certainty is not the standard in this matter, because it cannot be. "Men should be satisfied," Thorowgood asserts, "if they see Probabilitie, he that collected them is a man full of infirmities, and those to whose censure they are exposed, are not yet perfect" (4a). As long as knowledge is produced and evaluated by humans, it will remain an imperfect commodity. Even the dimmest conjecture, therefore, has a place in human reason. "If therefore what is set down be at all probable," he suggests, "they fulfill their promise" (4a). Rather than defend the merits of his evidence, Thorowgood attacks the proposition that evidence must produce iron-clad conviction. In assessing his work and the work of his critics, he suggests, readers need not arrive at a place of absolute certainty—indeed, they cannot expect to—but they must perform a rational calculation of what might be.

Thorowgood concludes this chapter by highlighting his own uncertainty regarding the origins of human life in the Americas. "These things I offered," he writes, "to shew some Probabilitie in the conception, I did not obtrude them for certainties, if any produce that which seems more sure, I shall thankfully embrace it; they have not yet so far prevailed with my self, as to convince me, that the Americans are without Controversie of the Judaical race, but it is probable they are Jews, or descended from them" (4a–5a). The syntax here is ambiguous. It is unclear whether the "any" capable of producing "that which seems more sure" refers to evidence that may be uncovered in the service of his own argument or a competing claim. The "they" in the second half of the sentence seems to refer to the "things" he has offered as evidence, suggesting that his own proofs have been insufficient to convince him of his thesis. But it also could refer to the "any" that might produce more substantial or different proofs. The upshot of this conclusion, though, is that Thorowgood admits that his conjectures have not produced, even for himself, an airtight argument. But his point is that they do not have to. For Thorowgood, all that matters is that "it is probable that they [Native Americans] are Jews, or descended from them," because if his thesis is probable, then it can form the basis for rational decision making. As it turns out, *Iewes in America* and *Jews in America* are both, at their cores, invested in a decision to be made by English and Anglo-American Protestants. The calculation of probability with respect to the Hebraic Indian theory, these books contend, is a matter of grave spiritual import.

Thorowgood's Wager

It is crucially important that the issue of American origins is not merely academic for Thorowgood. Within both of his books lies an urgent question: should English Protestants attempt to convert Native Americans to Christianity? As Cogley's work on John Eliot's missionary endeavors has shown, "Puritans had to determine if the Indians were Jews or Gentiles in order to locate their conversion in an anticipated sequence."[39] That "sequence" refers to the order in which Puritans believed the world's various populations would be converted to Christianity at the end of days. Although Puritans generally subscribed to a belief that the world would undergo mass conversion around the time of Christ's second coming, they were divided on the question of whether the conversion of Jewish peoples would precede or follow that of Gentiles. For Puritans such as John Cotton, who believed both that mass Jewish conversion would occur first and that Native Americans were the Gentile descendants of Tartars, there was no point in attempting to convert indigenous populations until after the world's Jewish people became Christians.[40] But if Cotton was wrong about American ancestry, and Native people were in fact the lost tribes, then (within the context of Puritan understandings of Judaism) they could be considered "Jewish," and their conversion thus might be the key to Christ's return to earth.

Cogley notes that Eliot was particularly vexed by this problem. He "had subscribed to the Tartarian origins view as late as November 1648," and for years he deemed his own mission to Native people in Massachusetts as a kind of preparatory, "civilizing" endeavor—one laying the groundwork for future conversion by Christ if not in itself producing true mass conversion.[41] After hearing from Edward Winslow about the claims of Thorowgood, Dury, and Manasseh, though, Eliot became less sure. In a 1649 letter to Winslow, published in 1651, Eliot writes that now that he has read more on the subject, "It seemeth to me probable that these people [Native Americans] are Hebrews, of Eber, whose sonnes the Scripture sends farthest East."[42] This letter, like many documents related to the Hebraic Indian theory, incorrectly conflates "Hebrew" people with "Jewish" people and treats all Native Americans as a singular culture. In doing so, though, it opens up the possibility that Native Americans occupy a place of primacy within biblical prophecies regarding the return of Christ. Speaking as Thorowgood does in the language of probability, Eliot entertains the idea that his conversion efforts may be more than an exercise in preparation for Gentile conversion and could, in fact, be inaugurating the millennium.

Thorowgood's sense that it is probable that indigenous Americans are "Jews" motivates him in both works to plead for funds to support American missionary efforts. His dedication to the Norfolk nobility in *Iewes in America* makes this plain. "By you is the following tract communicated to the world," he begins. "'Tis like you will finde in the probabilities so many Judaicall resemblances in America . . . and if they bee Jewes, they must not for that be neglected" ([i–v]). Readers admitting that his proofs are at least plausible should be inspired to action. "If it be probable that providence honored [England] with the prime discovery of that New World," he writes, "God hath disposed the hearts of many in . . . New England, that they have done more in these last few years toward their [Native Americans'] conversion, then hath been effected by all other Nations and people that have planted there" ([xi]). Here, probability combines with providence to set England apart from other nations. That destiny, of course, comes with a price—in fact, a literal price. "I wish prosperity to all the Plantations," Thorowgood asserts, "but those of New England deserve from hence more then ordinary favour" ([xii–xiii]). The "favour" he hopes for here is financial; *Iewes in America* is, among other things, a request for private support of New England missionary work. Importantly, though, even as Thorowgood argues that English Protestants should send money and goods to New England to speed the process of "Jewish" conversion in the service of millennium, he also contends that even if his theory proves incorrect, such support will not be wasted. "Or if the lost Tribes are not to be found in America," he writes, "of whatever descent and origination the poore Natives be, if they finde the Lord Christ, and the Nov-angles [New Englanders] be the Wisemen guiding them unto their peace, great cause shall wee have to lift up the high praises of our God in spiritual exultation" ([vii]).

Although he has set out to prove the Hebraic Indian theory, before he even lays out his evidence, Thorowgood contends that the accuracy of the theory is a moot point. "How should we cast our mite into this treasure, yea, our Talent, or Talents, if wee have them?" he asks, "for certainly the time is coming, That as there is one Shepherd, there shall be one Sheepfold" ([vii]). Give money for the conversion of Hebraic Indians, he argues, and if those "Indians" turn out to be other than "Hebrews," the end result will nonetheless curry divine favor. Whether the Hebraic Indian theory be true or false, in other words, Englishmen should behave as if it were true. Cast your mite, he pleads, because even if there is nothing to be gained, there is much, in all probability, to be lost in not casting it.

In arguing that English elites should act as if the premise of the Hebraic Indian theory is true, even though there exists a real possibility that it is not, Thorowgood anticipates a kind of probabilistic reasoning that later would be made famous by that master of aleatory calculation, Pascal. Indeed, I would suggest that *Iewes in America* and its sequel are organized around the kind of calculation that would come to be referred to as "Pascal's Wager."

Thorowgood could not have known about Pascal's Wager while composing either of his works. The Wager did not appear in print in any form until 1662 and was not published in its entirety until 1670, when it appeared as part of Pascal's *Pensées*.[43] Still, the Wager offers a useful context for thinking about how probability's aleatory properties combined with its evolving qualitative sense in this period to allow writers to manage the problem of religious uncertainty. In his study of the Wager, Hacking notes that "Pascal's thought shows that the mathematics of games of chance had quite general applications."[44] An early example of "decision theory"—the theory of how to make a choice in the face of uncertain outcomes—the Wager situates religious belief within the frame of rational decision making by positing it as the greatest, yet most certain, gamble of them all. It operates thusly:

1. God either exists or does not exist.
2. Every human must wager—believe or do not believe.
3. If you wager that God exists and win (because God does exist), you gain everything (eternal salvation). If you lose (because God does not exist), you lose nothing (mere death).
4. If you wager that God does not exist and win (because God does not exist), you win nothing (mere death). If you lose (because God does exist), you lose everything (eternal damnation).
5. Belief in God is rational, because it minimizes risk while maximizing reward.

As Justine Crump notes, this Wager argues for belief "not by proving that God actually exists but by providing persuasive evidence that a belief in God is rationally legitimate."[45] The Wager cannot settle the question of whether a premise is true or untrue; it exclusively determines whether the adoption of a premise is rational.

There is a large body of scholarship on Pascal's Wager, much of which is devoted to critiquing the logic of his premises and deductions.[46] The Wager in this form has many obvious limitations: it assumes a single (Christian) deity whose relationship to humans is structured exclusively around punishment and reward, and it does not address the potential dangers of believing in the "wrong" god (or gods). It also takes no position on how belief should structure practice and action. As it pertains to Thorowgood, though, the most compelling aspect of Pascal's Wager is its effort to combine aleatory with spiritual calculation, because that is precisely what Thorowgood is attempting in his expositions of the Hebraic

Indian theory. In the decade before Pascal formulated his now famous Wager, Thorowgood was hedging a bet of his own. Native Americans either are or are not the lost tribes of Israel. To believe that they are not, he contends, is to risk everything in the hope of gaining nothing, but to believe that they are is to risk very little in the hope of gaining eternity.

The idea that only the merest probability that the Hebraic Indian theory is true should be enough to justify its acceptance as rational is, finally, the wager that allows Thorowgood to assemble his texts. In abandoning certainty in favor of probability, Thorowgood offers a set of evidences that may not be especially convincing, but that do lay out the stakes of a grand gamble. This explains, I would suggest, why both *Iewes in America* and *Jews in America* incorporate so much material by those who disagreed not only with Thorowgood's conclusions regarding the import of the Hebraic Indian theory but also, in some cases, with his very premises. Although Thorowgood cites numerous sources related to the colonization of the Americas and apparently read many works (in several languages) about the western hemisphere, two of the most important sources of evidence for his Hebraic Indian theory are Roger Williams and John Eliot. Williams and Eliot not only lived among Native American populations, but they also corresponded directly with Thorowgood. Although both men entertained the notion of American Hebraism and wrote to Thorowgood to express their interest in it, they also both ultimately took issue with Thorowgood's version of the theory, rejecting and refining it as they saw fit.

Williams was one of the earliest figures to engage with Thorowgood about the Hebraic Indian theory, as the two men corresponded fifteen years before *Iewes in America* was published. During the few months when Williams had been banished from the Massachusetts Bay Company but was still living in Salem—the order for his banishment having been stayed because winter was approaching—he replied to a query from Thorowgood regarding the origins of American peoples.[47] The original letter has been lost, but Thorowgood cites passages from it in *Iewes in America* and dates it to December 20, 1635, in his text's margin.[48] According to Thorowgood, Williams "was desired to observe if he found any thing Judaicall among them [Native Americans]," and "He kindly answers . . . in hac verba [sic],"

Three things make me yet suspect that the poore natives came from the southward, and are Jewes or Jewish quodammodo [in a certain way], and not from the Northern barbarous as some imagine 1. Themselves constantly affirme that their ancestors came from the southwest . . . 2. They constantly and strictly separate their women in a little Wigwam by themselves in their feminine seasons, 3. And beside their God Kuttand . . . they hold that Nanawitnawit (a God over head) made the Heavens and the Earth, and some tast of affinity with the Hebrew I have found. (*Iewes*, 6)

This list actually contains four "proofs," with linguistic "affinity" folded into a dubious claim that Native Americans worship a deity similar to the one depicted in the Hebrew Bible. Thorowgood's reproduction of Williams's letter, though, laid the groundwork for future engagements with the theory. As I will discuss more in later chapters, European interpretations of Native histories, stories of the separation of menstruating women, and ostensible language similarities became mainstays in expositions of the Hebraic Indian theory. Williams's brief and admittedly thin assent in his letter to Thorowgood thus took on a life well beyond *Iewes in America*. His letter is crucial for Thorowgood, because it offers a first-hand, English account of Native American life. Although Williams does not wholly endorse the theory in his letter, the fact that his observations do not discount its possibility entirely is enough for Thorowgood.

Whatever Williams believed in 1635, he was unwilling to wholeheartedly endorse the Hebraic Indian theory when he published his *Key into the Language of America* in 1643. In the preface to that work, Williams acknowledges the competing theories regarding the origins of human life in the Americas, but he draws no conclusion about which theory might be most accurate. "From Adam and Noah that they spring," he writes, "it is granted on all hands. But for their later Descent, and whence they came into those parts, it seems as hard to find, as to finde the wellhead of some fresh Streame, which running many miles out of the Countrey to the salt Ocean, hath met with many mixing Streames by the way."[49] This is a lovely metaphor for human lineage—fresh streams intermingling as they wind toward a salty sea—but it does not exactly present a clear picture of American history. Williams is careful throughout his preface to avoid occupying a single position on the question of

Native American origins. "Wise and Judicious men . . . maintain their Originall to be Northward from Tartaria," he writes, but also notes that "it pleased the Dutch Governor . . . to draw their Line from Iceland." Of his own take on the question, Williams asserts, "I shall present (not mine opinion, but) my Observations to the judgement of the Wise."[50] For Williams, the distinction between "observation" and "opinion" is crucial, as he presents a list of cultural traits that could produce different conclusions. Like his letter to Thorowgood, Williams's *Key* asserts that Native people "constantly separate their Women (during the time of their monthly sickness)," and it further asserts that they "anoint their heads as the Jewes did" and "give Dowries for their wives, as the Jewes did."[51] Still, a reader seeking confirmation of the Hebraic Indian theory in the *Key* will be disappointed. Though Williams notes that "others (and my selfe) have conceived some of their words to hold affinitie with the Hebrew," he also contends, "Yet againe I have found a greater Affinity of their Language with the Greek Tongue."[52] In the decade that intervened between his letter to Thorowgood and his writing of the *Key*, Williams became less etymologically certain. Following this observation, he offers some affirmative (and, as always, dubious) comparisons between Native American and Greek cultural practices. The Hebraic Indian theory, though present in the *Key*, is neither the sole nor even the most central focus of Williams's account.

Thorowgood read Williams's *Key*, and although it does not fully endorse his theory, he cites its account of the Dutch governor's theory of Icelandic origins (which Thorowgood denounces) in *Iewes in America*.[53] Thorowgood's willingness to refer to the *Key* may stem from the fact that, although Williams presents the Hebraic Indian theory alongside other theories and even undercuts it, he does leave it in the realm of possibility. Having listed several theories of American origins and asserted, "I dare not conjecture in these Uncertainties," Williams concedes, "I believe they are lost, and yet hope (in the Lords holy season) some of the wildest of them shall be found to share in the blood of the Son of God."[54]

Williams's evocation of "lostness" is quite strategic. Williams never says that he believes Native Americans to be the lost tribes of Israel. Indeed, his preface leaves unanswered the question of what it means for American peoples to be "lost." Their condition of "lostness" appears in the text more figurative and spiritual than literal or historical. "I know there is no small preparation in the hearts of Multitudes of them," Williams writes. "I know strong Convictions upon the Consciences of many of them."[55] Rather than appearing in the *Key* as a civilization missing from history, Native peoples may merely have been absent from the spread of Christianity across the Old World. Their "discovery" may not solve a biblical mystery, but it might, Williams suggests, render them once again visible to the divine. "I know not with how little Knowledge and Grace of Christ the Lord may save," he writes, "and therefore neither will despaire, nor report much."[56] Native Americans may be "lost" in the sense that they are not Christians, but Williams asserts that he has no way of knowing for sure what, if any, plan the divine might have to "find" them. Williams manages the controversy over American Hebraism, in other words, by converting the "lost" in "lost tribes" into a metaphor. In this way, he can believe that indigenous peoples are lost without asserting that they have been missing. In the space Williams leaves between "lost" and "lost tribes," Thorowgood finds enough probability to maintain his argument.

If Williams was ambivalent about Thorowgood's lost tribes version of the Hebraic Indian theory, Eliot was more explicit in his revision of it. Although Eliot opens his epistle to Thorowgood by asserting that upon reading *Iewes in America* he "saw some ground to conceive, that some of the Ten Tribes might be scattered even thus far, into these parts of America," his "learned conjectures" mainly contend that the primary source of human life in the Americas was a migration predating the formation of the Kingdom of Israel. "I have some cogitations, as well as others," he explains, "of the first peopling of America by the posterity of Sem, though in sundry particulars, I have some different thoughts touching the story of those first times."[57]

The "Sem" in question here is Noah's son, more commonly referred to as "Shem." In the Genesis account, Noah and his family, including his sons Ham, Shem, and Japhet, survive the great flood by building an ark at God's command. The story of Noah's family received varied attention and interpretation through the Middle Ages, but over time Europeans developed a reading of the story in which Noah's sons became the patriarchs of a tripartite world—with Shem "fathering" Asia, Japheth Europe, and Ham Africa. This interpretation was convenient for white Christians, because the ninth chapter of Genesis describes

Ham seeing his father drunk and naked, at which point Noah, oddly, curses Ham's son: "Cursed be Canaan; a servant of servants shall he be unto his brethren" (Genesis 9:25). Readings of this verse that combined a racialized conception of Noah's descendants with emerging notions of continental geography allowed some European Christians to justify the enslavement of African peoples. Indeed, the idea that the "curse of Ham" was perpetual, race-based slavery persisted into the nineteenth century.[58] Benjamin Braude's study of the shifting meaning of the Noah legend shows that this interpretation of the story was not universal and emerged in conjunction with several developments in Europe, including the print technology that standardized biblical texts, European incursions into Sub-Saharan Africa, and the emergence of early modern notions of race and nation.[59] Braude explains, "As even the most cursory reading of Genesis 9 and 10 immediately demonstrates, the connection between the biblical account of Noah and his offspring and the modern interpretation . . . is tenuous. Not only does the conflict between the misbehavior of Ham and the cursing of Canaan defy simple explanation, but there is the more basic problem of the identities of Ham, Shem, and Japhet and their offspring."[60] Noah's lineage, provided in Genesis 10, "is repetitive, contradictory, and manifestly incomplete: it lists sons without daughters; not surprisingly, it is accompanied by no map; [and] most of the names are unidentifiable."[61] The Bible, in short, assigns neither territories nor anything like racial identities to Noah's descendants. Nonetheless, the notion of a tripartite world populated by the "sons of Noah" was commonplace by the seventeenth century, and it is this notion that undergirds Eliot's letter to Thorowgood.

Where Thorowgood asserts that the scattering of Israel sets the stage for human life in the western hemisphere, Eliot draws his origin story out of Noah's genealogy. Specifically, he argues, "I conceive that the first planters of America, to be not only of Sem, but Ebrews of Eber, even as Abraham and Israel were, though not in the same line" (2). Here Eliot refers to biblical verses that describe Shem as "the father of all the children of Eber," and Eber as Shem's great-grandson (Genesis 10:21). Eliot's argument hinges on an apocryphal story about Eber, whose name sometimes is spelled "Heber" and is linked to the word "Hebrew." Eliot does not provide citations for his account of Eber, and I cannot locate a specific source for his claims. It is clear, however, that his epistle to Thorowgood builds on a longstanding exegesis of Genesis. Eber receives scant attention in the Bible, appearing only in lists of Noah's descendants, and he never is depicted doing anything. But as James VanderKam notes, the verses that mention him have for centuries held "several points of interest for interpreters, not the least of which was the fact that the chronology of Eber's life entailed that it overlapped with the time when the tower of babel was built and destroyed."[62] This is crucial, because the Babel story depicts the confounding and diversification of human language.

A full accounting of the history of the Eber story is beyond the scope of this chapter, but it is essential that a handful of Christian texts produced in the fourth century CE suggest that at some point there existed a now-lost text about Eber. VanderKam notes that the descriptions of that missing work appearing in these early Christian texts share a narrative trajectory:

- Eber alone among the people of his time refused to join in building the tower [of Babel].
- He was rewarded by escaping the confusion of languages.
- He preserved the original Hebrew language and transmitted it to his descendants, among whom was Abraham.[63]

Though the Eber text is lost, a trace of it remains in Christian mythology. Eliot clearly encountered this story somewhere, because he asserts that "there being now [in the aftermath of Babel] several languages in the earth, the Fathers thought good to call the holy language . . . by the name of Eber, who was then in his flower and stood against Nimrod [the builder of Babel]" (11). This notion that Eber's line retains humanity's original language, now called "Hebrew," because of his heroism in the face of the builders' arrogance, makes Eliot's claim that the original Americans were "not only of Sem, but Ebrews of Eber" all the more significant. Though the migration he will track is not that of the lost tribes, it is of a people whose history is biblical and Hebraic.

Having established Eber as the bearer of both the Hebrew language and a divine plan, Eliot makes the case that this figure's descendants are the most likely to have migrated to the western hemisphere. He writes that "whereas all former expeditions [by Noah's descendants] for plantations were westward, now they make an expedition Eastward, and send for the a great familie, the grandchildren of Eber, to possesse the Easterne world . . . [H]ere is a great familie that like to travel Eastward for their inheritance" (16). He probably drew this cardinal location from Genesis 10:30, which describes the descendants of Eber's son Joktan thusly: "Their dwelling was from Mesha, as thou goes unto Sephar, a mount of the east." Extrapolating from this verse, Eliot imagines an eastward migration that leads Eber's line across the Asian continent and into a new hemisphere. In making this case for the eastern location of Eber's line, Eliot draws a somewhat radical conclusion: "And thus it appeareth by the holy story, that as the whole Easterne world is the portion of Sem, so all the Easterne world eastward of Elam is the portion of Eber. . . . Hence therefore we may, not only with faith but also with demonstration, say, that the fruitful India are Hebrews, that famous civil (though idolatrous) nation of China are Hebrews, so Japonia, and these naked Americans are Hebrews, in respect of those that planted first these parts of the world" (17). In Eliot's imagining of postdiluvian migration, all people east of present-day Iran are the descendants of Eber; and thus they are, at least in this respect, Hebrews. Correctly speculating that humans must have migrated into the western hemisphere via Asia, Eliot offers the possibility that the scope of Hebraism is broader than even Thorowgood has imagined, and that many different populations might trace their lineage to a Hebraic source.

In locating a potential migration to the western hemisphere in Genesis, Eliot creates a space in which to entertain Thorowgood's lost tribes theory. The main link Eliot draws between his own conjectures and those of *Jews in America* is language. Unlike Williams, Eliot asserts, "It seemeth to me, by that little insight I have, that the grammatical frame of our Indian language cometh neerer to the Hebrew, than the Latine, or Greek do" (19). For Eliot, though, linguistic similarity itself is not a reason to accept the lost tribes theory. Rather, he is concerned with how such similarity might reveal a divine order. If the descendants of Eber brought the Hebrew language into the Americas, Eliot speculates, then "the dispersion of the Ten Tribes to the utmost ends of the Earth eastward, into the Easterne world . . . hath less severity of punishment in it, being dispersed into the countries of Sem, and among the posterity of Eber, whose language and spirit was not wholly strange unto them" (19). Embedded in this argument that the ten tribes received "less severe" punishment than the Kingdom of Judah (which would suffer exile in later periods) is an anti-Jewish notion that the descendants of the Kingdom of Judah—the world's known Jewish population—are implicated in the death of Jesus, while the Kingdom of Israel, due to its early disappearance from the Bible, is not. "Judah," Eliot explains, "when they were dispersed, it was westward, to the uttermost ends of the Westerne world, and among a people whose language was utterly strange to them" (19).

This notion that the lost tribes, though scattered as punishment for their sins, have escaped the perils of history becomes an important aspect of the Hebraic Indian theory in later periods, and I will explore it in more detail in the third chapter of this book. Here it is merely important to note that Eliot reconciles perceived similarities between Native American languages and Hebrew by positing that if the lost tribes made it to America, they would have been greeted by people like themselves. And that, he argues, would be great consolation to a displaced people. "Hence why ought we not believe," Eliot asks, "that the ten Tribes being scattered Eastward, as scattered to the utmost ends of the Easterne world? and if so, then assuredly into America, because that is part of the easterne World, and peopled by Easterne Inhabitants" (20). Reading backward from Thorowgood's theory, Eliot finds the origins of America in Genesis, and he posits that if the lost tribes traveled all the way east, when they arrived, because God still loved them, they were met with the sound of home.

Though the writings of Williams and Eliot present challenges to Thorowgood's theory, they nonetheless remain essential sources in both *Iewes in America* and *Jews in America* because they leave open enough space for him to make a case that the theory is probable. In the end, of course, Thorowgood's interest in the history of the Americas has essentially nothing to do with Native Americans, and neither is he concerned with actual Jewish people. Thorowgood's wager on the origins of human life in the Americas is a wager on the future of English Protestantism at home and in the colonies. The conversion of Native Americans operates in both of his books as means for England to solidify its distinction from Catholic nations and shore up the differences among its own Christian sects—to prove its worthiness to the divine and be spared future punishment. *Jews in America* thus concludes as it begins, with a defense of those Protestants who opted to depart from England and settle in North America. "I love not to dip my pen in the commemoration of these matters," he writes of the violence of Reformation and England's late civil wars, "but this little may shew what great cause many had to bethink themselves of new Habitations, forseeing plainly, if such violence continued, their old houses would be too hot for them" (66). If Native Americans are the lost tribes of Israel, then the terror of religious war was not merely terror; it was a divine hand leading England to a great destiny. Those who left, in this interpretation, were neither cowards nor traitors but an instrument of God's will. Though it is impossible to know with perfect certainty whether the theory is true, English Protestants should behave as if it is. "Oh that we all could be Christian Patriots once," Thorowgood implores, "effectually endeavoring the preservation of our land, and Religion. . . . I wish wee could weep over our sinnes and dangers . . . yet with the Britons pious devotion: Thou art our King O God, command deliverances for us" (66). The financial and moral support of missionary endeavors such as Eliot's, Thorowgood contends, is a material manifestation of such devotion. In betting on the Hebraic Indian theory, English Protestants are betting on themselves. They may have nothing to gain from this bet, but they may have everything to lose in not making it. For Thorowgood, that is enough reason, if not to believe in American Hebraism, then to wager on its probability.

2

"A Complete Indian System"

James Adair and the Ethnographic Imagination

If there is a single text responsible for the Hebraic Indian theory's persistence beyond the colonial era, it is James Adair's massive 1775 work, *The History of the American Indians*. A trader who lived for forty years among various nations in what is now the southeastern United States, Adair produced one of the earliest and most comprehensive English-language accounts of Native American cultural practices. His book is structured as a prototypical version of what would come to be called participant observation ethnography.[1] Stories of Adair's life as a self-styled "English Chikkasah" are interspersed among detailed descriptions of the Cherokee, Chickasaw, Choctaw, Katahba, and Muskogee nations.[2] The *History* thus has been a source of much useful information for historians and anthropologists interested in the cultural history of the region. First published by Edward and Charles Dilly at the recommendation of Benjamin Franklin, the text has appeared in numerous editions over the past two centuries. Its appeal to first popular and then scholarly audiences makes sense, given its unique perspective and surprisingly sophisticated methodology. Adair's descriptions of the people he encountered and places he lived are admirably thick—Geertzian before Geertz, even—and in retrospect they frequently are accurate.[3] What is more, he draws on a staggering amount of source material, citing everything from biblical and classical writings to European colonial texts to Native American oral traditions. And unlike many of his contemporaries, Adair typically (though not always) treats the cultures he describes with respect. His book defends Native practices against charges of savagery and highlights the hypocrisy of white settlers who encroach upon lands, break treaties, and then cry foul when they suffer retaliation. In tune with the machinations of competing colonial powers, Adair also notes how the ever-shifting relations among European and American nations have an impact on all peoples residing in the region. His book thus stands as a colonial text at once invested in and suspicious of the workings of colonialism. He is certain of the worth of his project, but he remains uncertain of the context out of which that project emerges.

Despite its importance in the period and ongoing use by historians, Adair's *History* has received almost no attention from literary critics. There are several possible reasons for this. The *History* is not precisely literary, for one thing, and it might be a stretch to call it an enjoyable read. What is more, Adair himself remains an opaque figure. Though he at times appears as a participant in scenes his book describes, his life is an almost complete mystery because he did not leave much beyond his *History* in the way of records. The likeliest explanation, though, for the lack of attention to Adair is the fact that his *History* is framed entirely by the argument that the Americas were initially populated by ancient Israelites. The first half of the text is comprised of twenty-three arguments regarding aspects of different Native American cultures, each of which is designed to support Adair's Hebraic Indian thesis. For all its accuracies, then, Adair's *History* is founded upon a fundamental inaccuracy. This makes the text easy to dismiss and challenging to take seriously. But Adair's text was serious, and its approach to ethnography reinvigorated the Hebraic Indian theory by infusing it with much more empirical data than previous expositions had offered.

This chapter's first section will explore the *History* in detail, focusing on how Adair constructs his inquiry as a "scientific" endeavor, partly building on Thorowgood's earlier efforts to demonstrate the probability of American Hebraism but also situating himself as an expert witness. Though Adair at times draws upon older accounts of the peopling of America, he derives his conclusions primarily from first-hand experience with Native populations, detailing his observations and deducing his conclusions from them. Particularly, his notion that a culture's past could be extrapolated from the conditions of its present became the standard mode of argument in Hebraic Indian theories, and his carefully rendered accounts of American practices provided other writers with the evidence their own theories required. Adair's *History*, in other words, infused this old theory with new evidence, and his methodology allowed the figure of the Hebraic Indian to reemerge long after it had all but fallen out of public discourse and right when it otherwise might have fallen entirely away.

In the century that intervened between Thomas Thorowgood's 1660 publication of *Jews in America*, which is discussed at length in the previous chapter, and the release of Adair's *History*, the Hebraic Indian theory had declined into near obscurity. This is perhaps the case because, despite Thorowgood's efforts to frame the theory in terms of the probable, many readers found it quite improbable. As Richard Cogley notes, by the end of the seventeenth century, Thorowgood and his thesis had become jokes even among devout Christians. "In 1691," he reminds us, "Cotton Mather wrote that John Eliot . . . had 'Thorow-good reasons' for hoping that the native peoples of the New World were descended from the lost tribes of Israel."[4] Mather believed no such thing, perhaps because he found Eliot's and Thorowgood's reasoning lacking, but also perhaps because European settlement in the Americas, though certainly transformative of the world order, had not produced a Christian millennium. The theory, in short, had not fulfilled its religious promise.

When Adair revisits the theory in the mid-eighteenth century, he does so not out of a sense of religious urgency but instead to refute emerging accounts of the origins of life in the Americas. Adair's goal is to argue for monogenesis—that is, he wishes to demonstrate that indigenous Americans are the products of the same creation as the earth's other inhabitants. Thorowgood took up the theory partly in response to the crisis of religious war in England, but Adair adopts it in the face of polygenism. His anthropological investment in the American past means that Adair focuses mainly on ethnographic "proofs" for his theory, and that he does not take a position on the broader implications his thesis holds for an American future. Adair's argument begins and ends with American origins.

Because Adair, unlike Thorowgood, appears certain about the evidence he presents but, also unlike Thorowgood, is not inclined to speculate broadly about the implications of that evidence, the *History* became a crucial source for later writers concerned with the Hebraic Indian theory. The second section of this chapter will explore how two very different proponents of the theory put Adair's work to different ends, focusing on how his ethnographic approach lent credence to later theological writings. Examined first is the work of Ethan Smith, a millennialist Congregationalist minister who viewed the Hebraic Indian as a sign of the end of days. Structuring his own book around Adair's arguments, Smith deems the Hebraic Indian proof of divine favor for the United States. I then turn to the work of Mordecai Manuel Noah, the Jewish statesman who attempted to establish an American utopia in the 1830s. For Noah, Adair's *History* did not contain evidence of an impending Christian millennium, but it did suggest that the "gathering of Israel" was imminent. The possibility that indigenous peoples were the descendants of ancient Hebrews made questions of US policies regarding the world's Jewish people, rather than Native nations, a central concern in Noah's work. Although Adair produced his work before the American Revolution and primarily was interested in describing and analyzing the cultures of Native peoples, for Smith and Noah the *History* speaks directly to the political and religious concerns of the antebellum United States.

At stake in this evaluation of Adair's enduring influence on the Hebraic Indian theory is a reassessment of the boundaries between what might be called sacred and secular reasoning. In the past decade, the study of secularism as something other than the mere absence of religion has reshaped the study of US literature in particular, as well as of culture more generally.[5] One of the main results of this line of inquiry has been a recognition of the often porous and always mutually constitutive relationship between religious and secular epistemologies. As the theologian Guy Collins puts it, the "truth of the sacred and the secular distinction is that it is an entirely artificial one. . . . [T]he profane needs the sacred, just as much as the sacred requires the profane."[6] The challenge of theorizing the secular and the religious in conjunction with one another is revealed in Collins's syntax. The distinction between the two is "artificial," yet they "need" and "require" one another in a way that only distinct entities can. In Adair's case, the need for a "secular" assessment of Native cultures both emerges from and reinvents a "sacred" dilemma, as the question of American origins is inseparable from questions regarding the Americas' absence from the Bible.

Adair himself was acutely aware of the limits of sacred reasoning when it came to explaining life in the Americas. In the *History*'s dedication, addressed to three other prominent traders in the region, he explains, "You often complained how the public had been imposed upon, either by fictitious and fabulous, or very superficial and conjectural accounts of the Indian nations—and as often wished me to devote my leisure hours to the drawing up [of] an Indian system" (59). From its outset, Adair presents the *History* as a remedy to an epistemological problem. True knowledge of American nations requires a systematic account derived from careful observation. Nonetheless, within Adair's assertion of the importance of empirical study lies the sacred. "Should my performance be in the least degree instrumental to promote an accurate investigation and knowledge of the American Indians," he explains, "I shall rejoice" (59–60). At the end of his project, in other words, lies the promise of joy tinged with praise. For Adair and those who would follow him, the question of American origins simultaneously required the systematic assessment of evidence and held implications of biblical proportions. When his "Indian system" was complete, Adair was not the only one who would rejoice.

An English Chikkasaw: Adair and the Power of Observation

The preface to Adair's *History* lists two "grand objects" for its project: "to give the Literati proper and good materials for tracing the origin of the American Indians—and to incite the higher powers zealously to promote the best interest of the British colonies, and the mother country" (62). He deems the former goal especially pressing, because he has "with inexpressible concern . . . read the several imperfect and fabulous accounts of the Indians, already given to the world" (62). The fabulous account of most concern to Adair is Henry Home, Lord Kames's *Sketches of the History of Man*, a sweeping work of proto-anthropology first published in 1774. Adair completed most of his *History* several years before its publication, so he clearly updated it to address Kames's work. *Sketches* covers a vast amount of material: three decades worth, which Kames collected and read in the interest of writing "a natural history of man."[7] A comparative assessment of everything from language to property rights to artistic production, the book charts a teleological trajectory in which all human civilizations begin as loose units of hunter-gatherers, evolve into first animal-herding and then agricultural groups, and culminate in civil societies precisely like those of Europe.

The small body of scholarship on Kames tends to focus on his impact on the disciplines of history and anthropology, or his relationship to other Scottish Enlightenment figures such as David Hume and Adam Smith.[8] For this chapter, the most significant feature of Kames's work is the one that inspired Adair's ire: namely, Kames's embrace of polygenism. Adair was particularly galled by Kames's accounting of the origins of indigenous American civilizations, and he wanted to counter the claim that, in Kames's words, "America has not been peopled from any part of the old world" (2:256). One way to read Adair's *History*, then, is as an effort to shift the Hebraic Indian theory out of the theological context in which it typically had been presented and reframe it in the terms that had begun to structure polygenic accounts of American peoples. In reacting to new theories of the origins of humankind, Adair reinvented the Hebraic Indian theory for the Age of Enlightenment.

Kames was not the first to propose a polygenic history for humankind, though his version of that theory differed somewhat from previous accounts. David Livingstone deftly has explored the history of the notion of pre-Adamic creation, showing that "alternative world chronologies" circulated in Western thought at least as early as the fourth century, complicating the linear Genesis narrative.[9] Theories of distinct human creations gained popularity in Europe in the sixteenth and seventeenth centuries, as men traversing the globe encountered people whose histories and ways of life did not fit easily into the biblical narrative. Livingstone notes that "the encounter with the New World threw into yet sharper relief the growing tensions between geography and the Mosaic record."[10] If all humans owed their origins to a single pair, then what could explain the vast diversity of human life?

Writers from Montesquieu to George Buffon explained human difference in terms of climate: over time, this position held, humans had adapted differently to their material circumstances and developed a variety of physical characteristics.[11] This explanation did not satisfy Kames, who writes that "we cannot doubt of the authority of Moses, yet his account of the creation of man is not a little puzzling" (1:47). The puzzle Kames wishes to solve is the existence of what he deems "savage" nations. He writes that "Adam, as Moses informs us, was endued by his Maker with an eminent degree of knowledge; and he certainly must have been an excellent preceptor to his children and their progeny, among whom he lived many generations. Whence then the degeneracy of all men into the savage state?" (2:47–48). This is a question climate cannot answer. Because Kames begins with the assumptions that humans were created in the image of the divine and that their history is progressive, the existence of people who continue to occupy the role of hunter-gatherer poses a theological as well as historical problem. The only solution, he concludes, is that some great "convulsion" must have thrown men into a state of savagery, from which not all have recovered. The convulsion on which Kames focuses is the story of Babel. "By confounding the language of men," Kames writes, "and scattering them abroad upon the face of all the earth, they were rendered savages. And to harden them for their new habitations, it was necessary that they should be divided into different kinds, fitted for different climates" (2:48). Here, Kames cleverly inverts the relationship between climate and human difference while skirting the edges of Christian orthodoxy. Creation may have begun with Adam, he contends, but that does not mean all humans derive from the same source. In the confusion of Babel, Kames finds the origins of race.

Although Kames's study begins with a biblical problem, it moves quickly to empirical observation for the solution to that problem. His investment in demonstrating the possibility of racial discreteness explains why a study of human civilizations begins with a rather odd description of the process by which animals are distinguished from one another. "Animals are formed of different kinds," Kames explains, "resemblance prevailing among animals of the same kind, dissimilitude among animals of different kinds. And, to prevent confusion, kinds are distinguished externally by figure, air, manner, so clearly as not to escape even a child" (1:13). Appearance and behavior separate one species from another. Contra theories of acclimation, Kames asserts that the important reason for the distinctions among species is that "no animal nor vegetable is equally fitted for every climate"; it follows that all beings are created to suit their location rather than adapt to it (1:15).

The racialist logic of this zoological argument snaps into focus when Kames moves to the subject of animal mating, taking issue with Buffon's contention that all humans belong to the same species because "a man and a woman, however different in size, in shape, in complexion, can procreate together without end" (1:17). Interspecies breeding, Kames suggests instead, is perfectly in line with the laws of nature. A "he-goat and a ewe produce a mixed breed which generate for ever," he asserts. "The camel and the dromedary, though nearly related, are however no less distinct than the horse and the ass . . . and yet these two species propagate together, no less freely than the different races of men and of dogs" (1:17–18). The production of fertile offspring, for Kames, thus does not offer proof of species similarity. The roots of racist pseudo-science are evident in this work, and I do not want to downplay the impact that *Sketches* had on later theories of racial difference that furthered the goals of white supremacy. Of greatest importance here, though, is that Kames attempts to solve a biblical problem—gaps in the Mosaic record—with a scientific solution. Subordinating the Pauline assertion that God "hath made of one blood all nations of men for to dwell on all the face of the earth" (Acts 17:26) to secular accounts of human difference, Kames invents an extra-biblical creation story ostensibly legitimized by empirical fact.[12]

Kames offers a series of arguments to prove that "America has not been peopled from any part of the old world," the first being that the Americas show signs of cultural degeneration radiating out from two clear sources (2:556). "When America was discovered by the Spaniards," he writes, "Mexico and Peru were fully peopled; and the other parts less and less, in proportion to their distance from these central countries" (2:556). Deeming Aztec and Incan city-states more advanced than other American nations, Kames argues that the dispersal of peoples out from these creation points accounts for their "savagery": "In travelling northward, the people are more and more ignorant and savage. . . . In travelling southward, the Patagonians, the most southern of all, are so stupid as to go naked in a bitter cold region" (2:556).[13] The sparseness of populations, combined with a kind of cultural amnesia, Kames contends, explains why North American peoples have not built cities on par with their southern counterparts. Despite the numerous observable differences between, say, Aztec and Choctaw societies, Kames insists that they spring from the same source. His primary evidence for this is phenotypical similarity. "They are widely different in appearance from any other known people," he says of indigenous Americans. "Excepting the eye-lashes, eye-brows, and hair of the head, which is invariably jet black, there is not a single hair on the body of any American: no appearance of a beard. Another distinguishing mark is their copper colour, uniformly the same in all climates, hot and cold; and differing from the colour of every other nation" (2:556–57).

That a racist, eighteenth-century European writer would attribute variations in hair and skin color to species difference is no surprise. But Kames's work offers a useful window into Enlightenment efforts to find scientific solutions to religious problems. "America emerged from the sea later than any other part of the known world," he asserts, "and supposing the human race to have been planted in America by the hand of God later than the days of Moses, Adam and Eve might have been the first parents of mankind, i.e. of all who at that time existed, without being the first parents of the Americans" (2:559–60). Here, Kames threads the needle between Christian orthodoxy and what will become racial science, embracing a polygenism that does not undercut Genesis.

In refuting Kames's polygenism, Adair also confronts the line between sacred and secular reasoning. Deeming the *Sketches* "contrary both to revelation, and facts," Adair highlights his project's dual purpose: to present accurate descriptions of Native American cultures and to situate those cultures within a biblical context (66). His facts will show that the western hemisphere and its original inhabitants fit within the scope of revealed religion. For Adair, proof of a singular creation lies in empirical observation, and he is quick to assert that his decades of life among Native peoples have produced sounder conclusions than have Kames's decades of reading. Although he "was separated by his situation, from the conversation of the learned, and from any libraries," Adair promises a truer account than any currently available (66, 62).

As Kathryn Holland Braund has shown in her excellent edition of the *History*, Adair's claims of insufficient access to reading materials is belied by the stunning range of works he cites. In addition to Kames's text and other English-language accounts of life in colonial America, Adair was familiar with works produced in French and Spanish, as well as classical histories, religious treatises, and even Hebrew works. Still, he downplays the role that research has played in his assessment of American origins, choosing instead to highlight his reliance on ethnographic study. Countering the *Sketches'* assertion that "there is not a single hair on the body of any American," for example, he writes that Kames's argument is "completely destitute of foundation, as can be attested by all who have had any communication with [Native peoples]" (66).

Adair's *History* thus makes a claim as much about epistemology as about American history. Having stood close enough to see the hair on American bodies, Adair also has seen the error in Kames's reasoning. At the same time, however, Adair is quick to add that "to form one creation of whites, a second creation for yellows, and a third for the blacks, is a weakness of which infinite wisdom is incapable" (66). Although his purpose stands in stark opposition to Kames's, Adair is threading the same needle. Engagement with Native American peoples provides him with the evidence to counter arguments for polygenism, but such evidence ultimately is unnecessary in the face of divine omnipotence. Empiricism merely proves what any good Christian already should know.

Adair's privileging of personal engagement with a subject seems sensible enough, but things take a strange turn when he counters Kames's assertion that Americans' "copper colour" sets them apart from the rest of humanity. "We are informed by the anatomical observations of our American physicians, concerning the Indians," he explains,

> that they have discerned a certain fine cowl, or web, of a red gluey substance, close under the outer skin, to which it reflects the colour; as the epidermins, or outer skin, is alike clear in every different creature. And experience, which is the best medium to discover truth, gives the true cause why this corpus mucosum, or glueish web, is red in the Indians and white in us; the parching winds, and hot sun-beams, beating upon their naked bodies, in their various gradiations of life, necessarily tarnish their skins with the tawny red colour. Add to this, their constant anointing themselves with bear's oil, or grease, mixt with a certain red root, which, by a peculiar property, is able alone, in a few years time, to produce the Indian colour in those who are white born, and who have even advanced to maturity. These metamorphoses I have often seen. (67)

In this instance, and many others, Adair becomes a case study in the dangers of empiricism. Although his conclusion—that American peoples are as human as anyone else—is correct, his assessment of phenotypical difference is as odd as anything else in the period. Still, what matters is

Adair's insistence that differences among humans result mainly from the influences of climate and culture and, thus, are mutable. This notion of human change over time owing to environmental and social factors not only undercuts Kames's theory of multiple origins but also sets the stage for Adair's larger claim that American peoples bear a Hebraic past that they cannot remember, but that lingers on their bodies and in their cultures.

Before turning to the *History*'s extensive evidentiary proofs, I should note that Adair's construction of Hebraism is, as it is in most articulations of the theory, flexible. As Braund notes, "Adair does not dogmatically trace the Indians from the Ten Lost Tribes but from Hebrews in general, whom he refers to variously as Jews, Hebrews, and Israelites" (480, n. 21). Indeed, his timeline for American settlement traces back to several possible beginnings. "From the most exact observations I could make in the long time I traded among the American Indians," he writes, "I was forced to believe them lineally descended from the Israelites, either while they were a maritime power, or soon after the general captivity" (74). He makes no distinction between the Israel ruled by Solomon until roughly 922 BCE and the Kingdom of Israel conquered by Assyria in 722 BCE. His "Hebrews" are a vaguely Jewish conglomerate with an imprecise history, defined mainly by a set of stereotyped cultural practices. This is not atypical for expositions of the Hebraic Indian theory, which tend to engage loosely with Hebrew or Jewish history and rely on broad stereotypes to encompass as many indigenous American customs as possible. Adair's belief that American nations all derived from a single source shapes his account, as he frequently conflates different groups and treats specific cultural practices as evidence of uniformity. Adair's Americans are at once discrete national entities (Choctaw, Creek, Muskogee) and a single nation (Israel), displaying a culture simultaneously ancient and modern, Hebrew and Jewish. The *History* thus goes beyond exposing the fault lines of polygenism, blurring the most basic distinctions of time and space—past and present, there and here, this group and that—and contracting the Americas into a point where colonial politics collides with ancient prophecy.

The *History* is thorough in its cataloging of ethnographic and anecdotal evidence, but a handful of Adair's arguments laid the groundwork for a wide range of variations on his thesis. His assessment of Native

American languages directly influenced many later expositions of the Hebraic Indian theory. Acknowledging the contemporary belief that "there is no language, in which some Hebrew words are not to be found" and that "probably Hebrew was the first, and only language, till distance of time and place produced a change," Adair suggests that the similarities between Hebrew and American languages offer proof of monogenism (94). He admits to possessing "small acquaintance with the Hebrew, and that acquired by his own application," but he hoped to "make up the deficiency of Hebrew, with plenty of good solid Indian roots" (94).[14] What Adair lacks in knowledge, he makes up for in creativity. He observes, for example, that there "is not, perhaps, any one language or speech, except the Hebrew and the Indian American, which has not a great many prepositions" (95). In addition to a dearth of prepositions, Hebrew and Native languages share, according to Adair, a flair for exaggeration. "The Hebrew language frequently uses hyperboles, or magnifying numbers, to denote a long space of time," he writes, and "the Indians, accordingly, apply the words Neetak akroobah, 'all days,' or, in other words, 'for ever,' to a long series of years" (95).

In both structure and style, Adair detects a Hebrew echo in America. As he does throughout the *History*, Adair assumes a singular origin for indigenous cultures, and thus he does not take differences among American languages into account. Nor does he entertain the possibility that other languages might form the root of American speech. His comparisons do not always withstand scrutiny: the description of long spans of time as "forever," for example, is not a feature unique to Hebrew or any indigenous language. Adair's interpretation of speech rests on the assumption that similarity indicates unity of origin. In the present, Adair hears the past; in that past, he discovers a singular human destiny.

Language serves both as a site of inquiry for Adair and a way into other proofs of cultural overlap. One of the *History*'s main claims is that Native Americans worship the same god as Jewish people. His central proof of this similarity is the name of that god. In a chapter outlining the ostensible monotheism of Americans, Adair writes, "The Hebrew nation were ordered to worship at Jerusalem, Jehovah the true and living God, and who by the Indians is stiled Yohewah" (78). Charles Hudson notes that Adair probably heard "the long, drawn out syllables of YO-He-Wah" during Creek Indian tea ceremonies and interpreted them as invocations of a familiar deity.[15] The translation of "Jehovah" and "Yah-weh" into "Yohewah" runs through the *History*, as Adair uses the terms interchangeably and often substitutes the latter for the former. In one quite startling passage, he even revises the Hebrew Bible to produce linguistic equivalence: "With the Muskóhge, Algeh signifies 'a language,' or speech: and, because several of the Germans among them, frequently say Yah-yah as an affirmative, they call them Yah-yah Algeh, 'Those of the blasphemous speech;' which strongly hints to us that they still retain a glimpse of the third moral command delivered at Sinai, 'Thou shalt not take the name of the Lord thy God in vain,' or apply the name of YOHEWAH, thy ELOHIM, to vain, or created things" (117).

There are a number of impressive interpretive feats in this passage. Adair converts "language" into "blasphemy," merges the second and third (Protestant) commandments into a single injunction against swearing and idols, and seamlessly attaches "Yohewah" to "Elohim." The layers of translation are vertigo inducing, as Adair hears Muskogee Indians hearing the German "yah" as the first syllable of the Hebrew "Yahweh." A local nickname referring to a settler group's manner of saying "yes" becomes proof of latent Judaism among Native Americans.

Language is the audible trace of Hebraism in America, but Adair also sees evidence of Native origins all around him. One evidentiary claim that would come to hold significance in the nineteenth century was his observation that Israelites and Indians alike built "Cities of Refuge, or places of safety, for those who killed a person unawares, and without design; to shelter them from the blood-thirsty relations of the deceased, or the revenger of blood" (191). Adair extrapolated this notion from the Book of Joshua, in which God decrees that the Israelites should "appoint out for you cities of refuge . . . [t]hat the slayer that killeth any person unawares and unwittingly may flee thither: and they shall be your refuge from the avenger of blood" (Joshua 20:2–3). The offer of sanctuary to those who commit an offense but not a crime, Adair claims, lies at the heart of both Hebrew and Native American morality. Over time, though, the purpose of the sanctuary city has grown faint and warped within American cultures. "The Cheerake, though now exceedingly corrupt," he explains, "still observe that law so inviolably, as to allow their beloved town the privilege of protecting a willful murtherer: but they seldom allow him to return home afterwards in safety" (192). One may seek refuge in America, in other words, but safety is bound to be short-lived. "In almost every Indian nation," Adair writes, "there are several *peaceable towns*, which, are called 'old beloved' . . . [T]hey seem to have been formerly 'towns of refuge,' for it is not in the memory of their oldest people, that ever human blood was shed in them; although they often force persons from thence, and put them to death elsewhere" (193). The implication is that Native Americans have forgotten the purpose of these cities of refuge. They refuse entry to or drive out the guilty party, allowing execution just beyond the city limits. Left alone in America, the city of refuge has been reduced to a hollow vestige of a once great culture. But in the vague memory of its past glory, Adair discovers the key to American history.

In addition to these broad similarities of language, law, and ritual, Adair recognizes Hebraism in ordinary American life. His ninth argument, for example, asserts that "the Hebrews offered daily sacrifice. . . . The Indians have a similar religious service. The Indian women always throw a small piece of the fattest of the meat into the fire when they are eating" (157). Similarly, he asserts in the following chapter, "Their frequent bathing, or dipping themselves or their children in rivers, even in the severest weather, seems to be as truly Jewish, as the other rites and ceremonies which have been mentioned" (160). Discarding fatty meat and bathing, read within the right context, are "truly Jewish."

Like earlier proponents of the Hebraic Indian theory, Adair takes notice of one particularly gendered practice. His eleventh argument holds that "the Indians have customs consonant to the MOSAIC LAWS of UN-CLEANLINESS." Alluding to the Levitical command that "if a woman have an issue, and her issue in her flesh be blood, she shall be put apart seven days," Adair writes that Americans "oblige their women in their lunar retreats to build small huts at as considerable a distance from their dwelling-houses, as they imagine may be out of the enemies reach, where during the space of that period they are obliged to stay, at the risque of their lives" (164). Setting aside the adorableness of the phrase "lunar retreats," it becomes possible to see the way that Adair treats America as the amber in which ancient practices have been suspended. His aim is to debunk Kames's polygenism, but his assumptions about indigenous people are similar—namely, that they enact a culture that, having stalled out on its developmental trajectory, retains observable ties to its past. Adair's America, in other words, is not a space of radical newness; it is an old world, playing out an old history, even as other continents have moved forward in time.

Although Adair goes to great lengths to make his case for the Hebraic Indian theory, he draws essentially no conclusion about what his thesis means for the Americas and their inhabitants. Prior expositions of the theory (and later ones) generally tied the "discovery" of American Hebraism to the fulfillment of biblical prophecies and treated it as the event that would inaugurate profound global change. Adair makes no such leaps, and readers hoping to discover the implications of his claim will be disappointed. The *History's* appendix, tantalizingly titled "Advice to Statesmen," leaves the question of American origins behind in favor of a critique of English colonial policy. "Though Great Britain hath been many years invested with the Mississippi possessions," he writes, "little hath been done to improve them" (435). The cultural decline that most concerns Adair, in the end, has nothing at all to do with Judaism or indigenous peoples. "If Britain feels a decay of her former American trade, on account of attempting to introduce among her colonies, illegal and dangerous innovations," he asserts, "it is high time to retract" (436). Chief among Adair's concerns is British mismanagement of American ports, which he deems a threat to the development of the southeastern economy. "The court sophistry of extending the prerogative of the crown," Adair warns, "will never do in America" (438).

There is nothing startling about this argument on its face; it rehearses much of the rhetoric circulating in the colonies in 1775. But it is a strange conclusion to a text almost entirely focused on proving a thesis with potentially far-reaching religious as well as civil consequences. Perhaps Adair deemed the debunking of polygenesis a complete project, or he may have thought the Hebraic Indian theory's consequences were self-evident. There is no way to know for sure. What is certain, though, is that the *History* became one of the most important proof texts for later proponents of the Hebraic Indian theory, because it offered a great deal of empirical evidence for its claims but drew no grand conclusions. Although its assertions about Britain and her North American colonies became obsolete on the heels of its 1775 publication, Adair's *History* moved into the nineteenth century as a text capable of proving a wide range of conjectures not only about the Americas' past but also, and more importantly, about their future.

A Land Shadowing with Wings: Adair's *History* and the Many Gatherings of Israel

Despite its relative silence on theological issues, Adair's *History* is without doubt a Protestant document. This is most evident in its unabashed anti-Catholicism, as Adair's ire toward French and Spanish colonists extends well beyond pragmatic nationalism. Adair rails against "the infernal French catechism," parodying its format: "Who killed Christ? Answer, The bloody English" (129). More significantly, his antipathy toward Catholics translates into disbelief of Spanish accounts of Mesoamerican cultures and a rejection of narratives countering his belief in the continent's uniform origin. Spanish depictions of cannibalism in Aztec society were especially troubling to Adair, who claims that there "is not the least trace among their ancient traditions, of their deserving the hateful name of cannibals, as our credulous writers have carefully copied from each other" (173). Adair's insistence on the absence of cannibalism in the Americas is a marvelous rhetorical feat. He first notes that American peoples' "taste is so opposite to that of the Anthropophagi, that they always over-dress their meat, whether roasted or boiled," suggesting that insufficient seasoning is a hallmark of cannibalism. But in the following paragraph, Adair notes that he has heard from some Muskogee Indians who had wartime contact with "the Indians of Cape-Florida" that Muskogee prisoners of war "could never be informed by their captives [the Indians of Cape-Florida], of the least inclination they ever had of eating human flesh, only the heart of the enemy—which they all do, sympathetically (blood for blood) in order to inspire them with courage" (173).

My aim here is not to assess cannibalism in the Americas, a complex topic in its own right, but rather to show that Adair uses Catholicism as an irrational counterpoint to his Protestant empiricism. Responding, for instance, to a Native legend that itself suggests polygenesis, Adair writes that the "story sprung from the innovating superstitious ignorance of the popish priests, to the south-west of us" (221). When French and Spanish accounts line up with his conclusions, Adair tacitly accepts them; when they do not, he treats their sources' Catholicism as easy proof of their falsehood. Although the *History* by and large eschews direct engagement with theological or doctrinal particulars, it positions itself quite clearly within a Protestant paradigm.

Adair's commitment to situating the Americas within sacred history and his rejection of Catholicism made him a useful source for evangelical Protestants with a stake in the Hebraic Indian theory. Typical of this kind of engagement with Adair is Ethan Smith's *View of the Hebrews*, which was published in two editions—1823 and 1825—by the printing firm Smith & Shute, the proprietor of which was Ethan's son, Stephen Sanford Smith. Adair is a primary source for Ethan Smith, who cites him throughout his treatise on the lost tribes theory.

Smith was a Congregationalist minister who served in several churches in New England and upstate New York over the course of his career. From 1821 to 1826, during the period in which he wrote and published *View of the Hebrews*, he was pastor of the Congregational church in Poultney, Vermont. His residence in Poultney overlapped with that of Oliver Cowdery, who traveled to western New York just a few years after the publication of *View of the Hebrews* and served as a scribe for Joseph Smith Jr. as he produced *The Book of Mormon*—perhaps the most famous text to present biblical origins for indigenous American peoples. (Joseph Smith and Ethan Smith were not related.) Cowdery was the first baptized member of what would become the Church of Jesus Christ of Latter-day Saints, and he was one of that church's most important early members. The possibility that he was acquainted with Ethan Smith has generated much controversy in studies of *The Book of Mormon*. Some argue that Cowdery must have read *View of the Hebrews* and shared its contents with Joseph Smith, laying the groundwork for the latter's development of *The Book of Mormon*'s Hebraic Indian plotlines.[16] Others contend that it is unlikely Cowdery ever interacted with Ethan Smith—indeed, to date no archival evidence has surfaced to link them directly—and highlight the numerous differences in style and content between *View of the Hebrews* and *The Book of Mormon*.[17]

This book's fourth chapter discusses *The Book of Mormon*'s relationship to the Hebraic Indian theory in great detail, though it does not take a position on whether Joseph Smith was acquainted with Ethan

Smith's version of the theory. The temporal and geographic proximity of these two books, if nothing else, highlights the flurry of interest in Native American genealogy that was operant in the 1810s and 1820s. This chapter is concerned with how Ethan Smith combined his Christian millennialism with Adair's empirical observations to make a case for American Hebraism.

View of the Hebrews opens with a rather complex accounting of its own project. "Few historical events have been of such interest to the world, as the destruction of Jerusalem by the Romans, about forty years after the ascension of our blessed Lord," Smith writes in his preface, "But when it is admitted that the event was a striking fulfilment of denunciations of wrath uttered by Christ on his persecutors, and by ancient prophets on the same people; also that it furnished a most brilliant type of the final destruction of the Antichrist in the last days; it becomes far more interesting."[18] Here, Smith positions the destruction of the Second Temple—destroyed in 70 CE by the Romans during the Siege of Jerusalem—as an event simultaneously occupying several temporal planes. It exists in a fixed historical time, to be sure: "about forty years" following the death of Jesus. It also, however, reaches into the past to evoke biblical prophesies and points toward to an unrealized future by serving as "a most brilliant type of the final destruction of the Antichrist."

Smith's aim with this anecdote is twofold. On the one hand, it situates his argument within an eschatological theory of time, in which all events drive toward a predetermined end. On the other, it establishes a framework through which Christian readers may situate their present with a sacred timeline and recognize the imminence of that end. Interest in the Second Temple's destruction "must be felt at this period," Smith asserts, "when the great events of the last days connected with the restoration of the Hebrews, are in a train of incipient fulfilment. The signs of the times are important on this generation" (iii). From its opening lines, *View of the Hebrews* lays out the urgency of its own project: the world as we know it is ending, and all Christians must prepare for "the battle of that great day of God Almighty," which will produce "the millennial kingdom of Christ" (iii). The Second Temple is long gone, but the echo of its destruction reverberates into the present.

The destruction of the Second Temple and its connection to the "last days" is of the utmost significance to Smith's articulation of the Hebraic

Indian theory, because, in his accounting of it, "The restoration of God's ancient people is to be as 'life from the dead' to the Gentile world" (iii). Like many Protestants of this and earlier periods (and, indeed, in some corners today), Smith accepts the notion that, as he puts it, "The Hebrews are to have a literal restoration" (67). By this, he means that both the world's known Jewish populations and the missing Kingdom of Israel will convert to Christianity in the end of days, when Jesus returns and lays claim to the earth. For this mass conversion to occur, though, there must first be a "gathering" of the descendants of Abraham, Isaac, and Jacob. For many Christians, the promise of this gathering can be found in biblical prophecies, particularly in Isaiah, which asserts, "And it shall come to pass in that day, that the Lord shall set his hand again the second time to recover the remnant of his people, which shall be left, from Assyria, and from Egypt, and from Pathros, and from Cush, and from Elam, and from Shinar, and from Hamath, and from the islands of the sea. And he shall set up an ensign for the nations, and shall assemble the outcasts of Israel, and gather together the dispersed of Judah from the four corners of the earth" (Isaiah 11:11). In some Christian traditions (and especially within millennialist Protestant traditions), the "that day" referenced in Isaiah is the inauguration of the end of human history, and the assembly of Israel described is a "literal restoration" of the lost tribes to the rest of the world. The upshot of Smith's exegesis is that the end has begun, and thus the return of "the outcasts of Israel" must be imminent. A good Christian should be able to read these "signs of the times" and recognize them as "a train of incipient fulfilment." For Smith, this means recognizing the veracity of the Hebraic Indian theory and the mass conversion that must follow on the heels of such recognition.

Throughout *View of the Hebrews* Smith makes clear his indebtedness to Adair and justifies that indebtedness by positioning Adair as a credible source. "Mr. Adair was a man of established character, as appears from good authority," Smith writes. "He lived as a trader among the Indians, in the south of North America, for forty years" (82). The "good authority" on which Smith bases his estimation of Adair, it turns out, is Elias Boudinot, whose 1816 work on the Hebraic Indian theory, *A Star in the West*, clearly inspired Smith's own text. I discuss Boudinot's work at length in the following chapter of this book, and so will not rehearse his arguments here, but it is important to note that his assertions regarding

Adair's good character held weight for later writers who used the *History* in their own expositions of the Hebraic Indian theory. Smith is particularly invested in demonstrating Adair's use value for his text, because, he says, "the evidence given by Mr. Adair seems in some respects the most momentous and conclusive" (83). Thus Smith writes, "I shall adduce a testimonial on his behalf" (83).

What follows is a lengthy citation of *A Star in the West,* which describes Boudinot's efforts to ascertain Adair's trustworthiness as a reporter. "That venerable man [Boudinot]," Smith tells us, "says . . . Mr. Adair . . . brought ample recommendations, and gave a good account of himself" (83). Boudinot's satisfaction with Adair's account is enough for Smith himself, and it should be enough for his readers. "The character of Mr. Boudinot (who was for some time President of the American Bible Society,) is well known," Smith writes. "He was satisfied with the truth of Mr. Adair's history, and that the natives of our land are the Hebrews, the ten tribes" (84). Adair's *History* does not merely provide evidence for the Hebraic Indian theory; it offers "the most momentous and conclusive" evidence. And it is all the more conclusive, Smith contends, because Adair's character is beyond reproach. A reliable source with forty years of observations to offer, Adair is the ethnographer who will solve a biblical riddle.

Having established Adair as a reliable source, Smith moves through a series of "proofs" of American Hebraism, mainly relying on the cultural similarities Adair identifies in his *History.* Throughout *View of the Hebrews,* Adair's evidence is presented at face value and as if the sole conclusion one could draw from it is that Native Americans are the lost tribes of Israel. In a section entitled "*Their language appears clearly to have been Hebrew,*" for example, Smith notes that "Mr. Adair is confident of the fact, that their language is Hebrew" (88, italics original). Another section claiming that "the Indians have had their imitation of the ark of the covenant in ancient Israel" asserts that "Mr. Adair is full in his account of it. It is a small, square box, made convenient to carry on the back" (93).

On the question of Native American religious practices, Smith writes, "Mr. Adair . . . assures that 'none of the numerous tribes and nations . . . have ever been known to attempt the formation of any image of God'" and that "Mr. Adair is very full in this, that the Indians have but one

God, the Great Yohewah" (95–96). In addition to their ostensible mono-theism, Smith writes, indigenous Americans share with Jewish people a sense of divine favor: "The Indians thus please themselves (Mr. Adair assures us) with the idea that God has chosen them from the rest of mankind as a peculiar people" (97). Smith also notes that "Mr. Adair describes the Indian feasts, and speaks of them as bearing a very near resemblance of the stated feasts in ancient Israel," and that "their reckon-ings of time, Mr. Adair viewed as evidently Hebrew" (115). Smith's aim throughout *View of the Hebrews* is to convince readers that the gathering of Israel is nigh. His evidence for its proximity, though, is secular as well as biblical—ethnographic as well as exegetic. Biblical prophecy may set the stage for Smith's millennialist views, but Adair's empirical observa-tions become the "signs of the times" that all Christians must learn to read.

Adair's *History* is threaded throughout Smith's text, and it is not this chapter's purpose to catalog every citation of his work. It is, however, notable that Adair appears as the most compelling source of "secular" evidence for the religious claims laid out in *View of the Hebrews*. In an appendix iterating both his own main points and the major claims of Adair's *History*, Smith again notes, "The most important evidence in relation to the Indians being the descendants of Israel, the reader will perceive, is James Adair, Esqr." (173). "Recollect," Smith writes, "he had lived among them as an intelligent trader, 40 years.—That his charac-ter was well established; and his accounts well authenticated by collat-eral evidence, by a gentleman, member of congress, who had resided a number of years as an agent of our government among those Indians where Mr. Adair resided. Dr. Boudinot assures us that he examined this congress member, without letting him know his design; and that from him he found all the leading facts mentioned in Mr. Adair's history fully confirmed his own personal knowledge" (173).

Smith already has provided all this information in the main body of his text. He even cites himself in this moment, directing readers to "see page 83rd of this book" at the end of his reiteration of Adair's trustwor-thiness (173). Smith also has incorporated the bulk of Adair's evidentiary points into his own proofs throughout *View of the Hebrews*. Nonethe-less, following this restatement of Adair's credentials—that his work is backed up by "40 years" of personal experience as well as the testimonies of good men—Smith devotes six pages of his appendix to summarizing Adair's *History*. It is almost as if Smith imagined *View of the Hebrews* as having two kinds of readers: one who would read the body of the text but not the appendix, and one who would read the appendix exclusively. In either case, though, a reader would encounter Adair as the work's most convincing source of information about Native Americans and their ostensible link to Israel.

Where Adair stopped short of drawing religious significance from his evidence, Smith identifies not only general "signs of the times" in the *History* but also a specific message for Christians in the United States. Much of *View of the Hebrews* is devoted to analysis of what he calls "an interesting address . . . in the 18th chapter of Isaiah to some people of the last days; calling them to have a special agency in the recovery and restoration of the ancient people of God" (131). Smith asserts that there was a time when he believed the address to be "to the people of God in Great Britain" but goes on to say, "I have since become of a different opinion; and now apprehend it to be an address to the Christian people of the United States of America" (131).

Smith's interpretation of this portion of Isaiah rests in part on a translation of that book produced by the Anglican Bishop Robert Lowth in 1778 and later revised by the Anglican theologian George Stanley Faber. Although the first verse of Isaiah 18 appears in many English versions of the Bible, including the King James version, as "woe to the land shadowing with wings," Lowth's translation changes "Woe" to "Ho!" and thus transforms a warning into a hail.[19] "Our translators render this address, 'Wo to the land,'" Smith notes, but quickly asserts, "This is manifestly incorrect, as the best expositors agree . . . the whole connexion and sense decide, that the word here is a friendly call" (138). That call, he asserts, is for assistance with the restoration of the Israelites. Rendered as "friendly" rather than chastising, Isaiah "lands the prophetic vision at the point of the western continent," Smith claims, "where the two great wings of North and South America meet, as at the body of a great Eagle" (138). But the call is not merely hemispheric; it is more targeted than that. "And those two great wings shall prove but an emblem of a great nation then on that continent," Smith writes, "far sequestered from the seat of antichrist, and of tyranny and blood; and whose asylum for equal rights, liberty, and religion, shall be well represented by such a national coat of arms,—the protecting wings of a great Eagle" (138). Adair could not have read Lowth before writing his *History*, and neither could he have known that the United States, a nation that did not exist when he produced his text, would take the eagle as its emblem. His evidence, though, points to a divine destiny for that nation. To see the Hebraic origins of America, Smith contends, is to discover in the Bible not simply America but more specifically the United States.

It is imperative that American Christians realize that they live among the lost tribes, Smith concludes, because only then will they achieve their grand destiny. "If it be a fact, as is apprehended," he writes, "that the aborigines of our continent are indeed descended from the ten tribes of Israel; our nation, no doubt, must be the people addressed to restore them; to bring them to the knowledge of the gospel, and to do with them whatever the God of Abraham designs shall be done" (132). It is not enough to recognize the veracity of the Hebraic Indian theory; that recognition is the "friendly call" that should inspire action.

There was debate among Christian proponents of the Hebraic Indian theory about what form such action should take, and the following chapter examines the work of two Christians whose views differed from Smith's on that question—Boudinot and William Apess. In Smith's case, the notion that the "address of Heaven must be to our western continent" makes the role of American Christians at the end of days crystal clear. "Ye friends of God in the land addressed," he asks, "can you read this prophetic direction of the ancient prophet Isaiah, without having your hearts burn within you?" (146). His answer is swift: "Surely you cannot" (146). Those Christians whose hearts burn with the knowledge of American Hebraism must restore Israel by working to convert both Jewish and indigenous peoples to Christianity. "By prayer, contributions, and your influence," he concludes, "be prepared to aid every attempt for the conversion of the Jews and Israel. . . . Look at the origin of those degraded natives of your continent, and fly to their relief.—Send them the heralds of salvation. Send them the word, the bread of life. You received that book from the seed of Abraham. Restore it to them" (148–51). Convinced by Adair's evidence, Smith lays out a case for reading the Americas into Isaiah and for the systematic conversion of Native Americans to Christianity.

For Christians such as Smith, Adair's evidence of a Hebraic American origin produces a singular set of conclusions: the second coming of

Christ is imminent; indigenous peoples will be included in the literal restoration of Israel; and the United States will play a central role in the fulfillment of biblical prophecy. Secular reasoning, in other words, has sacred implications. But Adair's *History* was not used exclusively by Christian writers. In leaving unanswered the question of what his observations meant, Adair created the possibility for other appropriations of his text. Much as his work fit into certain fundamentalist Christian understandings of sacred time, it also created space for thinking about the history and potential futures of global Judaism. Thus Adair also caught the eye of Manuel Mordecai Noah, the most prominent Jewish figure in the antebellum United States.

Studies of Noah have tended, with good reason, to focus on his extraordinary achievements and equally extraordinary failures. In addition to serving as US ambassador to Tunis—and negotiating the release of enslaved American sailors while occupying that position—Noah was a celebrated playwright and travel writer, a sheriff, a judge, and an occasional participant in duels. Today, Noah is most commonly remembered for his effort to establish a Hebrew "city of refuge" on Grand Isle, near Buffalo, New York. As has been well documented, Noah named the city "Ararat" (after himself) and presided over a spectacular inauguration ceremony in Buffalo on September 15, 1825. Dressed in a borrowed costume from a Shakespeare production, and accompanied by a band playing the march from Handel's *Judas Maccabeas*, Noah declared himself a "judge of Israel" and led a procession through the city to its Episcopal church, where Ararat's cornerstone was positioned on the communion table. Noah then read a "Proclamation to the Jews," declaring that the city would serve as a home for the world's Jewish populations, governed by Hebrew law but protected by the US Constitution. The city never materialized beyond that cornerstone, but throughout his career Noah promoted the idea of a Jewish homeland—both within and beyond the United States. The small body of scholarship on Noah has illuminated the myriad reasons for the failure of Ararat, as well as Noah's own vexed position as a Jewish patriot.[20] My aim here is more modest, as I will focus on Noah's use of Adair's *History*, a book that lent itself as easily to Jewish state planning as to Christian plans for the end of all nations.

Noah's proclamation at the founding of Ararat includes an invitation for the world's Jewish population to emigrate to his new city. "The Jews have been destined by Providence to remain a distinct people," he asserts. "Though scattered over the face of the globe they still retain their homogenousness of character—the peculiarity of their tenants, the identity of their faith."[21] Laying out a plan for this deliberate gathering of Israel, Noah proposes the "establishment of emigration societies throughout Europe" and declares that "passages in all cases should be taken for New York" (*Writings*, 123). But there is, of course, one population that will not require assistance in relocating—the indigenous peoples of the western hemisphere. "The discovery of the lost tribes of Israel, has never ceased to be a subject of deep interest to the Jews," he writes, "and if, as I have reason to believe, our lost brethren were the ancestors of the Indians of the American Continent, the inscrutable decrees of the Almighty have been fulfilled in spreading unity and omnipotence in every quarter of the globe" (*Writings*, 122). A central feature of Ararat's mission, then, will be the reconversion of these "Jewish" populations and a welcoming of them into the city of refuge. "If the tribes could be brought together, could be made sensible of their origins, could be civilized, and restored to their long lost brethren," Noah exclaims, "what joy to our people, what glory to our God, how clearly have the prophecies been fulfilled, how certain our dispersion, how miraculous our preservation, how providential our deliverance" (*Writings*, 123). In the Hebraic Indian, Noah finds proof not of an impending Christian millennium but of an enduring covenant. "It shall be my duty to pursue the subject by every means in my power," Noah says. To awaken indigenous America from its religious slumber, for Noah, is to deliver Jewish people at long last from the burden of history. In establishing Ararat, Noah created a site on which the prophecies of Jewish reunion could be fulfilled, but the success of his mission rested as much on the revelation of the lost tribes in America as it did on the enthusiasm of potential Jewish transplants from Europe.

Noah's proclamation offers a comprehensive list of his reasons for accepting the Hebraic Indian theory. It reads like a thumbnail sketch of Adair: "The Indians worship one Supreme being . . . Like the Israelites of old, they are divided into tribes . . . They consider themselves as the select and beloved people of God . . . Their words are sonorous and bold, and their language and dialect are evidently of Hebrew origin. They compute time after the manner of the Israelites . . . They have their prophets, high priests, and their sanctum sanctorum . . . They have their towns and cities of refuge" (*Writings*, 122). Although Noah does not directly reference Adair in this piece, he makes his reliance on the *History* expressly clear in later writings. In his *Discourse on the Evidences that the American Indians Being the Descendants of the Lost Tribes of Israel*, first published in 1837, Noah describes Adair as one "in whom I repose great confidence, and who resided forty years among" indigenous peoples.[22] For Noah, as for Smith, Adair's lengthy experience and observational prowess—rather than his superior religious knowledge—lend credence to his work. Noah even admits that Adair and other proponents of the theory know very little about Judaism. "All the missionaries and travelers among the Indian tribes since the discovery of America—Adair, Heckwelder, Charliveux . . . have expressed opinions in favour of their being of Jewish origin," he explains in the *Discourse*. "The difficulty, however, under which they all laboured was simply this; they were familiar with the religious rites, ceremonies, traditions and belief of the Indians, but they were not sufficiently conversant with the Jewish rites and ceremonies, to show the analogy. It is precisely this link in the chain of evidence that I propose to supply" (*Discourse*, 9). Adair's weakness lies in his lack of experience with Jewish customs. Positioning himself as the necessary "link in the chain of evidence," Noah makes the case that a better understanding of Judaism will support rather than undermine Adair's claims.

Despite his correct assertion that Adair knew little about Jewish people and Jewish practice, a fact Adair himself would not have disputed, Noah ultimately concludes that the *History*'s main contention is correct. His own "proofs" often draw directly from Adair's work. To give just one example of several in the text, Noah fully accepts Adair's account of indigenous languages. He notes that Adair "says, these Indians pay their devoir to Lo-ak (Light) Ish-ta-hoola-aba, distinctly Hebrew, which means the great supreme beneficent holy Spirit of Fire who resides above . . . but they have another appellative, which with them as with us, is the mysterious essential name of God, which they never mention in common speech" (*Discourse*, 10–11). Here, Adair's reasoning melds with Noah's, as the former's argument about Hebrew slides into the latter's observation regarding the prohibition against speaking the sacred name of the divine.

Noah does not seem to notice weaknesses at play in Adair's analyses of Native languages, nor does he seize on Adair's admittedly thin understanding of Hebrew. For the purposes of the *Discourse*, Adair's experience and logic are sound enough. But this is the case because Noah's own sense of the march of history depends on Adair's claims being correct. His presentation of cultural overlap—"with them as with us"—simultaneously asserts distinction and similarity. Noah's Hebraic Indians are like Jewish people because, he claims, they are Jewish people, but centuries of isolation have divided them from their brethren. Following from Adair's deductions, Noah asserts the necessity of effacing that divide. "If the Indians of America are not the descendants of the missing tribes," he asks, "from whom are they descended?" (*Discourse*, 33). His answer is that no other possibility makes enough sense. "The Indians have distinct Jewish features," he concludes. "I have endeavored to show this by their traditions, by their religion, by their ceremonies, which retain so much of the ancient worship" (*Discourse*, 33). Positioning himself as an expert, by virtue of experience, on Jewish rather than indigenous customs, Noah aligns himself with Adair to make the case for American Hebraism.

Building out from Adair's argument, Noah, like Smith before him, reinterprets prophecies regarding the tribes through the lens of the Hebraic Indian. In his *Discourse on the Restoration of the Jews*, which he delivered as an address in 1844 and then published in 1845, Noah makes the case for Christian assistance in the formation of a free and independent Jewish nation (he was at this point mainly interested in purchasing a portion of Syria for colonization). Also like Smith, he seizes upon Isaiah. "Has it ever occurred to you, my friends," he asks, "that the eighteenth chapter of Isaiah might possibly be a reference to America in connexion with the restoration of the Jews? Indulge me a moment in examining that short but singular chapter. 'Ho to the land' (it is translated wo, but evidently erroneously: it is Ho, or Hail)—'Hail to the land, shadowing with wings, which is beyond the rivers of Ethiopia'" (*Writings*, 143). Noah, it seems, was reading the same Lowth translation as Smith. "The arms of no country are so emphatically 'wings' as those of the United States," he asserts. "It is an eagle in the act of flying with outspread wings, peculiarly conspicuous as an armorial ensign and living description of our land, which, under the shadow of her wings, offers a shelter for the persecuted of all nations" (*Writings*, 143).

This is a lovely thought, and its similarity to Smith's view is uncanny. In Noah's work, though, this passage has little to do with Native Americans; it is prophecy about the nation's ideal relationship with the world's actual Jewish populations. "I am right in this interpretation," Noah insists. "What a glorious privilege is reserved for the free people of the United States . . . selected and pointedly distinguished in prophecy as the nation which, at a proper time, shall present the Lord his chosen and trodden-down people, and pave the way for their restoration to Zion" (*Writings*, 144–45). The revelation of the lost tribes in the Americas, then, does not prompt Noah to consider the US federal government's relationships with Native nations. Rather, it becomes the pressing occasion for the formation of a Jewish state—either within US borders or, failing that, in Palestine—assisted by the chosen, magnanimous, eagle-winged United States. Indigenous American populations fall within the scope of Noah's plans as stateless Jewish people rather than discrete nations with legitimate claims of sovereignty. Federal policy toward Native Americans will be rendered moot, as sacred history overrides profane concerns. "There is no fanaticism in it," Noah writes of his colonization plan. "It is easy, tranquil, natural, and gradual" (*Writings*, 145). In language reminiscent of romantic renderings of Indian Removal, Noah presents the gathering of Israel, with its requisite effacement of ethnic particularities, as a seamless process that will commence as soon as the United States recognizes its sacred destiny.

Read with Caution: Adair and the Limits of Observation

That Adair was an invaluable source for proponents of the Hebraic Indian theory is undeniable, but it would be disingenuous to pretend that the *History* made it through the nineteenth century without generating controversy. As early as 1812, Thomas Jefferson referred to Adair's notions as a "kink," and warned John Adams that the *History* "contains a great deal of real instruction . . . only requiring the reader to be constantly on his guard against the wonderful obliquities of his theory" (qtd. in Braund, 43). In 1859 John Henry Logan—a physician and educator who would become a surgeon for the Confederate army—published

A History of the Upper Country of South Carolina, which includes an entire chapter about Adair. Logan praises Adair's "valuable and now rare book," describing it as the source from which "the world has derived most that is known of the manners and customs of the Southern Indians."[23] He attributes the value of the *History* to the fact that Adair "was for forty years, a trader among the Cherokees and Chickasaws . . . and displays in his writings much good sense, and rare powers of observation" (1:345). But if Adair's method lends credence to the *History*, its conclusion gives Logan pause. "It is to be regretted, however," he writes, "that an observer so intelligent, and so admirably situated for obtaining the minutest information, in a field becoming every day more and more interesting, should have collected and used it mainly to illustrate the single idea which Adair appears to have fondly cherished, that the Indians of America were descended from the ancient Israelites" (1:346). For Logan, the content of Adair's "single idea" is not the problem. Rather, the presence of any "single idea" within an empirical text is an affront to the scholarly endeavor. "His arguments in proof . . . are exceedingly plausible and well arranged," Logan explains, "but the value of the history would have been greatly enhanced if [Adair] had presented his facts free from the bias and prejudices of any pre-conceived notion" (1:346–47).

It is impossible not to read Logan's charge against Adair without a tinge of irony, given the fact that the former's own study deems the Atlantic slave trade the work of divine providence. Still, it is worth noting that readers often recognized the *History*'s out-of-order deductive mode and found its backfilling of "proof" in service of a predetermined outcome empirically suspect. The anthropologist Livingston Farrand's *Basis of American History, 1500–1900* (1904), for example, cites Adair's book but describes it as "marred by certain absurd general theories" and notes that it "should be read with caution."[24] For these writers, the *History* operates as an important proof text not for the Hebraic Indian theory but for the perils of history writing itself.

The problem of how to read Adair, how to reconcile his meticulous ethnography with his ardent belief in American Hebraism, has persisted into current reckonings with the *History*. In her edition of Adair's *History*, Braund makes the case that Adair's work retains much value, not only because it remains one of the best primary source documents for information regarding the region's cultures but also because "Adair's framework . . . can be viewed as a strength" (45). Drawing on the anthropologist Charles Hudson's claim that "Adair's Hebrew theory helped him understand the culture and society of the Indians more than it hindered him," Braund suggests that the search for "parallels between Hebrew and Indian culture . . . led him to record careful and detailed information about Indian societies" (46). Thus the *History* persists as a source for the scholar of American history not despite but because of its faulty line of reasoning.

This is a compelling possibility, and I agree with Braund that the inaccuracy of Adair's theory does not diminish the significance of his study. But the *History* is not simply important for what it can teach us about eighteenth-century Native American customs and histories. Adair's work reveals much about the porous boundary between what we imagine to be secular reasoning and the religious concerns that often invisibly structure the terms of that reasoning. Adair was looking for something very specific, it is true, and so he looked in such a way as to find it. His *History*, in turn, provided empirical proofs for those who followed him, looking in their own ways for the truth of their own beliefs. In its own writing as well as its afterlives, the *History* reminds us that the question, "Where did Americans come from?" never has been a secular question, and neither has it ever merely been a question about the past. It reminds us, too, that a gulf separates observation and interpretation—and the bridge spanning that gulf might be constructed, without the observer's realizing it, out of theology.

3

Elias Boudinot, William Apess, and the Accidents of History

The conclusion of William Apess's autobiography, *A Son of the Forest*, is not, it turns out, a conclusion at all. "Believing," Apess writes, "that some general observations on the origin and character of the Indians, as a nation, would be acceptable to the numerous and highly respectable persons who have lent their patronage to this work, the subscriber has somewhat abridged 'his life' to make room for this Appendix."[1] What follows is a document nearly as long as the narrative itself. In fact, when revising the 1829 version of the text, Apess cut sections from his life story, "which some persons deemed objectionable" (mainly his critique of the Methodist Episcopal Church), and added about seven pages of new material to the appendix (3). As a result, in the 1831 edition of the book, Apess's memoir outnumbers his appendix by a mere four pages. By his own account, in both editions the near equivalence of the narrative and appendix is a product of design: Apess "somewhat abridged" the former to "make room for" the latter. The appendix thus appears more primary than subsidiary in his text, operating within *A Son of the Forest* as the broader history to which he has deliberately yielded some of his life story.

Apess's appendix promises a macro-history of indigenous America. But readers expecting information about specific Native American nations or their histories quickly learn that the "origin" to which he refers is singular and sacred. Drawn largely from Elias Boudinot's 1816 book *A Star in the West*, which Apess rearranges and cites at length (often without attribution), the appended text contends that the western hemisphere's first inhabitants were "none other than the descendants of Jacob, and the long lost tribes of Israel" (53). In this way, although the appendix presents itself as addressing a gap in the story of Apess's life, it produces a sense of incompleteness in two different ways. First, it does not provide much in the way of context for understanding Apess himself, or the history of the Pequot people, or even nineteenth-century Native peoples in North America. Second, it reminds readers of the longstanding absence of the lost tribes from history. The tribes have been missing from sacred and profane records for nearly three millennia, and the numerous documents positing their existence in the Americas have failed to result in anything approaching wide-scale cultural change or millennial apocalypse. By the time Apess wrote *A Son of the Forest*, the Hebraic Indian theory was over two hundred years old, and it had fulfilled none of its promises. And yet, this is the history of Native America that Apess appends to his narrative, a history of the absence of history—the history of a revelation that has not been revealed.

Apess's decision to cite Boudinot heavily makes a great deal of practical sense: *A Star in the West* was one of the most thorough, recent treatises on the Hebraic Indian available when Apess was composing his memoir, and Boudinot had been more sympathetic to the plight of Native Americans than many of his white contemporaries. As Meghan Howey notes, unlike earlier expositions of the theory, *A Star in the West* offers the Hebraic Indian as proof not only of a divine plan for the Americas but also of the innate and eternal goodness of indigenous populations. In Boudinot's view, the "Jewishness" of American peoples, however latent, is proof that they are a chosen people. Thus he uses the Hebraic Indian theory to argue for the reform of US policies toward Native nations. Most significant for my purposes, though, is Boudinot's specific configuration of providential history in *A Star in the West*.

This chapter's first section explores how Boudinot's exposition of the Hebraic Indian theory centers on a notion of providential history contingent upon inadvertence.[2] Presenting his "discovery" of the lost tribes of Israel as the product of an accident, Boudinot situates his argument for the Hebraic Indian theory within a theological tradition holding that the truth of divine intent could be found in the space of human error. Within the historical frame constructed by *A Star in the West*, the accident becomes, in retrospect, proof of godly design. Although Boudinot's work begins by articulating the consequences of a single, small mistake, it ultimately is concerned with the larger "accidents" of colonial history. Configuring white imperialism and the United States' commitment to Indian removal as the terrible consequences of faulty interpretation, Boudinot urges readers to see the signs of sacred time erupting into the present, recognize divine interest in indigenous Americans, and adjust US policies accordingly. Through Boudinot's accident, in other words, *A Star in the West* synchs the timelines of sacred and profane history, setting whites and Native Americans alike on a shared path to glory.

Indebted as it may be to *A Star in the West*, *A Son of the Forest* offers a very different picture of providential history, and this chapter's second half explores how Apess's appropriation of Boudinot's work effects a significant revision of *A Star in the West*'s main claims. Although lost tribes mythology pervades Apess's writings, it has until recently attracted relatively little critical attention. This is perhaps the case because it can be read as a capitulation to white discourses that degrade Native American cultures. Indeed, in one of the few sustained inquiries into Apess's use of the Hebraic Indian theory, Sandra Gustafson notes that the "figure of the Hebraic Indian participates in an important sense in a discourse of domination: it legitimates non-European, non-Christian societies in Judeo-Christian rather than autochthonous terms."[3] Apess's self-identification as a latent Israelite, therefore, has generated some critical ambivalence. In a recent study, Rochelle Zuck argues that "the rhetoric of the lost tribes operates as more than just an expression of Christian orthodoxy or a reaction to white narratives of American exceptionalism; it provides a means to challenge 'Vanishing Indian' narratives with stories of sovereignty and continuing presence."[4]

Frankly, I am sympathetic to both readings. On the one hand, Gustafson is correct: Apess uses Boudinot's caricature of Judaism—and its corresponding assumptions about the potential Christianity of Jewish peoples—to make the case for indigenous rights. On the other, as Zuck notes, a Hebraic Indian cannot vanish. But Apess's use of the theory need not be a zero-sum game, and Gustafson's and Zuck's approaches to his work are both essential to understanding his project. Here I would suggest that, in appending Boudinot's work to his text, Apess accepts the terms of the Hebraic Indian theory but disrupts the temporal logic essential to *A Star in the West*'s configuration of providential history. This temporal reorientation allows him to assert an indigenous identity that always has been Christian and Israelite yet never has been Jewish.

Repackaged by Apess, Boudinot's work becomes proof not of colonialism's essential function within providential history but instead of its irrelevance to Native American Christianity. Apess uses the Hebraic Indian to situate his own Christianity outside of European and US colonial practices—to reach back to an alternative historical source for his religious identity. The theory thus enables him to present Native American Christianity as occupying a timeline distinct from that of white Christianity and to reject the colonial teleology that threatened his existence as both a Native American and a Christian. It also allows him to distinguish his own Christian practice from both the organized Methodism with which he associated and the orthodox Presbyterianism to which Boudinot subscribed. Apess's reconfiguration of Boudinot's book into an appendix, in other words, is part of a broad project of atemporality in *A Son of the Forest*, one that enables the Pequot to lay claim to a primal Christianity by claiming to be a lost Israelite.

Quite Accidentally: Elias Boudinot's Providential Error

Scholars of the early United States have all but forgotten Elias Boudinot, but he was a central figure in the development of the nation's political and religious cultures. A major underwriter of the American Revolution, he served as president of the Continental Congress and, after the Revolution, first director of the US Mint. Boudinot was a patron of Alexander Hamilton and an advocate for the publication of James Adair's *History of the American Indians*. His fingerprints are all over early US politics, and his influence arguably grew when he left politics to establish the American Bible Society (ABS). Richard Popkin has suggested that Boudinot "passed into oblivion, probably because his religious views seemed out of keeping with the prevailing deism and liberal Christianity of his time."[5] Indeed, his evangelical Presbyterianism still challenges critical accounts that would downplay the role of orthodox Protestantism in early national politics. In discussing his work, I wish in part to recover this piece of the story of the early republic—a story of emergent Christian fundamentalism and of a politics directly shaped by millennialist concerns.

Boudinot was a literalist; he believed in a future, material fulfillment of biblical prophecies. A year before publishing *A Star in the West*, he produced *The Second Advent*, a lengthy meditation on what he deemed signs of an impending millennium unfolding before him in real time. Reading human history through the lens of biblical prophecy, Boudinot asserts that "God shall descend, and this earth be on fire; and the trumpet shall sound; and the tribes of mankind shall be assembled."[6] For Boudinot, the return of Christ is imminent, but it will not arrive in the absence of hard work. The "many and clear prophesies concerning the things to be done at Christ's second coming," he writes, "are not only for predicting, but also for effecting a recovery and reestablishment of this long lost truth and setting up a kingdom, wherein dwelleth righteousness."[7] Good Christians, in other words, do not merely await the end of time; they produce it. According to Boudinot, this entails "the preparation of the bride, or the conversion of the Jews."[8] The hope of the second advent lies in the effort to bring all peoples to Christ. The Hebraic Indian theory thus presented Boudinot with an enticing project for Christians in the United States. If Native Americans were in fact the lost tribes of Israel, then their conversion would ignite the fire of millennium.

A Star in the West, the last of Boudinot's book-length religious works, directly links his sense of the proximity of the second coming to the founding of the United States. The book not only contends that the Americas originally were populated by the Kingdom of Israel, but it also explicitly connects that point of origin to a notion of American exceptionalism that positions the nation as the engine of Christian eschatology. Within Boudinot's cosmology, "The restoration of this suffering and despised nation to their ancient city and their former standing in the favour of God . . . are [believed to be] expressly foretold . . . as immediately preceding the second coming of our Lord and Saviour Jesus Christ."[9] Discovering the location of the tribes is not an intellectual exercise; the fate of the world depends upon the veracity of his theories, and, according to those theories, the United States will play an integral role in the return of Christ.

The realization that the lost tribes inhabit the Americas, Boudinot explains, referring to himself in the third person, is "in his opinion of the utmost consequence to the present generation in particular, as that era in which the latter times, the last times of the scriptures, or the end of the Roman government, seem to be hastening with rapid strides" (27). American Christians, Boudinot fears, are running out of time to fulfill their destiny. "What could possible bring a greater declarative glory to God," he demands, "than a full discovery, that these wandering nations of Indians are the lost tribes of Israel[?]" (280). Such discovery is crucial, as is missionary work among Native peoples, because "thus wonderfully brought to the knowledge of their fellow men, [Native Americans] may be miraculously prepared for instruction, and stand ready, at the appointed time, when God shall raise the signal to the nations" (280). Here Boudinot imagines a kind of partnership between American Christians and the divine. The appointed time is near, but it will not arrive until the gathering of Israel commences. To set that gathering in motion is the sacred calling of those who finally realize they have been living among the lost tribes all along.

Despite the urgency of its topic, A Star in the West begins with an error. Describing his interest in locating the ten lost tribes of Israel, Boudinot explains that he has spent nearly forty years attempting to solve one of the Bible's most perplexing mysteries, because of a chance encounter with one of its most mysterious texts. Again referring to himself in the third person, Boudinot writes that "soon after, reading (quite accidentally) the 13th chapter of the 2d apocryphal book of Esdras . . . his ardour to know more of, and to seek further into the circumstances of these lost tribes, was in no wise diminished. He has not ceased since, to improve every opportunity afforded him" (28). That phrase, "quite accidentally," is offset by parentheses, the punctuation of simultaneous emphasis and erasure. Like a whisper, it cannot be ignored, though its manner of appearance invites ignoring. Indeed, Boudinot's assertion of accidental reading captivated some of his nineteenth-century critics. A reviewer for the 1818 edition of The Portico notes that Boudinot "attributes [his work] principally to an accidental reading," and expresses incredulity that "he who appears so orthodox, could consider the figurative language of the prophets, as literally implying such an event."[10] In a similar vein, an 1829 account of Israel Worsely's View of the American Indians, appearing in the Eclectic Review, unfavorably compares Worsely to Boudinot, noting that the latter "appears to have been greatly biased by accidentally stumbling upon this passage."[11]

Contemporary dismissal of Boudinot's text stemmed both from the outlandish nature of his thesis and the means by which he arrived at it. This is probably the case because his supposed accident seems quite improbable. While it might be possible to read a few biblical verses without exercising much agency, the imagination strains at the thought of someone involuntarily perusing an entire chapter with enough attention to use it as the basis for a theological treatise. Quite frankly, even if one were to begin reading 2 Esdras inadvertently, it is easy to stop reading it. Boudinot's "accident," in other words, seems no accident at all. And, in fact, his account of unintentional reading becomes, by *A Star in the West*'s conclusion, important proof of his claims. Through this moment of ostensible inadvertence, *A Star in the West* teaches its readers to view the American landscape with an eye for the error and to rethink the improbable as a marker of divine providence. Denying his own agency, Boudinot makes himself a vehicle of divine fiat, and his reading of 2 Esdras provides a blueprint for white American Christians to follow when considering the status and future of the nation's indigenous populations.

In presenting an accident as the initiating force behind his work, Boudinot situates *A Star in the West* within an epistemological tradition that deemed accidents crucial sources of information about the world and its relationship to the divine. The idea that accidental occurrences could be considered sources of knowledge emerged, Michael Witmore shows, in the early modern era and marked a significant revision of ancient notions of chance.[12] Where Aristotle had declared that "regarding the accidental, there can be no scientific treatment of it" (because accidental events, by their very nature, must be singular and thus resist classification), later thinkers influenced by Protestant theology, a developing scientific method, and even innovations in theatrical production came to view accidents as windows into a grand design.[13] As Witmore puts it, "Accidents transformed from an epistemological dead end into a source of knowledge in the early modern period, whether that knowledge was of God, nature, or the hidden plots of individuals."[14]

Witmore's work provides a detailed picture of the way shifts in theatrical conventions combined with notions of scientific experimentation to reconfigure the accident as site of discovery rather than confusion. Most relevant to my understanding of Boudinot, though, is Witmore's observation that within early Protestant traditions, "Calvin and others repeatedly point out the way in which a latent knowledge of God's providential presence is uncovered in encounters with accidents."[15] Indeed, Calvin asserts in his *Institutes of the Christian Religion* that "the Providence of God, as taught in Scripture, is opposed to fortune and fortuitous causes. By an erroneous opinion prevailing in all ages, an opinion almost universally prevailing in our own day—viz. that all things happen fortuitously, the true doctrine of Providence has not only been ob-scured, but almost buried."[16] Within this logic, accidents are significant precisely because they never are accidental. The accident shifts from an object that resists systemization to proof of the very existence of a grand system. This is the vein of thinking that undergirds Boudinot's presenta-tion of his reading of 2 Esdras. The accident does not threaten the order of *A Star in the West*'s argument; it authorizes it.

Given the gravity of his mission, it is both surprising and utterly sen-sible that Boudinot would turn, however inadvertently, to 2 Esdras. It is surprising because 2 Esdras is, as Boudinot admits, an apocryphal text. A group of books of contested theological value, the apocrypha occupy a vexed position within various Christian traditions. The Catholic Church treats some but not all of the books as scripture; some Protestants deem the texts historically significant though not sacred, while others reject them altogether. For most evangelical Protestants, the apocryphal books are *libris non grata*.

Despite their controversial position, the apocryphal books were printed in the 1611 King James Bible and appeared in some printings of that version of the text into the nineteenth century. They often were sandwiched between the Old and New Testaments or clustered together at the end of the book to indicate their dubious status. The British and Foreign Bible Society (BFBS), which was founded in 1804 and served as the blueprint for the ABS, produced bibles both with and without the apocrypha. Boudinot had access to bibles printed by the BFBS, and this might be how he encountered 2 Esdras (though he does not offer a specific explanation). For its own part, the ABS typically did not in-clude the apocrypha in its bibles. As Jeffrey Makala notes, soon after its formation, "The ABS received an offer from an Albany printer for 'a set of stereotype plates for an octavo edition of the Bible.' It contained 1,171 plates, including the Apocrypha . . . [T]he ABS concluded that the type size was too small and the Apocrypha not needed."[17] It did print at least one Spanish edition with those texts, mainly to appease Catholic officials who otherwise might have blocked the distribution of bibles in Latin America. In 1828, however, the ABS officially announced that it no longer would print bibles containing the apocryphal books.[18] Boudinot's admission that his interest in the tribes stems from a reading of 2 Esdras thus injects some controversy into *A Star in the West*. Rather than omit this detail, though, he frames his inquiry around the book and his accidental perusal of it.

Inclusion in the apocrypha makes 2 Esdras a dubious text to begin with, but even beyond that, it is a troublesome artifact. Narrated by the scribe Ezra (of the eponymous book of the Hebrew Bible) and dating itself to around 450 BCE, 2 Esdras actually was composed much later, and it is a composite of three different texts. The book's middle chapters were produced first, by an unknown Jewish writer at the close of the first century. They constitute a freestanding apocalypse in the form of a dream sequence experienced by Ezra and interpreted by an angel named Uriel. Christian writers added the introductory and concluding chapters perhaps a century later (no one knows precisely when). Scholars believe that the apocalypse—which includes the chapter Boudinot discusses— originally was written in either Hebrew or Aramaic, then translated into Greek, then translated from the Greek into Latin. Both the primary text and the Greek translation have been lost. The other chapters probably were composed in Greek, but those documents, too, no longer exist. The Geneva Bible was the first to offer the work as a singular composite in English, and most English bibles that include 2 Esdras have followed suit. The 2 Esdras Boudinot accidentally read, then, is a translation of a translation of a lost translation of lost originals—a fantastic simulacrum asserting false unity and impossible origins. This might explain why he professes to have read it accidentally. It is not the sort of text a serious Protestant would read on purpose in the antebellum United States.

Boudinot is aware of 2 Esdras's potential to unravel his argument. Anticipating critique by fellow Protestants, he writes, "This Jew [the author] seems to be a serious and devout writer, on a subject he appears to be acquainted with, and from his situation and connections, might be supposed to know something of the leading facts. And whether he wrote in a figurative style, or under the idea of similitudes, dreams or visions, he appears to intend the communication of events that he believed had happened, and as far as they are corroborated by subsequent facts, well attested, they ought to have their due weight in the scale of evidence" (72–73).

Trepidation about his source is evident in his diction: the author "appears to be acquainted" with the facts and "might be supposed" to be credible, despite the text's multifaceted weirdness. But though it might just seem like Boudinot is papering over his apocryphal dabbling, herein lies the core of *A Star in the West*'s logic: 2 Esdras is so beyond the pale of canonical scripture that no self-respecting Protestant could possibly take it seriously. And yet, in "accidentally" reading it, Boudinot has stumbled upon the key to unlocking the secrets of millennium—thus his accident becomes, in retrospect, proof of a divine hand at work in his discovery. No other text could serve this function. It would not be remarkable for a man in Boudinot's position to read Isaiah or Revelation. The significance of 2 Esdras lies precisely in its fraught status. Only the unintentional reading of a suspect text could make Boudinot so certain of his conclusions.

Despite its murky provenance and dubious status as scripture, 2 Esdras contains the most unambiguous prophecy regarding the lost tribes of Israel. Therefore, Boudinot's reading of it is as sensible as it is strange, and his accident turns out to be a happy one. The tribes appear late in the apocalypse portion of the text, when Ezra dreams of a man who descends from a mountain and calls out to a multitude of people. "And there came much people unto him," Ezra explains. "Some were glad, some were sorry, and some of them were bound, and other some brought of them that were offered" (2 Esdras 13:13). When Ezra asks Uriel to interpret the dream, the angel replies that the man in the vision is the son of God and that the multitude is "the ten tribes, which were carried away prisoners out of their own land in the time of Osea the king, whom Shalmaneser the king of Assyria led away captive" (2 Esdras 13:40). Uriel tells Ezra that the tribes "took this counsel among themselves, that they would leave the multitude of the heathen, and go forth into a further country, where never mankind dwelt. . . . Then dwelt they there until the latter time; and now when they shall begin to come, the Highest shall stay the springs of the stream again, that they may go through" (2 Esdras 13:41–47). Although some canonical books of the Bible, such as Isaiah, can be interpreted as predicting the return of the lost tribes, this account is unique because it mentions them by name and explicitly aligns them with impending millennium. In this way, 2 Esdras offers seekers of the tribes something no other text does: a clear assertion that the Kingdom of Israel still exists as a coherent nation on the globe, and that its return will coincide with that of Christ.

In addition to providing the most explicit prophecy regarding the eventual return of the tribes, 2 Esdras holds a special place for seekers because it names the tribes' location. Describing them as traveling "a year and a half," the book places the tribes in a land called "Arsareth" (2 Esdras 13:45). As Zvi Ben Dor Benite notes in his history of the lost tribes, "The word Arzareth, first coined in Esdras, became a ubiquitous code for the search for the tribes."[19] Though it is most likely a portmanteau of the Hebrew phrase *"eretz ahereth,"* meaning "another place," Arzareth morphs into a physical space in imaginings of the lost tribes—a land just beyond the known world, where the tribes are always on the verge of being discovered. It thus stands, Benite writes, as "a stunning example of place making at work."[20]

Where 2 Kings listed locations that could not be found on the globe, 2 Esdras provided a label that could be affixed to any as-yet-unexplored territory. Indeed, Arzareth appeared as a real place on some early European maps of the world, occupying space just beyond familiar regions. The German cartographer Sebastian Münster labeled it "Arsare" and "located it in the northeasternmost corner of Asia" in his 1544 *Cosmographia*.[21] The Flemish geographer Abraham Ortelius followed suit, labeling the same site "Arsareth" in his *Theatrum Orbis Terrarum* of 1570, one "of the most authoritative atlases, and certainly the most popular."[22] Appearing just inside the Arctic Circle, the Arzareth of these sixteenth-century maps was real in a material sense yet beyond the reach of ordinary Christians.

As exploration of the globe extended the boundaries of first European and then American geographical knowledge, the imaginative and physical space available for Arzareth shrank, and it became necessary for those seeking the tribes to reconfigure the landscape of 2 Esdras's prophecy. For Boudinot and other proponents of the Hebraic Indian theory, Arzareth remains a discrete territory but no longer exists beyond the boundary of Western colonialism. Overlaying Uriel's pronouncement that "the Highest shall stay the springs of the stream again, that they shall go through" onto nineteenth-century understandings of the globe, Boudinot concludes that the prophecy of 2 Esdras describes the migration of the tribes across a frozen Bering Strait, from northern Asia to the westernmost portion of North America. "The distance between the most northeastwardly part of Asia and the northwest coast of America," he writes, "is determined by the famous navigator capt. Cook, not to exceed thirty-nine miles" (118).[23] Asserting that the Bering Sea is "very shallow" in this region and "often filled with ice, even in summer and frozen in winter," Boudinot suggests that it "might become a safe passage for the most numerous host to pass over in safety" (118). Though perhaps not as spectacular as the parting of the Red Sea, the freezing of the Bering Sea serves as a plausible explanation for why the tribes have not been located in even the furthest reaches of the Asian continent and why they must, therefore, inhabit the American hemisphere. 2 Esdras provides Boudinot with something no other biblical text can: a description of how the tribes came to the Americas, and the explicit promise that their discovery will bring about a Christian new world order.

Having established his work as the effect of accidental reading, Boudinot lays out an argument in which nothing about the lost tribes is an accident. Much of his text is dedicated to outlining apparent similarities between Native American and ancient Hebrew cultures. Like other writers of the period, Boudinot draws much of his evidence from James Adair's 1775 book, *A History of the American Indians* (which is explored in detail in this book's second chapter), but he was well read on the subject of the Hebraic Indian and offers readers a veritable catalogue of cultural parallels drawn from several sources. In a section of *A Star in the West* devoted to Indian origin stories, which he interprets as refracted versions of Bible stories, Boudinot writes that "Father Charlevoix, the French historian, informs us that the Hurons and Iroquois . . . had a tradition among them that the first woman came from heaven and had twins, and that the elder killed the younger" (114). Similarly, he notes an account by "a Dutch minister" who wrote that a Mohawk woman informed him that "the great spirit once went out walking with his brother, and . . . a dispute arose between them, and the Great Spirit killed his brother" (114). Boudinot deems this "plainly a confusion of the story of Cain and Abel," attributing the differences between it and the original to "the ignorance of the minister in the idiom of the Indian language" (114).

Boudinot hears echoes of Genesis in every instance of indigenous mythology. Citing Sir Alexander MacKenzie, he notes that the Chipewyan "describe a deluge, when the waters spread over the whole earth, except the highest mountains, on the tops of which they preserved themselves" (112). Further proof of America's sacred origins lies in Charles Beatty's *Journal of a Two Months Tour in America*, which includes testimony by a "christian [sic] Indian" that "a long time ago, the people went to build a high place to reach up a great way; and that, while they were building it, they lost their language" (113). Of primary importance here, though, is the fact that Boudinot concludes this catalog of shared mythology by asking, "Can any man read this short account of Indian traditions, drawn from tribes of various nations . . . *and yet suppose that all this is either the effect of chance, accident, or design*, from a love of the marvelous or a premeditated intention of deceiving?" (116, italics mine). For the incredulous reader, in other words, only two options are available. Either all these good men independently have risked "ruining their own well-established reputations" for a shared flight of fancy, or all these instances of cultural overlap are meaningless coincidences. The former option is unthinkable, the latter impossible within the frame of providence.

For Boudinot, proof of America's Hebraic origins lies not only in accounts of indigenous history but also in observations of the indigenous present. In this, he is much like Adair, extrapolating American history from contemporary cultural practices. I do not wish to outline all of Boudinot's "proofs"—mainly because most of them are drawn directly from Adair—but it is worth mentioning a few. In a chapter devoted to American religious rites, for example, Boudinot ascribes indigenous aversion to idolatry, spiritual pride, and amenability to theocracy to latent Judaism. "Their religious ceremonies," he insists, "are more after the Mosaic institution, than of pagan imitation" (190). As further proof, he notes that "the Cherokees and Choctaws have some very humble representation of . . . cherubimical figures, in their places of worship, or beloved square," which he suggests is an imitation of the Hebrew tabernacle and mercy seat. And religion is not the exclusive location of Hebraism in American nations. In a chapter detailing the treatment of women in various nations, Boudinot repeats Adair's observation that "southern Indians oblige their women, in their lunar retreats, to build small huts at a considerable distance from their dwelling houses . . . where they are obliged to stay at the risque of their lives." This ritual is presented as proof of a kind of Jewishness, as "the conduct of the women seems perfectly agreeable . . . to the law of Moses" (277). As he did in his discussion of mythology, Boudinot argues that these similarities "form a coincidence of circumstances in important and peculiar establishments, *that could not, without a miracle, be occasioned by chance or accident*" (244, italics mine). The syntax here is telling: Boudinot asserts that only a miracle could produce the accident required for all these similarities to line up. But a miracle is never, by its very status as miracle, an accident. The only force that could produce such a marvelous instance of chance is a deliberate and divine will.

Perhaps the most convincing proof of the Hebraic Indian theory, in Boudinot's rendering of it, lies in the ostensible similarities between Hebrew and American languages. *A Star in the West* offers numerous examples of these similarities, including a chart containing English words, and then phonetic renderings of those words in three indigenous languages and Hebrew. Like Adair before him, Boudinot most clearly hears Hebrew in American religious rituals. "When they meet at night," he explains, "it is professed to be to gladden and unite their hearts before Y. O. He. wah. They sing Y. O. He. wah. Shoo. . . . The first word is nearly in the Hebrew characters, the name of Joshua or Saviour" (228). The echo of Genesis, then, is found not only in the content of Native speech but also in its very form, the phoneme operating as the trace of a forgotten past. Unlike Adair, though, Boudinot is quick to assign theological significance to his findings. "We say such a consideration will show an almost miraculous intervention of Divine Providence," he writes, "should a clear trace of the original language be discoverable among the natives of our wilderness" (97). The preservation of Hebrew in America can only be proof of holy design because, Boudinot asserts, languages are unstable markers of identity.

By the end of his study, Boudinot concludes that his notion of providence is accurate. "Is it possible," he asks, "that the languages of so many hundred nations of apparent savages, scattered over a territory some thousands of miles in extent, living excluded from all civilized society, without grammar, letters, arts or sciences, for two thousand years, should, *by mere accident*, be so remarkable for peculiarities, known in no other language, but the Hebrew—using the same words to signify the same things—having towns and places of the same name?" (283, italics mine). The question is rhetorical, of course, and it rests on several inaccurate and racist assumptions about American nations, their histories, and their cultures (as well as a paltry understanding of Hebrew). Nonetheless, though phrased as a question, this passage asserts not only that history cannot be the product of chance but also that what may at first appear to be a contingency ultimately will be revealed to have been divinely ordered. In Boudinot's teleological rendering of the Americas, all lines converge, and all pasts become a singular present.

Like previous proponents of the Hebraic Indian theory, Boudinot interprets the signs of American Hebraism as pointing toward a divinely ordered future for his nation. The specific conclusions he draws from his analysis, however, are a bit surprising. As I have discussed elsewhere, A Star in the West ends not with grandiose pronouncements of US exceptionalism but rather with a stark warning to white American Christians.[24] "If it is then plain, that the Israelites have heretofore suffered the just indignation of the Almighty," he asks, "for their and all his threatenings and fury have literally and most exactly been poured out upon them, according to the predictions of his servant Moses, what have not their enemies and oppressors to fear, in the great day of God's anger, when he cometh to avenge his people, who have been dear to him as the apple of his eye?" (296–97). The Israelites are God's chosen people, and God has caused them to suffer immensely for millennia. The biblical narrative reveals this much. So how much more terrible, Boudinot demands his readers consider, will be the sufferings of the Israelites' tormenters? The project of Indian Removal and the brutal treatment of Native peoples by the United States, this passage suggests, have placed the nation on the road to destruction. The earthly gain available through cruel national policy will be short-lived in the face of millennium. "If his word has been yea and amen, in punishing the people of his choice, because of their disobedience," Boudinot warns, "what hope can those gentiles have, who are found to continue in opposition to his positive commandments[?]" (297). His answer is simple: none. There is no hope for the nation that does harm to Israel. The only option available to the United States, A Star in the West concludes, is repentance and reform. Otherwise, the United States' cruelty to Native Americans, now revealed as the Israelites they have been all along, will double back upon the nation and justify its destruction.

Considered in retrospect within this structure, 2 Esdras morphs from a text that never should have been read (or, for that matter, written) into a necessary guide for the end times, and Boudinot becomes an agent of God in the very moment he acts without agency. 2 Esdras enters A Star in the West as a problematic artifact but becomes, by the end, conclusive proof of Boudinot's thesis; the accident lights the millennial fuse. The following section of this chapter will explore what happens when Boudinot's own text enters, and is transformed by, the work of William Apess. Like 2 Esdras before it, *A Star in the West* begins its intertextual life as a proof text, supporting evidence for a major claim. Refracted through Apess's unique reordering of time, however, Boudinot's teleological arguments fray, and *A Star in the West* becomes part of a larger project aimed at moving indigenous Americans beyond the purview of white Christian eschatology. Apess's American future is, like Boudinot's, a Christian one; but it is not a white one. Colonialism, in Apess's rendering, has not brought Christianity to America's shores, because Christianity already was there, in nascent form, brought by Hebrew settlers a millennium ago. In the Hebraic Indian, Apess finds the origins of an American Christianity operating independently of, and thus uncorrupted by, those bent on the destruction of indigenous peoples. The appendix to *A Son of the Forest* converts Boudinot's accident into Apess's design.

Greatly Improved: William Apess's Atemporal Appendix

Where *A Star in the West* opens with a scene of accident, *A Son of the Forest* begins with an assertion of intent. In the preface to the book's second edition (1831), Apess informs readers that "the present edition is greatly improved; as well in the printing, as in the arrangement of the work, and the style in which it was written" (3). Having noticed flaws in his original, Apess asserts, he has taken greater care with his book's reissue. "The first edition," he explains, "was hurried through the press. . . . It has been carefully revised . . . and in its improved form, it is now submitted to the public, with the earnest prayer of the author, that it may be rendered a lasting blessing to every one who may give it even a cursory perusal" (3).

It is possible to read this preface simply as a standard apologia—the kind common in writings by both women and members of racial minority groups in the period, and, indeed, also present in the first edition of Apess's work.[25] Interestingly, the scene of reading this edition evokes is not unlike the one described by Boudinot: in giving the text a "cursory perusal," the perhaps indifferent reader discovers a "lasting blessing." Here, though, the similarity between Boudinot's and Apess's works begins and ends. For a central component of the "blessing" offered by

A Son of the Forest is its presentation of history that refuses to unify white Christian and Hebraic American timelines. Where white evangelists such as Boudinot configured the Hebraic Indian as the lynchpin between sacred and secular time, Apess deploys it as a figure of recurrence, continuously rewinding and replaying rather than synching American history with a divine temporality

Like many Native writers, Apess received relatively little attention from scholars of American literature until the end of the twentieth century. His early exclusion from the canon is no surprise, given the field's early (and ongoing) privileging of works by white authors, but as Carolyn Haynes reminds us, Apess's longtime absence from critical accounts of the period is striking, because it persisted "despite the fact that his literary output was among the most prolific of any Native American writer in the early nineteenth century and that he led the only successful Indian revolt in New England prior to 1850."[26] In the past few decades, though, scholars recognizing Apess's literary and historical significance have explored everything from his role in the Mashpee Revolt of 1833 and his work to preserve his own Pequot identity to his engagements with Methodist reform movements and his reconfiguring of American colonial history.[27] Reassessment of Apess has taken place simultaneously with a shift in the field that Mark Rifkin identifies as an effort to "[focus] on forms of Native political self-representation, as against the tendency to treat Native peoples as another racial minority excluded from the national peoplehood of the United States."[28] In Apess's specific case, recognition of his commitment to Native American claims of national sovereignty over US citizenship has allowed critics to see the radical politics underpinning his depictions of his own life and of Native history. Apess's appropriation of Boudinot could thus be considered as a formal strategy aimed at reorienting white conceptions of American history and the role of indigenous populations within it. While other scholars have acknowledged Apess's engagement with the Hebraic Indian theory and identified strains of both assimilation and resistance to white and federal supremacy within it, I would like to explore how Apess's decision to append Boudinot's work to his memoir contributes to a larger project of temporal distortion that allows Apess to separate Native history from colonial history and his own Christianity from established Protestantisms.

Apess's embrace of Christianity has occupied a somewhat vexed position within scholarship dedicated to his work, because it simultaneously gives force to and, perhaps, works against his assertions of indigenous sovereignty. Some of the earliest critical work devoted to Apess positioned his Methodism as a capitulation to white cultural values. Arnold Krupat's assessment of Apess, which asserts that his ministerial ordination marks him as one "wish[ing] to be the licensed speaker of a dominant voice," is illustrative of this perspective.[29] Krupat's point is not without validity. Apess does not merely convert to Methodism: he situates that conversion at the center of his life story, and he details his real and hard fight for ordination. Christianity is not an auxiliary feature of Apess's identity; it is as important to his narrative as is his status as a Pequot, and it is in many respects inseparable from that status. Although it is impossible to know for sure what Apess truly believed, his writing suggests that he was sincere in his devotion. Describing his search for salvation as a teenager, for example, Apess writes, "I ceased not to pray for the salvation of my soul. Very often my exercises were so great that sleep departed from me—I was fearful that I should wake up in hell" (20). This is not an expression of religion as a negligible biographical factor. And as Hanes has shown, *A Son of the Forest* not only foregrounds Apess's Christianity but also bears all the formal properties of a Protestant conversion narrative, describing "(1) life before the conversion process; (2) the awareness of one's sinfulness (or the conviction); (3) the conversion proper; (4) the immediate rewards of the conversion; and (5) further temptation and subsequent renewal."[30] In perfectly copying the conventions of the conversion narrative, Apess demonstrates a high level of familiarity with the genre. He is not a casual Protestant. *A Son of the Forest*, then, speaks the language of American Protestantism and marshals its formal conventions in the service of an indigenous life story. Apess refuses to distinguish his claims to Christian piety from his arguments regarding Native sovereignty. This conflation of identity markers that might seem at odds with one another is one of the most challenging features of Apess's memoir. Both Pequot and Christian, Apess grounds his claims to one identity formation in the terms of the other.

For many critics, the "problem" of Apess's Christianity never actually stood as a problem at all, though, because of his embrace of Methodism over other possible sects. As Hanes puts it, "Apess's ability to engage in cultural criticism would not have been possible . . . with [just] any form of Protestant rhetoric; Methodism . . . was uniquely suited to his needs."[31] Methodism was, in fact, unique among nineteenth-century Protestant-isms. Its doctrine of universally available grace—as opposed to the no-tion of predestination that dominated Calvinist sects—decentralized its institutional power. Where orthodox Protestants such as Presbyterians and Congregationalists historically had emphasized the importance of election and membership within a religious community, Method-ism embraced an evangelism that relied heavily on itinerant ministers and enthusiastic worship practice. This made it particularly appealing to women, people of color, and members of economically marginalized groups. Even the more well-off, white Methodists typically were outsid-ers in the nineteenth-century United States. Mocked by establishment Anglicans and members of dissenting low-church sects alike, Method-ists were not "dominant" by any means in this period.[32]

Laura Donaldson has suggested that Methodism's formal proper-ties may have proven as appealing to Native converts as its potential for social justice did. The sect's privileging of "thick orality," she notes, "attracted Apess (and many other American Indians) in ways that thin Christian literacy never could," because it correlated with the story-telling traditions of many American nations.[33] Methodist Christianity stood not as a mark of assimilation or capitulation in the nineteenth century, but rather as a powerful tool for social change. Apess makes it clear that the sect appealed to him because it differed from the or-thodoxy practiced by the whites who mistreated him. I am most inter-ested here, though, in how, refracted through the Hebraic Indian theory, Apess's Methodism becomes an indigenous religious form, distinct from that practiced by white Americans.

Although it does seem that Apess chose Methodism because of its progressive potential, A Son of the Forest presents that choice as a prod-uct of historical contingency rather than transcendent truth. Following his removal from his grandparents, Apess was indentured in the homes of Calvinist Protestants (mainly Presbyterians and Baptists) who were neglectful at best and abusive at worst. A Son of the Forest presents their religious practice as a mirror of the hopeless drudgery of Apess's inden-ture, as is evident in his depiction of Judge William Hillhouse's Pres-byterianism: "He never neglected family prayer, and he always insisted on my being present. I did not believe or, rather, had no faith in his prayer, because it was the same thing from day to day, and I had heard it repeated so often that I knew it as well as he. Although I was so young, I did not think that Christians ought to learn their prayers, and knowing that he repeated the same thing from day to day is, I have no doubt, the very reason why his petitions did me no good" (15). Here Apess rehearses a familiar critique of Orthodox Protestantism: its compulsory devotional forms are hollow; its rote repetition forecloses the possibility of authentic religious experience; its appeals to the intellect impoverish the emotional life of the practitioner.

Unmoved by these forms, Apess gravitates toward an alternative devotional practice. The Methodists, in contrast to these staid Calvinists, "were earnest and fervent in prayer" and bore hearts "warm in the cause of God" (12). Most important here is the fact that Apess frames Methodism's appeal as formal more than theological—the Methodists' spontaneous preaching and enthusiastic singing draw him to their services. Although *A Son of the Forest* begins with Apess's decision to embrace Methodism, it does not end there. In laying claim to an ancient Hebrew origin, Apess situates his Christianity beyond the purview of Protestantism, Methodism included, and reaches back to a religious origin operating apart from white colonialism. Presenting readers with time out of joint, *A Son of the Forest* disrupts the arc of Boudinot's teleological history and reorients the standard conversion narrative. At once a new Methodist and an old Hebrew, Apess appears, by the end of his memoir, an original Christian who, by virtue of an ancient covenant, never needed white religion.

My thinking about temporality in *A Son of the Forest* owes much to recent assessments of the operation of time within the frame of settler colonialism and is particularly indebted to the work of Mark Rifkin. Although time often is depicted in Western cultures as a neutral and universally experienced measure of existence—in which all subjects inhabit a single plane of sequence and synchronicity—Rifkin notes that the operation of time should be understood as plural and relative in culture, just as it is in physics.[34] As he puts it, "U.S. settler colonialism produces its own temporal formation, with its own particular ways of apprehending time, and the state's policies, mappings, and imperatives generate the frame of reference (such as plotting events with respect to their place in national history and seeing change in terms of forms of American progress).["35] Within settler colonial time, Native Americans are configured as inhabiting both a distant past (where their cultures are suspended as if in amber) and an approaching future (where they ultimately will vanish) but not a present synchronous with that of whites. "These kinds of elisions and anachronizations," Rifkin asserts, "can be understood as a profound denial of Native being. They perform a routine and almost ubiquitous excision of Indigenous persons and peoples from the flux of contemporary life, such that they cannot be understood as participants in current events, as stakeholders in decision-making, and as political and more broadly social agents with whom non-natives must engage."[36] Against the grain of this rendering of Native peoples as exclusively historical beings, Rifkin does not argue for the mere expansion of some universal present but rather asserts the need for a recognition of the plurality of time. "Adopting sovereignty and self-determination as normative principles guiding the approach to time," he suggests, "opens the potential for thinking Indigenous temporalities—temporal multiplicity—in ways that exceed the forms of presentness imposed through dominant modes of settler time."[37]

Rifkin's work provides an apt frame for considering Apess's radical religious project in *A Son of the Forest*. Where Boudinot deemed the Hebraic Indian a lynchpin between sacred and human history, the recovery of which would set in motion a teleology concluding with the salvation of white Christians, Apess lays claim to American Hebraism to assert a different kind of temporal sovereignty within millennial Christianity. The Hebraic Indian theory is not, for Apess, a means of inserting himself into the linear timeline of American Christianity. Rather, it serves as a site for claiming a past unavailable to white Christians and thereby moving beyond the reach of colonial time.

A Son of the Forest presents readers with temporal distortions in several different ways. First, Apess achieves his aim formally, simply by converting the text *A Star in the West* into an appendix to which he assigns nearly equal significance as his memoir proper. In his explicit assertion of abridgement in service of appendance, Apess complicates longstanding notions of the function of the appendix, which dictionaries and common practice alike treat as documentation designed to complement but not complete, to support but remain detachable from the main body of a text.[38] Though Gérard Genette does not define them particularly as such, appendices are "paratexts" in that they are "accompanying productions"—textual artifacts that appear with but not within the main body of a book. As Genette notes, a paratext is an "'undefined zone' between the inside and the outside, a zone without any hard and fast boundary on either the inward side (turned toward the text) or the outward side (turned toward the world's discourse about the text)."[39] This is perhaps most true of the appendix, which typically brings an "outside" text "in," to aid or guide interpretation of a book's body text.

The appendix nearly always marks a moment of intertextuality, a simultaneous gesture of drawing in and reaching beyond. For my purposes, most significant is the fact that an appendix also "harbors a lie" similar to that which Gayatri Spivak identified in prefaces. To write a preface, she asserts, requires "a pretense at writing *before* a text that must be read *before* the preface can be written."[40] If a preface is that which appears first but was written last, an appendix is that which concludes a book only by virtue of predating it. To read an appendix, in other words, is to end in the past. Although most appendices bear this temporal oddity, not all foreground it. Apess deliberately highlights the temporal distortion produced by his appendix by labeling its beginning an "Introduction" and by promising readers an American history that turns out to be a biblical exegesis. To finish Apess's book, in other words, is to rewind beyond his own origin and begin anew.

Apess's appendix reaches back not only through biblical history but also to the beginning of *A Son of the Forest*, addressing an issue raised but not explained in the book's opening pages. The narrative begins, as many memoirs do, with a genealogical account: "My grandfather was a white man," Apess writes, "and married a female attached to the royal family of Philip, king of the Pequot tribe of Indians, so well known in that part of American history which relates to the wars between whites and the natives. My grandmother was, if I am not misinformed, the king's granddaughter. . . . This statement is given not with a view of appearing great in the estimation of others . . . [W]e are all the descendants of one great progenitor—Adam" (4). There are two temporal oddities at play in this genealogy, perhaps the most obvious being that it ends with a beginning—with *the* beginning, as it were. Arriving at the end of Apess's ancestral line, readers find the ostensible origin of all human lines.[41]

This is not a quirk in the text. Apess evokes Adam twice more, using him to assert a more authentic "originality" for indigenous Americans than for other humans. "The proper term which ought to be applied to our nation, to distinguish it from the rest of the human family," he writes, "is that of 'Natives'—and I humbly conceive that the natives of this country are the only people under heaven who have a just title to the name, inasmuch as we are the only people who retain the original complexion of our father Adam" (10). Here, Apess rehabilitates the term "Native," converting it from a moniker assigned retrospectively by white colonists into an assertion of transcendent racial primacy. He makes the same assertion later in the text, writing that he believes "our nation retains the original complexion of our common father, Adam" (34). Barry O'Connell has noted that these references to Adam mark the entry of the Hebraic Indian theory into the text, previewing what Apess's appendix will make explicit. Adam's cameos destabilize the chronology of *A Son of the Forest*, forcing readers to confront early on Apess's jagged and recursive history. Although he articulates a "common" origin for all peoples, Apess simultaneously makes it clear that his people were the first to spring from that origin. To be "Native," then, is not merely to precede white settlers in the realm of secular time and space. Rather, it is to precede everyone, everywhere, at all times—to operate beyond the mere contingencies of human history.

Apess's concluding reference to Adam creates a kind of loop in his genealogy, but the ostensible beginning of his family line produces a more radical rupture in the text. Although on its face Apess's linking of his grandmother to "Philip, King of the Pequot tribe of Indians" seems like a simple chronology (perhaps designed, despite Apess's assertion to the contrary, to lend status to his family), its presentation of familial origin is quite complex, because King Philip was not the king of the Pequots. He was, rather, a Pokanoket Wampanoag, and his war with the English began nearly forty years after the conclusion of the Pequot War. The "error" has puzzled scholars, especially because when Apess revised the 1829 edition of *A Son of the Forest* for republication, he compounded it. The 1829 edition does describe Apess as "a descendant of one of the principal chiefs of the Pequod tribe, so well known in that part of American history called King Philip's wars," so the error is present in that text, but it does not list King Philip specifically as Apess's ancestor. By 1831, though, Apess's grandmother has become "the king's granddaughter," and King Philip's history has merged not just with that of the Pequots but also with that of Apess himself.

Charting the history not only of this oddity in the text but also of critical engagements with it, Roumiana Velikova notes that scholars typically treat it as little more than "a result of confusion."[42] Importantly, that "confusion" may have resulted from Apess's reading of Boudinot, who describes King Philip in *A Star in the West* as "an independent sovereign of the Pequods" (156). Situating Apess within the context of both Puritan and Romantic historiographies, Velikova shows that the Pequot War often appears in white accounts of colonial history as the preceding model for King Philip's war, and thus conflation of two nations and wars is not unique to Apess. For Velikova, Apess's rehearsal of Boudinot's error reflects his "impulse to attach King Philip, a well-known chief, to the Pequots, the most prominent New England tribe, according to Boudinot," in an "attempt to restore the faded glory of the Pequots and to refashion their historical record."[43] This seems plausible, though the precise location of Apess's refashioning of King Philip on the spectrum between accident and design is unknowable. The effect of Apess's use of Boudinot's error here, though, is in line with much of *A Son of the Forest*'s temporal work: from its outset, Apess offers readers an impossible historical trajectory, simultaneously evoking multiple timelines and disrupting any easy sense of linearity. His genealogy begins with an impossible line of descent from an ancestor who cannot exist and then is revealed, at its end, as a loop back to universal origins.

The at times jarring conflation of American and biblical histories is not confined to Apess's account of his family of origin. His distillation of Boudinot strategically deploys those portions of *A Star in the West* that blur the lines between past and present, east and west, secular and sacred. Although he already has linked the Pequots to both Adam and the Wampanoag King Philip in his opening chapter, Apess constructs, via Boudinot, yet another line of descent for them in his appendix. He writes, "Dr. Boudinot says that this tribe (the Pequots referred to above) 'were a principal nation of the east, and very forcibly reminds one of the similarity of the same name in Jeremiah 50:21, where the inhabitants of Pekod are particularly mentioned; and also in Ezekiel 23:23. The difference in spelling one with a k and the other with a q is no uncommon thing; the Indian languages being very guttural, k is generally used where an Englishman would use the q'" (56). The word "Pekod" does appear in those verses of the King James Bible. It most likely is an alternate spelling of "Puqudu," which refers to a group of Aramean people who inhabited a region in southern Babylon and were, like the lost tribes, conquered by Assyria. It is worth noting that the incorporation of the Puqudu people into Assyria took place before the conquest of Israel. Thus in linking the Pequot to the Pekod, Apess and Boudinot mutually draw a timeline distinct from the one connecting the Kingdom of Israel to the Americas. For the Pequot to be the Pekod, they must reach back to a new moment in a history that is more secular than sacred. The substitution of the "k" for the "q" is the substitution of one conquest for another, one timeline for another.

Though Apess follows Boudinot in complicating the timeline of Pequot history by inserting the biblical Pekod, he makes one significant alteration to Boudinot's text here, substituting "forcibly" where Boudinot uses "naturally." This perhaps seems a small change, but it speaks to the difference between the two men's projects. In *A Star in the West*, American history merges organically with sacred history, and the discovery of Israel in the United States is a joyful progress narrative. Boudinot is frank about the suffering of Native peoples at the hands of whites, but that suffering operates in the service of the great and divine order of Christian ascendance. The "reminder" of the "Pekod" past in the face of a Pequot present is, for Boudinot, simply "natural." In contrast, *A Son of the Forest* even takes pains to remind readers that the convergence of timelines—whether sacred, secular, national, or racial—always is a product of force.[44] Apess's process of biblical remembrance is violent. Although Boudinot appears in *A Son of the Forest* almost whole cloth, Apess's citations of him are not mere copies. The substitution of force for nature calls the project of *A Star in the West* into question. Although Apess accepts Boudinot's proofs of the Hebraic Indian theory, *A Son of the Forest* undercuts *A Star in the West*'s conclusions by highlighting the trauma of temporal overlap within the frame of settler colonialism.

The confounding of both familial and national chronologies that structures *A Son of the Forest* allows Apess to replace contemporary white accounts of the vanishing Indian with an indigenous account of the lost Israelite. In his analysis of Apess's final work, the *Eulogy on King*

Philip (which, importantly, does not assert a familial link between the writer and the king), Eric Wolfe reminds readers that Euroamerican colonial discourses typically are structured around a logic of melancholic mourning that paradoxically presents the demise of indigenous populations as both an inevitable future and a lamentable past. Noting, for example, Andrew Jackson's 1830 assertion that "humanity has often wept over the fate of the aborigines of this country"—an assertion made during his administration's active campaign against Native nations—Wolfe argues that such statements "posit this extinction as literally still-to-come," though "rhetorically they treat it as though it has already occurred."[45] Apess, in contrast, "reopens the past to point toward a potentially different future."[46]

While I agree with Wolfe's assessment of the melancholy at play within the discourse of Indian disappearance, I would argue that when Apess evokes the lost tribes of Israel, he is doing so not to argue for a more robust understanding of the past or even for a better present but rather to posit a sacred future that will unfold beyond the contingency of national events. As he writes in his appendix, "Mr. Boudinot says that there is a possibility that these unhappy children of misfortune may yet be proved to be the descendants of Jacob; and if so, that though cast off for their henious [*sic*] transgressions, they have not been altogether forsaken, and will hereafter appear to have been in all their dispersion and wanderings, the subjects of God's divine protection and precious care" (53). This almost verbatim rendering of Boudinot furthers Apess's project in several ways. The syntax collapses the distinction between lost Israelite and indigenous American, as that ambiguous "they" who have not been forsaken is both populations at once. This passage also produces the past in negation—God never abandoned the Israelites—in order to assert a futurity in which divine fiat rather than governmental policy will dictate the status of Native Americans. The convoluted verb phrasing, "will hereafter appear to have been," presents a future that is at once indeterminate (merely "hereafter") and as unalterable as the past. Native peoples are what they always have been, and their disappearance is not an inevitable condition to be mourned in advance by whites but rather a sacred truth to be revealed at the end of time.

In moving Native Americans out of the purview of white history, Apess crafts for them an important status within the trajectory of sacred time. In perhaps his most explicit original composition about the lost tribes theory—a sermon fittingly titled "The Indians: The Ten Lost Tribes"—Apess suggests that the people of America have lived out of time since the conquest of Assyria, and in living thusly, they have eschewed the pitfalls of human history. The "Indian tribes," he insists, "now melting away like dewdrops in the morning's sun, are no less than the remnant of that people, the records of whose history has [sic] been blotted out from among the nations of the earth—whose history, if history they have, is a series of cruelties and persecutions without a parallel" (113). Apess deploys conditional language here to provocative ends. If the lost tribes have a history, which they may not, it is unknowable to the rest of the world. The significance of this state of living out of history becomes clear when Apess offers a history of Judaism in which the Jews "disdained [Jesus], simply because he did not come in princely splendor . . . and nailed the Lord of the universe to the cross" (114). Missing from this narration, but certainly obvious to a nineteenth-century audience, is the fact that the missing Israelites are long gone by the beginning of the New Testament, and thus do not appear in the Passion stories. Within this formulation of sacred history, then, Native Americans appear as Jews exempt from the story of Jesus' death, a chosen people who never forfeited their right to God's love and protection.

Within many of Apess's writings, European contact operates as the force that drives indigenous people back into profane chronology, with devastating results. "I think history declares," Apess asserts, "that, when this continent was first discovered, that its inhabitants were a harmless, inoffensive, obliging people. They were alike free from the blandishments and vices of civilized life" (114). History, in other words, declares Native Americans free from history—its burdens, its ugly effects. To be without civilization is not to be "savage." Rather, it is a function of having lived for centuries apart from the chronology governing the rest of the world; it is a function of having been lost. The nations that enact violence against indigenous bodies thus risk retribution, though not within the scope of human history. "They have all along been precious in the sight of God," Apess warns in his sermon "The Increase of the Kingdom of Christ." "Woe, woe to the nations who tread on the discarded jewels of Israel" (106). Vengeance for abuses leveled against Native Americans is a certainty in Apess's work, but the justice he awaits may come only at the end of time itself. "We fear the account of national sin, which lies at the doors of the American people," he writes, "will be a terrible one to balance in the chancery of heaven" (107). Human history will run its course, whatever that course may be, but there are other temporalities to consider.

Although it may be tempting to read Apess's warnings simply as strategies to spark reform in US policies, his work often eschews such quotidian concerns. "America," he asserts, "has utterly failed to amalgamate the red man of the woods into the artificial, cultivated ranks of social life" (107). But rather than frame this accusation as a national failure that might be redressed, Apess asks, "Has not one reason for this been that it was not the purpose of God that it should be done—for lo, the blood of Israel flowed in the veins of these unshackled, freeborn men?" (107). Colonialism and its brutalities link indigenous populations to the exiled of Israel and stand as proof of a divine plan unconcerned with the particulars of human history. "Suffice it to say, what is already known," Apess concludes, "that the white man came upon our shores—he grew taller and taller until his shadow was cast over all the land—in its shade the mighty tribes of olden time wilted away. A few, the remnant of multitudes long since gathered to their fathers, are all that remain and they are on their march to eternity" (115). Drafted in the era of Indian Removal, Apess's evocation of the "march" is especially poignant. But his Hebraic Indians are not walking west. Rather, they are moving as he claims they have moved for thousands of years: out of reach, because out of time.

4

The Book of Mormon's New American Past

Questions of authenticity have dogged *The Book of Mormon* ever since Joseph Smith Jr. first published it in 1830. As is well known by now, Smith claimed to have received a series of revelations leading him to a book buried in a hillside outside of Palmyra, New York.[1] A set of plates inscribed in a language Smith identified as "reformed Egyptian" (which he purportedly translated through divine inspiration), *The Book of Mormon* contained a sprawling narrative describing settlement of the western hemisphere by ancient peoples, mainly Hebrews fleeing Jerusalem during the Babylonian captivity. Like the bibles sitting in nineteenth-century homes, it was a composite text comprised of fifteen books narrated by different voices. Also like those bibles, the book described events spanning several centuries and included stories of captivity and flight, family discord, inter- and intragroup war, divine punishment for lapses in faith, spectacular martyrdom, and the resurrection of Jesus.[2]

Though the earliest converts to the faith deemed the book's similarity to the Bible to be proof of its veracity, skeptics viewed those qualities as proof of its fraud. Alexander Campbell's 1832 anti-Mormon treatise *Delusions*, for example, argues that Smith's text "is patched up and cemented with 'And it came to pass'—'I saith unto you'—'Ye saith unto him'—And all the King James' haths, dids, and doths—in the lowest imitation of the common version." A decade later, Daniel Kidder sardonically identified "a striking coincidence between the translation of certain uncouth hieroglyphics, engraven on metal plates some centuries ago, and the language of the King James Bible!" (290–91).[3]

The Book of Mormon thus offended its first critics not because it differed from the sacred texts they were accustomed to but because it so closely resembled them. In addition to deeming *The Book of Mormon* a poor imitation of the King James Bible, its detractors focused on its literary traits. Campbell, for example, declared the book a "romance" organized around "religious adventures," and Eber Howe argued that the book was a reworking of Solomon Spaulding's "Manuscript Story," a "found manuscript" tale of ancient American origins, written around 1812 but never published.[4] For Howe, *The Book of Mormon's* apparent similarity to contemporary fictions only increased its danger. "Fiction has its charms," he warns, "and when combined and presented to the mind in the mantel of inspiration, it is not singular that the credulous and unsuspecting should be captivated."[5] Here again, anxiety about *The Book of Mormon's* power stems not from its radical difference from other texts but from its relationship to them. *The Book of Mormon* emerged onto the nineteenth-century scene as an uncanny artifact, strange in its familiarity, unsettling at the moment of recognition.

This chapter is concerned with *The Book of Mormon's* uncanny relationship to the Hebraic Indian theory.[6] Like nineteenth-century skeptics before them, the book's recent detractors often contend that Smith merely cribbed from this existing mythology for his text.[7] In response, scholars affiliated with the Church of Jesus Christ of Latter-Day Saints[8] have highlighted *The Book of Mormon's* many and substantial differences from other works outlining this theory and cited those differences as proof of the book's veracity.[9] Debates over *The Book of Mormon's* authenticity are not a concern of this chapter, though I must acknowledge the fact that any effort to read it within a literary or historical context that is not ancient America might be deemed an effort to discredit it, so inseparable are the text's truth claims from its claims to ancient origins. Indeed, as the examples with which this chapter begins show, from the moment of its publication, efforts to prove *The Book of Mormon* a fraud also have been efforts to situate it within a literary context—the style of Elizabethan English, the mode of romance, or the convention of found manuscripts. But the question of legitimacy has proven tyrannical, and in many cases unproductive, in studies of *The Book of Mormon*. After all, whatever its origins, *The Book of Mormon* offers an intricate, alternative account of the original settlement of the western hemisphere. Elsewhere, I have discussed the book within the context of nineteenth-century antiquarianism to argue that in presenting record keeping as an impossible task, the text complicates both contemporary notions of biblical canonicity and progressive histories of American Protestantism.[10] This chapter is not a complete departure from that line of inquiry, as it also is invested in the challenges *The Book of Mormon* poses to prevailing notions of American history. My focus here, though, is the way in which the book refutes the lost tribes version of the Hebraic Indian and thereby calls into question the theory's place within millenarian eschatology.

Although it posits a biblical origin for the peopling of America, *The Book of Mormon* explicitly rejects the Kingdom of Israel as the source of that peopling, and where previous engagements with the idea of American Hebraism took the form of expository prose, *The Book of Mormon* is a narrative history.[11] Unlike earlier works discussed in this study, which attempted to demonstrate a Hebraic lineage for Native Americans through interpretations of biblical texts and analyses of cultural phenomena, *The Book of Mormon* offers itself as proof of the theory. It does not assess evidence; it is evidence. This is a crucial development in the trajectory of the Hebraic Indian theory. Where figures such as Thomas Thorowgood, James Adair, and Elias Boudinot adapted different empirical models to suit the theory—and also adapted the theory to fit those models—Smith's text in many respects renders such efforts moot by virtue of its existence. There is no need to catalogue contemporary Native American cultural practices alongside "Jewish" customs once a history of American Hebraism has been dug out of the ground. Neither is there any use in locating the Americas in the Bible once a bible has emerged in the Americas.

The Hebraic Indian theory does not fall completely away in the aftermath of *The Book of Mormon*'s publication, but it never holds real sway in mainline Christian circles again. In moving American Hebraism out of the realm of the probable or demonstrable and into the space of narrative, *The Book of Mormon* paradoxically alters the theory's course. On the one hand, the text propels the theory through the nineteenth century and, through the teachings of the Church of Jesus Christ of Latter-day Saints, into the present. On the other, it propels the theory beyond the interest of most American Christians and into, as this book's final two chapters will detail, the realm of fiction. If *The Book of Mormon*'s emergence offered believers absolute proof of the Hebraic Indian theory, it may have ruined the theory for those who did not believe its account of its own creation. The Hebraic Indian theory had invited epistemic innovation for centuries; *The Book of Mormon* seems to have innovated it out of American Protestantism.

The Book of Mormon offers readers a new key to the history of America, but it does not provide an answer to the question of the lost tribes' location. None of the migrations described in *The Book of Mormon* involve the Kingdom of Israel, and the text is explicit about its refusal to reveal their locations. This chapter's first section shows how *The Book of Mormon* offers readers a tantalizing array of stories depicting departures of people from the biblical narrative yet evokes the lost tribes only to deny their place within American history. The text mentions them directly only twice and only to remind readers that the populations depicted in its pages are not, despite their status as people missing from the Bible's narrative, members of the Kingdom of Israel.

The effect of *The Book of Mormon*'s engagement with and revision of the Hebraic Indian theory is twofold. First, in explicitly asserting that the lost tribes of Israel still exist but are not in the Americas, *The Book of Mormon* suggests that the "gathering of Israel" predicted by so many versions of the theory never was going to be initiated by European arrival in the Americas. Its Hebraic Indian theory, in other words, produces a deferral of the millennium rather than a prediction of its fulfillment. Second, and perhaps more important, *The Book of Mormon* effected a broader shift in the range of genres that could address the Hebraic Indian theory. In presenting its alternative picture of human life in the western hemisphere through narrative rather than expository prose, the book created space for different kinds of generic engagements with the Hebraic Indian theory. Its influence, then, was not restricted to its contents; its form, too, had a ripple effect on the theory.

Because *The Book of Mormon* accepts the proposition that the lost tribes are an essential component of a planned millennium yet denies the possibility that its own narrative will solve the mystery of their disappearance, writers affiliated with the Church have grappled with the question of the tribes' location for nearly two centuries. In the only extensive study of engagements with lost tribes mythology by Latter-day Saints, R. Clayton Brough identifies four main theories that have structured writings on the subject since Smith's death. These are the unknown planet theory, the North Pole theory, the hollow earth theory, and the dispersion theory.[12] The chapter's second section focuses on texts concerned with the first three of these theories, showing how each allows writers to maintain the Church's eschatological promises while simultaneously deferring the events required to set those promises in motion. As Brough notes, the "dispersion theory" now seems to be the most commonly accepted theory regarding the tribes among believers, and it "proposes that the Lost Ten Tribes have been totally scattered among the present nations of the earth, and are only lost as to their identity—not as to their location, and that they are presently being gathered into the Church through missionary labors."[13] This falls most in line with the thinking of contemporary historians, because populations conquered by Assyria typically assimilated into a variety of cultures.

The dispersion theory has not generated much in the way of narrative, for perhaps obvious reasons: gradual cultural adaptation over centuries may not be the stuff of gripping drama. It also is a later development in thinking on this topic, first appearing in Church documents, as Brough notes, around 1912.[14] The other theories, though, have produced a variety of literary engagements across genres. Such writings on the lost tribes not only reveal the religion's complex relationship to a longstanding biblical puzzle but also show how *The Book of Mormon* itself became an object of literary interest. Scholars of Smith's text, myself included, have tended to focus on *The Book of Mormon*'s place within specific literary or historical contexts. In the aftermath of its publication, though, the text became a site for new literary production, and the lost tribes literature it inspired is just one of many threads that writers drew out of its pages. The next logical step within the literary study of *The Book of Mormon*, therefore, might be to think beyond the contexts out of which the book emerged and consider the new literary contexts it produced in its wake.

Eternal Deferral: The Lost Tribes in (and out of) *The Book of Mormon*

The Book of Mormon's original title page declares that it contains two distinct narratives. The first is "an abridgment of the record of the people of Nephi, and also of the Lamanites, written to the Lamanites, who are a remnant of the house of Israel."[15] This narrative comprises the main portion of the text. It is a complex and sprawling story of the family of Lehi, which begins "in the commencement of the first year of the reign of Zedekiah, king of Judah" (1 Nephi 1:4). The temporal marker establishes Lehi as a contemporary of the biblical prophet Jeremiah, and Lehi's narrative initially follows roughly the same trajectory as that of Jeremiah. Lehi receives a vision of the destruction of Israel at the hands of Babylon, after which "he went forth among the people and began to prophesy and to declare unto them concerning the things which he had both seen and heard," but despite his best efforts, and like Jeremiah, "It came to pass that the Jews did mock him because of the things which he testified of them" (1 Nephi 1:18–19). Unable to convince his people that they are in grave danger of incurring divine wrath, Lehi finds himself at risk: "When the Jews heard these things," his son Nephi explains, "they were angry with him, yea even as with the prophets of old, whom they had cast out" (1 Nephi 1:20). He receives another divine order, to flee Jerusalem with his family and hide in the wilderness. Nephi later receives a holy vision himself, and a command from the Lord to "construct a ship after the manner which I shall shew thee that I may carry thy people across the waters" (1 Nephi 17:8).

Despite the divine origin of the instructions given to Lehi and Nephi alike, Nephi's brothers Laman and Lemuel continuously rebel. Following their resettlement in the western hemisphere, the brothers' feuding culminates in the family's division into two nations, the Nephites and the Lamanites. These groups spend most of the rest of *The Book of Mormon* engaging in all-out war. This narrative thread covers nearly a millennium and contains about a thousand characters, and it ends with the annihilation of the Nephites by the Lamanites. The last living Nephite, Moroni, collects and buries the records of the Nephite people, which is the book Joseph Smith claimed to unearth. In its central narrative, then, the text offers readers a story of Hebraic migration; Lehi and his family essentially walk out of the pages of the Book of Jeremiah and into those of *The Book of Mormon*. That migration, though, has nothing to do with the lost tribes of Israel, who have been missing for over a century when Lehi receives his vision.

Although the story of the Nephites and Lamanites occupies most of *The Book of Mormon*'s pages, embedded within this main narrative is another story of ancient migration to the western hemisphere. This story, though, predates the disappearance of the Kingdom of Israel as well as Lehi's departure. The Book of Ether, the penultimate text in *The Book of Mormon*, tells the story of the family of Jared and his (unnamed) brother, who escape the confounding of language after the fall of the Tower of Babel described in Genesis. Like Lehi after him, and like Noah before him, Jared receives a command from God to "work and build, after the manner of barges which ye have hitherto built . . . and they were built after a manner that they were exceedingly tight . . . and the bottom thereof was tight like unto a dish" (Ether 2:16–17). Once the barges are built and stocked with supplies, "The Lord God caused that there should be a furious wind blow upon the face of the waters, towards the promised land" (Ether 6:5).

As Lehi's family will centuries later, though, these people, called the Jaredites, discover that even chosen families bring old rivalries and weaknesses into new places. The Jaredites experience internal strife, and over the course of several generations, the civilization turns against itself. As in the stories of Lehi and Jeremiah, "There came also . . . many prophets and prophesied of the destruction of that great people except they should repent and turn unto the Lord and forsake their murders and wickedness. And it came to pass that the prophets were rejected by the people" (Ether 11:1). That rejection leads, as it will for the Nephites and Lamanites, to endless war. In this case, Ether is the sole remaining figure, left alone to write the history of his fallen people. Having acquired the Book of Ether, the last Nephite, Moroni, abridges it and includes it with his own story of the end of a civilization. The records that Smith claimed to have unearthed and translated, then, contain two parallel histories of oceanic migrations to the western hemisphere by families associated with biblical texts. Importantly, though, these stories bookend but do not contain the story of the Kingdom of Israel. As interested as it is in missing biblical populations, *The Book of Mormon* does not offer readers answers to questions regarding the fate of the nation whose disappearance is depicted in the Bible.

In addition to these longer narratives, *The Book of Mormon* provides glimpses of other biblical populations who relocated to the Americas during periods of strife. Perhaps the most striking of these stories is that of the Mulekites, which appears in the Book of Omni and forms a point of contact between the stories of the Nephites and the Jaredites. In Omni, the Nephites are described as being "admonished continually by the word of God, and . . . led by the power of his arm through the wilderness, until they came down into the land which is called the land of

Zarahemla" (Omni 1:13). Until this moment in the text, the Nephites had no idea that such a land existed. Upon arrival, they learn that Zarahemla's inhabitants "came out from Jerusalem at the time that Zedekiah, king of Judah, was carried away captive into Babylon . . . and they journeyed in the wilderness and was [sic] brought by the hand of the Lord across the great waters" (Omni 15–16). This brief account aligns the story of this people with that of Lehi's family; the Mulekite narrative, it turns out, has been running parallel to the rest of The Book of Mormon all along.

The Nephite and Mulekite stories do not merely share a temporal origin. The Nephites learn that the Mulekites "had fallen by the sword from time to time. And their language had become corrupted" (Omni 1:17). This is an important moment in the text, because it contains kernels of both the Nephite narrative and the Jaredite narrative. In many passages throughout the text, the Nephites, Lamanites, and Jaredites are described as having "fallen by the sword." Moroni, for example, complains bitterly (several times) in an epistle in the Book of Alma that the people have "fallen by the sword" (Alma 60: 5, 8, 12, 22). Likewise, in Ether readers learn that "many thousands fell by the sword" (Ether 14:4) in a battle between brothers. Unlike the Jaredites, the Mulekites suffer the confounding of their language, but even this difference evokes the story of the Tower of Babel, from which the Jaredites spring. Throughout each of these stories, The Book of Mormon suggests that transatlantic voyages were possible, and perhaps even common, for ancient peoples, because a divine force made them possible. It also makes the case that the Kingdom of Israel is not the only population to leave the biblical narrative behind and make its way to a new world.

The absence of the lost tribes from The Book of Mormon would be perhaps unremarkable were it not for the fact that the text directly refers to them twice, highlighting the fact that its narrative does not solve the mystery of their location. The tribes receive their first mention in 2 Nephi, a book mainly devoted to the recounting of visions and prophecies given to Nephi. The twenty-ninth chapter of the book contains a prophecy related to the nineteenth-century emergence of The Book of Mormon itself. Describing the book's future reception, God tells Nephi, "and because my words shall hiss forth, many of the Gentiles shall say: A Bible, a Bible, we have got a Bible! And there cannot be any more Bible!" (2 Nephi 29:3). This is, as it turns out, an accurate prediction. As David

Holland has noted, one of the many objections that other Christians have made to *The Book of Mormon* since its appearance is that the sacred canon is closed and complete. "The book," as Holland puts it, "thus repeatedly takes aim at a religious culture that offered a priori resistance to 'more' of God's words."[16] Rather than attempt to mitigate this objection, 2 Nephi offers a radical picture of a scriptural canon that both can and will be open to new texts. "For my work is not yet finished," God tells Nephi. "For behold, I shall speak unto the Jews, and they shall write it; and I shall also speak unto the Nephites, and they shall write it; and I shall also speak unto the other tribes of the house of Israel, which I have led away, and they shall write it; and I shall also speak unto all nations of the earth, and they shall write it" (2 Nephi 29:9, 12).

Here, not only the geographic but also the temporal scope of holy writ expands ever outward and forward. If the Jews will write the Bible with which Christians are familiar, and the Nephites will write *The Book of Mormon*, then what books are to be written by "the other tribes of the house of Israel" and "all nations of the earth"? And when will they write them? *The Book of Mormon* does not say. It merely asserts that such books shall be written and that in some unspecified future they shall be read. "And it shall come to pass," God continues, "that the Jews shall have the words of the Nephites, and the Nephites shall have the words of the Jews; and the Nephites and the Jews shall have the words of the lost tribes of Israel; and the lost tribes of Israel shall have the words of the Nephites and the Jews" (2 Nephi 29:13). *The Book of Mormon*'s own readers are invited to imagine the lost tribes of Israel writing a book that one day the rest of the world will read, and one day reading the complete Bible and *The Book of Mormon*. In conjuring this image, though, *The Book of Mormon* reminds readers that it is not the lost tribes' book, and it will not tell their story.

After predicting that the Kingdom of Israel will emerge with book in hand, *The Book of Mormon* links the writing of that book to the ultimate unification of God's people. "And it shall come to pass that my people which are of the house of Israel shall be gathered home unto the lands of their possessions. And my word also shall be gathered in one" (2 Nephi 29:14). This verse mirrors a prophecy in Isaiah, which often is interpreted as referring to the return of the lost tribes: "For a small moment have I forsaken thee; but with great mercies will I gather thee" (Isaiah

54:7). In *The Book of Mormon*, the predicted "gathering" is simultaneously human and textual. Playing on the dual meaning of "gathering," which can be both a collection of people and, in book-binding terminology, an assemblage of printed sheets, *The Book of Mormon* presents the future unification of all holy peoples as a kind of collaboration. The sacred canon will be complete only when the lost tribes return and only when their text is combined with those of "the Jews . . . the Nephites . . . [and] all nations of the earth." The rejection of new scriptures, *The Book of Mormon* asserts, is tantamount to a rejection of the divine itself. "And I will show unto them that fight against my word and against my people which are of the house of Israel," Nephi reports, "that I am God and that I covenanted with Abraham that I would remember his seed forever" (2 Nephi 29:14). This verse introduces an important slippage into the text, as it links rejection of *The Book of Mormon* to a rejection of "the house of Israel," suggesting to those who would say "there cannot be any more Bible" that to deny the veracity of the Nephite story is to one day deny the story of the lost tribes. Nonetheless, 2 Nephi's lost tribes exist only in an indeterminate future. Unlike the words comprising *The Book of Mormon*, the words written by the tribes have yet to "hiss forth," and they are present in the text only as an absence.

The second mention of the lost tribes in *The Book of Mormon* also configures them off-stage and absent, but it does so even more directly. In 3 Nephi, the resurrected Jesus appears to the Nephite people and instructs them in the practice of Christianity. This is one of the most important moments in the text for believing members of the Church of Jesus Christ of Latter-day Saints, in part because it is the moment that concretizes the western hemisphere's role in Christian sacred history. It is not simply the case that the Nephites descended from a biblical people; their history has ongoing significance within the larger story of Christianity. Jesus introduces the Nephites to the main tenets of his teachings, and the account of his visit reads a bit like an abridged reenactment of the synoptic Gospels. Jesus, among other things, baptizes the Nephites, cures the sick, instructs the people in the Lord's Prayer, delivers a version of the Sermon on the Mount, invites the little children to come to him, and shows the crowd his wounds.

There remains much to say about 3 Nephi, which is a rich and compelling text in *The Book of Mormon*. The most significant aspect of this scene for my purposes, though, is that as he prepares to depart, Jesus tells the Nephites, "But now I go unto the Father, and also to shew myself unto the lost tribes of Israel—for they are not lost unto the Father, for he knoweth whither he hath taken them" (3 Nephi 17:4). Here, the lost tribes operate not as an abstraction—writers furiously transcribing God's words from somewhere in the universe as they await a call to return—but as a real group of people about to be visited by Jesus. In this way, the text offers a solution to a problem within millennialist Christian thinking about the tribes: they are predicted to embrace Christianity when they return at the end of days, but if they have been separated from the rest of humanity, how are they to learn about the teachings of Jesus? The lost tribes, in Jesus' rendering of them here, "are not lost" both because God knows their location and because they are to learn about Christianity directly from its source. Their location is not revealed in *The Book of Mormon*, but Jesus' explicit plan to visit them suggests that they will Christianize like the Nephites. Rendered again as absent from the text in this passage, the lost tribes nonetheless retain their status as an important presence in the universe, fulfilling their divine calling in the service of millennium.

Even as Jesus announces his impending visit to the tribes, though, *The Book of Mormon* configures their relationship to Christian eschatology as one of deferral. Jesus tells the Nephites, "Now I go unto the Father, and also to shew myself unto the lost tribes of Israel," but he does not actually leave. Having announced his departure, the text informs readers, Jesus "cast his eyes round about again on the multitude, and beheld, they were in tears and did look steadfastly upon him, as if they would ask him to tarry a little longer with them" (3 Nephi 17:5). So Jesus changes his mind, telling the Nephites, "Behold, my bowels is [sic] filled with compassion towards you" (3 Nephi 17:6). Having decided to extend his stay, he calls the sick and injured to him for healing, and he prays for the Nephites. The seventeenth chapter of 3 Nephi concludes by noting that "the multitude did see and hear and bear record . . . and they were in number about two thousand and five hundred souls; and they did consist of men, women, and children," which would seem to draw this account of the visitation of Jesus to a satisfactory close (3 Nephi 17:25). The following chapter thus opens with a bit of a surprise, as it depicts Jesus initiating a reenactment of the Last Supper and introducing the communal sacrament to the Nephites. "Jesus commanded his disciples that they should bring forth some bread and wine unto him," it begins. "He took of the bread and brake and blessed it, and he gave unto the disciples and commanded that they should eat" (3 Nephi 18:3). Jesus then explains, "This shall ye do in remembrance of my body, which I have shown unto you" (3 Nephi 18:7). He repeats the action with a cup of wine, telling them, "You shall do this in remembrance of my blood" (3 Nephi 18:11).

This episode is a near copy of one presented in the Gospel of Luke, when the still living Jesus shares a Passover meal with his disciples before his arrest: "And he took bread, and gave thanks, and brake it, and gave unto them, saying, This is my body which is given for you: this do in remembrance of me" (Luke 22:19). It is one of the most significant moments in Luke, as it both depicts the ritual of communion—understood variously but nonetheless important to most Christian sects—and offers a blueprint for the continuation of Christian community in the absence of Jesus himself. The literal body of Jesus transforms into the figurative body of believers, and interpersonal interaction with a living deity transforms into the collective practice of "remembrance." In reenacting this gospel moment with the Nephites, Jesus completes their initiation into the community of Christ.

This is a crucial moment in the text, and yet it takes place only after Jesus informs the Nephites that he is leaving to visit the lost tribes and then, upon seeing their tears, opts to stay. The depiction of the communal ritual as something of an afterthought in the text is compelling and deserving of more critical investigation. My main interest here, though, is in the delay it produces in the text. Even as they are brought into Jesus' sphere in *The Book of Mormon*, the lost tribes remain beyond the margins of the text. Jesus says that he is leaving to visit them, but it turns out that they will need to wait. Their reception of Christianity and their reentry into history are equally deferred.

Highway from Heaven: The Lost Tribes in Latter-Day Saint Literature

Although *The Book of Mormon* offers no information about the location of the lost tribes of Israel, it is not the last word on the tribes within literature produced by members of the Church. Following the book's publication, a rich field of writing (some sacred, some not) emerged to address this ongoing biblical mystery. Although he never officially commented on the tribes' whereabouts, Smith did report two revelations regarding the tribes after the publication of *The Book of Mormon*. The second of these took place following the dedication of the Kirtland Temple in 1836 and also was experienced by Oliver Cowdery, the first baptized member of the Church and one of Smith's primary scribes for *The Book of Mormon*. The account initially was recorded in a journal of visions (the journal's handwriting belongs to Warren Cowdery, Oliver's older brother). This vision would later become the 110th section of *The Doctrine and Covenants*, a collection of revelations and declarations—many, but not all, attributed to Smith—that forms the theological backbone of the Church of Jesus Christ of Latter-day Saints. In this section, Smith and Cowdery state that "Moses appeared before them, and committed unto them the keys of the gathering of Israel from the four parts of the Eearth [sic], and the leading of the ten tribes from the Land of the North."[17]

This vision is significant for a few reasons. It confirms *The Book of Mormon*'s account of the tribes as an extant and cohesive body of people. More than that, though, it assigns responsibility for their recovery to Smith and Cowdery, placing the tribes within the purview of the Church. Finally, and for my purposes most significantly, the vision offers a clue to the tribes' location, even if it stops short of revealing it. The "Land of the North" is not the most specific geographic label, but it does eliminate vast portions of the globe. Subsequent discussions of the tribes by Church members would focus on their "northern" status, theorizing potential locations based on this admittedly vague directional marker. The tribes operate within this vision much as they do in *The Book of Mormon*; they are somewhere out of reach, but when the time comes, Smith and his followers will bring them home.

Smith's second vision regarding the tribes confirms an earlier and more detailed one he reported receiving in Hiram, Ohio, on November 3, 1831. The text of this revelation eventually became the 133rd section of *The Doctrine and Covenants*, though Smith detailed it early in his prophetic career. The vision was written down first in what is now referred to as Revelation Book 1, a manuscript book penned by several different scribes over the course of five years beginning in March of 1831.[18] It made its way into print as an appendix to the 1835 edition of the *Doctrine and Covenants of the Church of the Latter Day Saints.*

According to Smith, God revealed many things to him when he prayed for guidance, including a prophecy that "they who are in the north countries shall come in remembrance before the Lord, and their prophets shall hear his voice, and shall no longer stay themselves, and they shall smite the rocks, and the ice shall flow down at their presence. And an high way shall be cast up in the midst of the great deep. Their enemies shall become a prey unto them, and in the barren deserts there shall come forth pools of living water; and the parched ground shall no longer be a thirsty land."[19] This revelation echoes the promise in Isaiah that "there shall be an highway for the remnant of his people, which shall be left, from Assyria; like as it was to Israel in the day that he came up out of the land of Egypt" (Isaiah 11:16). Unlike Isaiah, though, and unlike the vision Smith later would share with Cowdery, the 1831 revelation offers tantalizing geographic specifics—the "north countries" that house the tribes are places of "rock" and "ice" on the edge of a "great deep." The apparent need, as in Isaiah, for a "high way" to be created for the tribes further suggests that they are out of reach yet not too far away. These clues narrow the scope of possible locations and make the recovery of the tribes a real possibility in an age of global exploration. As it turns out, of course, such details are open to interpretation, and over the course of the nineteenth century, members of the Church grappled with these prophecies that made the tribes appear so close even as it pushed them out of reach.

One of the earliest theories regarding the location of the lost tribes to emerge in this literature held that Israelites reside on either a separate planet or a portion of the earth that had been divided from the main body by divine order. The origins of this theory are murky, and there is no specific revelation or doctrine that officially sanctions it within the Church's theology. There are, however, several second- and third-hand accounts of Smith himself embracing such a notion. Per Brough, in an 1875 letter, Orson Pratt claimed that he once heard Smith "[advance] his opinion that the Ten Tribes were separated from the Earth; or a portion of the Earth was by a miracle broken off, and that the Ten Tribes were taken away with it, and that in the latter days it would be restored to the Earth or be let down in the Polar regions."[20] Pratt did not subscribe to this theory himself, but the idea that Smith had posited an extraterrestrial location for the tribes persisted among some Church members through the nineteenth century and remains an unsettled question.

It is not my aim to take a position on whether Smith received, invented, or subscribed to this planetary theory. For my purposes, the "unknown planet" serves two important functions in this literature. First, it explains the continuing absence of the tribes by linking them at least metaphorically to the biblical city of Enoch, a significant presence in Church theology. Second, in the decades following its emergence, the idea of an undiscovered planet allowed some writers to situate the lost tribes within evolving scientific understandings of the universe and thereby to align their religious commitments with an ever-shifting celestial landscape. The theory thus acted as a kind of lynchpin, connecting biblical exegesis to new empirical studies of heavenly bodies. Read in this light, the idea that an undiscovered planet might serve as the tribes' temporary home makes perfect sense; Church theology adapts to emergent science through the myth of the Israelites. This is not atypical in engagements with lost tribes mythology by Latter-day Saints. The tribes frequently are the site where scripture meets science.

Perhaps the most significant early engagement with the idea that the lost tribes resided on an unknown planet is Eliza Snow's poem "Address to Earth," which was first published in the periodical *Latter-Day Saints' Millennial Star* in 1851. It was republished as a hymn in several editions of *Sacred Hymns and Spiritual Songs for the Church of Jesus Christ of Latter-Day Saints*, first compiled by Brigham Young, Parley Pratt, and John Taylor in 1840, but updated and augmented well into the twentieth century. Snow's poem appears in that collection simply as "Hymn 322," and it occasionally is printed with the title "Thou Earth."

Snow was a popular and prolific poet, and she held high status among the Latter-day Saints. She was an early convert—joining the Church in 1835—and a close confidante of Joseph Smith, as well as one of his first plural wives. She married Brigham Young, Smith's successor, following Smith's murder in 1844. As Claudia Stokes notes in one of the few studies of Snow's poetry, Snow was "dubbed variously the Prophetess, Priestess, and Presidentess of Mormonism, as well as 'Zion's Poetess,'" and by the late nineteenth century, "Mormon primary-school teachers were advised to cultivate 'a reverence' for Snow in their young pupils."[21] Snow's poetry not only delighted readers but also, Stokes demonstrates, had a productive impact on the Church's developing theology. Despite her prominence in the period, though, she has received almost no attention from literary scholars. This is probably the case because she embraced a religion that remains marginalized within the study of US literature, though the unabashed sentimentality of her work also might have contributed to its nearly complete erasure from literary history.[22] There remains much to say about Snow's poetry, but for my purposes her "Address to Earth" is significant for its removal of the Kingdom of Israel from the planet. When Jesus departs to visit the tribes in 3 Nephi, he does not specify his destination. "Address to the Earth," though, fills in the blank with extraterrestrial specificity.

From its outset, Snow's poem presents readers with an incomplete globe. "Thou, Earth," she writes, "wast once a glorious sphere / Of noble magnitude / And didst with majesty appear / Among the worlds of God."[23] The past tense is striking. Earth "wast once" but is no longer "a noble sphere" (whether what has been lost is its nobility or its spherical shape or both is a bit unclear). The division of the planet, the poem asserts, was deliberate: "But thy dimensions have been torn / Asunder, piece by piece; / And each dismembered fragment borne / Abroad to distant space." Here, passive voice does not obscure the actor so much as indicate the vastness of the power at work. Even the earth's "magnitude" is no match for divine will. And for Snow, the violation of the planet's physical integrity serves a wonderful purpose: the protection of God's most favored people from worldly influence. The poem's third and fourth stanzas read as follows:

> When Enoch could no longer stay,
>   Amid corruption here;
> Part of thyself was borne away,
>   To form another sphere.
> That portion where his city stood,
>   He gained by right approved;
> And nearer to the throne of God
>   His planet upward moved.

The Enoch in question receives scant mention in the Bible—he is a descendant of Seth, Adam and Eve's third son, and the father of Methuselah. Genesis tells us only that "all the days of Enoch were three hundred sixty and five years," and that "Enoch walked with God: and he was not; for God took him" (Genesis 5:21–24).

For most Christians, Enoch is not a significant biblical figure. However, in the 1830s, Smith began an inspired new translation of the Bible, which included previously unrecorded books. Part of that translation included the "Prophecy of Enoch," which appeared in the *Millennial Star* in 1840 and then as part of Smith's Book of Moses, which was published in *The Pearl of Great Price* in 1851. God's taking of Enoch is rendered in literal terms, and his disappearance has deep theological significance. At God's bidding, the righteous Enoch and his people build the holy city of Zion, and to save that city from corruption, God lifts it off the earth. The Book of Moses parallels Genesis's description of Enoch's disappearance in its account of the city's departure: "And it came to pass that Zion was not, for God received it up into his own bosom; and from thence went forth the saying, Zion is Fled."[24] Thus Enoch and the City of Zion serve as a model for the removal of entire populations into outer space by divine fiat.

Snow uses Zion as a type to explain the disappearance of the Kingdom of Israel. She writes, "When the Lord saw fit to hide / The 'ten lost tribes' away; / Thou wast divided to provide / The orb on which they stay." This is not subtle: the Kingdom of Israel, like the city of Zion, is no longer part of the earth. The tribes thus cannot be located through mere human means, and their return will require a divinely ordered event. Importantly, for Snow, the future gathering of Israel will not only fulfill Christian millennial promises but also serve as a reckoning for Smith's murder. The poem concludes,

> Jesus, the Lord, thy surface grac'd
>   And fell a sacrifice;
> And, now within thy cold embrace!
>   Thy martyred Joseph lies!
> A "restitution" yet will come
>   That will to thee restore,
> By the grand law of worlds, thy sum

Of matter heretofore . . .
And thou, O Earth! will leave the track
Thou now art doom'd to trace—
The gods with shouts will bring thee back
To fill thy native place.

These stanzas have several remarkable features. First, Snow's situating of Smith's assassination between the description of Jesus' sacrifice and the assertion of a coming "restitution" places the prophet's story on par with that of the Christian messiah. Snow's earth has suffered several wounds that the tribes' return will heal: it has been broken into pieces to protect God's people; it has endured the crucifixion; and it has enveloped the body of the murdered Smith. Diminished and aimless, the planet has for thousands of years trod a lonely, cold ellipse. But someday, in some unknown future, the restoration of its missing pieces will allow it to break out of its orbit and make its way back to the divine. With "Address to Earth," Snow reveals exactly where the lost tribes are and predicts the radical changes that will be produced by their future return, but she also, most importantly, explains why human agency never will produce their recovery.

Although Snow's "Address to Earth" is not particularly concerned with the science of the missing tribes, the planetary solution it offers to the mystery was attractive to later Church members seeking to explain the tribes' continued absence in the era of global exploration. Variations on Snow's theme thus appeared in later writings. Perhaps the most compelling of these is the "narrow neck theory," which holds that the earth is not a discrete sphere but rather the center of three celestial bodies connected by tracts of land yet undiscovered by humans. This theory traces its roots to a diagram that Smith is purported to have drawn in 1842 and given to his friend Philo Dibble. Forty years later, Dibble made a copy of that diagram and gave it to Matthew W. Dalton, a convert who, like Dibble, had followed the sect to Utah. Dalton had his own copy of the diagram made by C. F. Wells Jr., and he included that copy in his 1906 book, *The Period of God's Work on this Planet; or, How Science Agrees with the Revelations of our Beloved Redeemer: A Key to this Earth.* Citing everything from scriptures and Snow's poem to Webster's dictionary and turn-of-the-century geography textbooks, Dalton attempts to align the sacred record with geological history and thereby prove the veracity of Latter-day Saints' beliefs.

The diagram, Dalton asserts, solves several biblical conundrums. The extra spheres are, for example, the perfect storage space for catastrophic flood waters. His most important goal, though, is to solve the riddle of the Kingdom of Israel. "The Ten Tribes are supposed to be in the north," he writes. "How is this possible when the explorers, by their discoveries and progress toward the pole have limited the unexplored parts around the North Pole to a space something like 400 miles across?"[25] His answer, of course, is that the earth is not one planet but three—a trinity awaiting reunification via divine order. If the extra spheres can house an earth's measure of water, then there is no reason why they cannot also serve as temporary housing for a missing population.

Dalton's text is significant for its overlaying of scientific reasoning onto revealed religion. For Snow in 1851, the City of Zion and the transfiguration of Enoch operated as a suitable model for thinking about the fate of the tribes. But by 1906, Dalton required a different kind of explanation. "It may be asked," he writes, "why it is not possible to see this other globe if the explorers have approached within 200 miles of the spot where the North Pole should be."[26] He offers material reasons for the invisibility of this massive land bridge jutting out into space. First, "an open sea [surrounds] the entire neck. . . . From this open sea, owing to the latent heat of the earth, arise mists of the greatest magnitude which effectively hide from view the land for any great distance."[27] What is more, the "northern lights, or aurora borealis, is caused by these continual mists," to further obscure the bridge's presence. Anticipating the argument that the spheres should at least be visible in the form of eclipses, Dalton asserts that "the shadow of the earth with its three spheres cannot be seen . . . because the earth is always in the same position at angle of 22½ degrees, and the two outer spheres are therefore outside the horizon, or outside the line of light which produces the shadow; therefore, only the shadow of the central sphere may be seen."[28]

Like Snow before him, Dalton is concerned with explaining why the tribes have not been found in an era of exploration, and the promised millennium seems as out of reach as ever. Although his explanation for their location might seem a bit extraordinary, his conclusion is as simple as Snow's: "All these things work upon natural laws," he writes, "and are

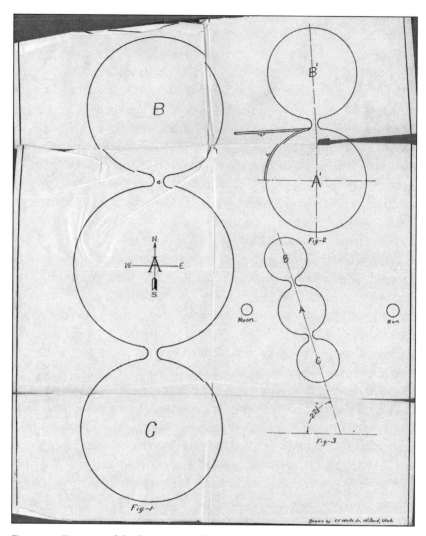

Figure 4.1. Diagram of the "narrow-neck" theory by C. F. Wells Jr. (1906). Source: C. F. Wells Jr., diagram for the frontispiece of Matthew Dalton's *Period of God's Work on this Planet; or, How Science Agrees with the Revelations of our Beloved Redeemer: A Key to this Earth* (1906). Image courtesy of General Research Division, the New York Public Library.

at the same time made to contribute to God's purpose so that everything shall be done in the season thereof."[29] The tribes have not been discovered, because the divine does not want them to be discovered. Human agency bears no part of this millennial story. The earth's other spheres will remain inaccessible until prophets are called to reveal them, and all any good Christian can do is wait.

In the absence of doctrinal certainty regarding the tribes, theories proliferated within literature by Latter-day Saints. But though they differed in their particulars, all attempted to square the Church's theology with the ever-expanding and more detailed secular knowledge of the globe. Though not always accurate, such writings about the tribes increasingly engaged in the kind of scientific speculation Dalton displayed in his defense of the alleged Smith diagram. This is perhaps clearest in the work of Elder Orson Pratt, one of the earliest and most influential members of the sect. A member of the Quorum of the Twelve Apostles, Pratt played an integral role in bringing the Church of Jesus Christ of Latter-day Saints to Europe, and he became one of the most important advocates for the doctrine of plural marriage. He also promoted scientific education, published a mathematical treatise, and worked diligently to systematize the Church's theology. For Pratt, then, the solution to the riddle of the tribes was both the simplest and the one supported by scientific reasoning: they had to occupy an as-yet-undiscovered terrestrial space, and the only possible candidate for that was the North Pole. In a sermon delivered in April of 1875 and recorded for the *Journal of Discourses*, Pratt asserts, "One thing I do know, from that which is reported by those who have tried to find a passage to the pole,"

> that there is a warmer country off there, and that birds of passage go north to find a warmer climate. That I know from the writings of intelligent men who have been on voyages of discovery. And I know, furthermore, that they have crossed by means of dogs and sledges a certain portion of this great band of ice and have come to an open sea, which proves there is a warmer country further north. There is a tract of country around the pole, some seven or eight hundred miles in diameter, that no man among the nations has ever explored. But how much of that land may be fit for habitation I am not prepared to say, for I do not know. I know it would be a very easy matter for the Lord God, by the aid of great mountain ranges

encircling them around about, to produce a band of ice which would prevent other nations and people very easily reaching them.[30]

As Dalton later would attempt to do, Pratt lays claim to epistemological certainty by linking his theory to secular accounts of the earth. The "writings of intelligent men," explorers with first-hand experience of the area surrounding the North Pole, allow him to literalize Smith's account of the "Land of the North" and explain the prophet's vision of rocks and ice. Needing to explain, though, why the tribes might not be found as the circumference of unknown polar territory shrinks, Pratt adopts the typical strategy of assigning divine intent to the tribes' ongoing obscurity. In this case, it is not a hidden neck of land that hides the tribes, but an untraversable "band of ice" fashioned for divine purpose. The tribes may still inhabit the earth, but that does not mean that humans will find them.

Pratt's theory that the North Pole would remain inaccessible without divine intervention provided fodder for fiction regarding the lost tribes. In 1903, Church member Otte J. S. Lindelof published *A Trip to the North Pole; or, The Discovery of the Ten Tribes, as Found in the Arctic Ocean.* Lindelof claims at the end of the novel to have received the manuscript from a dying fisherman he met in Europe. "To my surprise," he writes, "I found that it was in my own language. . . . It was written on poor paper . . . and it must also have been penetrated by salt water, for it was in bad shape and quite hard to decipher."[31] Nonetheless, Lindelof manages to transcribe its contents, which tell the story of a lost whaling ship that discovers the Kingdom of Israel at the North Pole. The manuscript's fictional narrator, Joe B. Lothare, details a great and implausible adventure involving pterodactyls, dirigibles, and a band of robbers. Most important for my purposes, though, is how Lindelof structures his narrative to situate the lost tribes within both Church theology and Pratt's speculation about life at the Pole. Describing the whaler's approach to the Pole, Lothare tells readers, "Wonders will never cease. We had been traveling through a temperature of one hundred and five to one hundred and ten below freezing point, when now, within two hundred miles of the North Pole, we found a climate comparatively mild" (7).

This is Pratt's "warmer country," the habitable region just beyond reach. "I had long believed the Pole was surrounded by a belt of ice,"

Lothare continues, "that, if it could be penetrated, would discover an open sea. . . . Should I ever be able to enlighten the scientific world in regard to the matter?" (8). Lindelof has reproduced almost verbatim Pratt's theory of polar geography and his notion that when the time is right, a divine order will reveal the region and its inhabitants to the world. Even in this fictional account, scientific reasoning forms the basis for human discovery of the tribes, but exploration alone will not reveal their location. Lothare fears that the secular world will never hear of his first-hand experience of temperate weather at the Pole and, thus, other explorers may miss an opportunity to find the tribes.

A Trip to the North Pole is deliberate in its linking of lost tribes mythology to the American history presented in The Book of Mormon. When the ship's first mate, Linder, falls in love with the governor's daughter, Koa, the two engage in extensive conversation about their mutual faith traditions. Much to Linder's surprise, Koa is familiar with the basic tenets of Christianity, and she seems to have received some introduction to The Book of Mormon. Linder asks if she believes in the scriptures, and she explains,

> There was a man who appeared amongst us many years ago, whom our chief men told us was the Son of God, crucified for the sins of the world, and who told us that we would yet be delivered from our sins and brought face to face with the tribes of Judah. And he also said this would happen in the near future. But before this happened, a great continent should be discovered in the West by a man inspired of God, and to this continent should we be brought by a man chosen from those people who would lead us back to our old Jerusalem. (92–93)

Although Linder takes the opportunity to explain that the "man" who visited the tribes was Jesus, and that the Israelites "have a portion of the Old Testament" but lack the "part [of the Bible] that should interest the human race more than any other," he does not acknowledge Koa's assertions about the discovery of a great continent in the west (93). This is perhaps because her story is ambiguous—the inspired man could be Lehi, or he could be Columbus. The slipperiness of Koa's account allows Lindelof to thread a theological needle, tying his story to a Latter-day Saints tradition while leaving enough space for other Christians to see their own conceptions of history at work within his narrative. Lindelof's Jesus, like the Jesus of *The Book of Mormon*, visits the tribes following his crucifixion. But the "near future" he promises them seems perhaps less "near" than "future." Like other accounts before it, *A Trip to the North Pole* attempts to keep the tribes intact and in play while still accounting for their relentless absence.

Theories of a polar home for the lost tribes persisted among both Latter-day Saints and some other Christians until the early twentieth century, when explorers finally reached the North Pole and found no one living there. But as late-nineteenth-century expeditions shrank the boundaries of the uncharted Arctic, another space remained open to the tribes: the earth's core. The idea that the earth was hollow was neither an invention of the Church nor its exclusive property. The following chapter of this book will examine the relationship between hollow earth and Hebraic Indian theories in more detail. Within the context of Latter-day Saints' writing, the hollow earth theory, like the separate planet and polar theories, facilitated a merging of scientific and theological reasoning in the service of deferring a promised millennium.

Interest in the idea of a hollow earth is nearly as old as the Church itself. The July 1832 edition of the *Evening and Morning Star*, for example, includes a brief synopsis of a report from the *Poughkeepsie Telegraph*, detailing the appearance of a large sinkhole in upstate New York. "An acre and a half . . . has sunk one hundred feet," the piece reads, "so that the tops of the highest trees growing upon it, are scarcely level with the surrounding surface."[32] According to the report, the likeliest cause of the sinkhole was a subterranean stream, but the *Evening and Morning Star* article concludes with, "If this be not a philosophical explanation, we must place the phenomenon to the credit of the theory of Capt. Symmes." The Symmes in question here is John Cleve Symmes Jr., who in 1818 developed a theory that the earth was comprised of concentric spheres, the center of which was habitable, and campaigned unsuccessfully for funds to support an expedition to the Pole to find a passage into the planet's interior. (Symmes's theory will be explored in more detail in the following chapter.) The reference to Symmes in the *Evening and Morning Star* might be bit tongue in cheek, but his cameo, which appears without further explanation, suggests that the paper's readers had some knowledge of and interest in theories regarding the earth's interior.[33]

The most explicit adoption of the hollow earth theory by an early Church member is Frederick Culmer's 1886 treatise, *The Inner World: A New Theory, Based on Scientific and Theological Facts, Showing that the Earth is a Hollow Sphere, Containing an Internal and Inhabited Region*.[34] Born in England, Culmer and his wife converted to the faith in 1852 and traveled to the United States in 1867. They joined a westward convoy the following year and eventually settled in Salt Lake City. *The Inner World* is like the writings of Dalton and Pratt, in that it attempts to marshal scientific reasoning to make the case for a theological claim. It bears the trappings of a scientific treatise, and Culmer was at least passingly familiar with theories related to chemistry and mechanics. However, his ideas are inconsistent with modern science, and their precise origins are hard to trace, because he refrains almost entirely from citing sources.

The clearest inspiration for his thinking is Sir Isaac Newton's *Philosophiæ Naturalis Principia Mathematica*, which first appeared in English in 1728 with the title *Mathematical Principles of Natural Philosophy*. Culmer draws (haphazardly) on Newton's notion of universal gravity to argue that every "particle of matter is charged with two primary forces, attraction and repulsion, which not only act, in opposition, in the molecule itself but the forces belonging to that molecule influence every other molecule to a degree established by known laws."[35] After aptly warning readers that "what follows is not at all orthodox," Culmer asserts that the forces of attraction and repulsion produce a condition whereby "the greatest density . . . cannot exist at the real centre of a mass, but in a globular outline approaching the centre in exact proportion to the specific gravity of the element of which it is composed" (5). Elements and molecules, he contends, are spheres with empty cores. And because gravity is a universal force, Culmer insists, the same must be true even for the largest of objects. "The form of the solar system is that of a hollow globe," he writes, "in which the sun and the planets form a material circumference and the centre is absolute space" (6). This is not correct, but it does allow Culmer to make his most important conjecture: "Are we, then," he asks, "to pursue this theory from infinitesimal proportions to those of the infinite, finding centres to be void of matter, whether they be in a molecule or in the universe, and not think seriously that our own earth, intermediate between the two extremes, may also be a hollow sphere?" (7).

At the heart of Culmer's reasoning lies a belief that the operations of the universe apply equally and with consistent results to all bodies, regardless of size or specific composition, and that the conditions of the invisible world may be deduced from those of the visible. For Culmer, of course, knowledge regarding the material condition of the world is not itself an end but rather a means to greater religious certainty. His empty molecules and solar systems are clues, divinely planted, leading to the truth beneath our feet.

Culmer's theory requires the earth's core to be not only hollow but also habitable, and so he ties his abstract postulations about attraction and repulsion to Symmes's notion of a world within the world. Culmer did not read Symmes, but rather encountered his theories in the 1885 issue of *Parry's Literary Journal*, which includes a translation of an 1882 French account of Symmes's work entitled "Le Trou de Symmes."[36] Culmer reproduces the translation, which asserts that "Symmes based his evidence upon proofs given, not by inanimate nature, but by nature animate and living," particularly by "the instincts of animals, which cannot mislead."[37] Contending that "an immense migration took place in the Autumn of each year among herds of bisons [*sic*] and reindeer, of white bears and foxes, as also game of all sorts . . . which moved in bands from the '*south to the north*,'" the piece asks readers, "Where had these animals passed the winter?"[38]

For the French author, this question is not settled, but the possibility that Symmes was correct "has seized upon the imagination of some scientific men, and if they do not give entire faith to his system, at least they do not laugh at this theory which is now already progressing."[39] For Culmer, however, the answer is clear; these herds are moving in and out of a habitable space within the earth. And if animals can survive in such a space, then so too must human beings be able to do. "The earth is a rotating crust of uneven surface," Culmer asserts, "open at the North and South, through which openings our sun shines by direct and refracted rays beyond their interior equatorial line and the light and heat thereof supplies the interior, the diurnal rotation causing every part to receive in its turn, the genial warmth and light. Thus they have their days and nights, their seed time and harvest, their summer and winter; and they have their sky overhead with its clouds, rain, waterspouts, thunder and lightning" (34–35). Gravity, light refraction, the water cycle—all operate to ensure that the hollow earth teems with life. Nonetheless, Culmer writes, "I do not believe there is any use in future explorations to discover either a Northwest passage or the 90th degree of North or South latitude" (9). His reasoning is simple: "The time is not yet come when the great secrets of the ice-bound regions of the North or South shall be unlocked" (11). Culmer's verb choice and passive voice are telling; for something to "be unlocked," it first had to be locked, by some agent, for some purpose. The ongoing obscurity of the North Pole and its secrets, for Culmer, can mean only that a force greater than human ambition has concealed the tribes for its own purpose.

Having established a scientific basis for his argument that the earth is hollow, Culmer moves into a theological case for the tribes' residence within it. For this, he relies heavily on Elder George Reynolds's 1883 book *Are We of Israel?*, which argues that the lost tribe of Ephraim migrated to northern Europe and that, consequently, some white Christians (conveniently and perhaps unsurprisingly, converts to the Church) are the literal descendants of that tribe.[40] Building on this conjecture and prophecies predicting the tribes' return from a northern region, Culmer asserts that at least a portion of them must have continued beyond Europe, first to the Pole and then deep into the earth.

The inner world's physical climate mirrors that of the outer world, but its political climate, according to Culmer, is even better. The tribes "can plant and eat the fruits thereof, can build and inhabit, with no nation to make war against them, no division of feeling, no political strife, no armies to maintain. Their lives, from infancy to old age, must be as in a heaven of peace. How different to the exterior earth, so full of violence and crime!" (32). Human life within the earth does not merely survive but reaches its maximum potential. And because the climate has been so hospitable to them, when they return, the tribes will overwhelm the earth's crust in fulfillment of biblical prophecy. "There will not be any part of hill or valley, plain or seaboard left unoccupied," Culmer asserts. "They will spread irresistibly through the land North, East, South and West. No Dominion of Canada nor United States can delay them. There will be few left to try. The boasted fifty-five millions of the United States will be but a drop in the bucket compared to the unnumbered millions of the Tribes of Israel. Then the proud and haughty that may be left in the land will cheerfully accept of a humility of which they never dreamed" (35). The grotesque horror of this scene seems to be lost on Culmer. That aside, it is important to note that his lost tribes are not the beleaguered and diminishing Americans of earlier writings. Nor have they been static in place all this time, holding on, waiting. These tribes, bolstered by a superior living situation, have been reproducing at lightning speed and are now poised to outnumber the humans living above them. They are locked in their sphere for now, but when the divine hand unlocks it, they will swarm like locusts and devour all nations in the service of God.

Interest in locating the lost tribes declined somewhat over the course of the twentieth century within the Church of Jesus Christ of Latter-day Saints. This decline was not unique to the Church, as the tribes came to occupy less and less space within Christian traditions in general. Successful expeditions to remote territories and advances in astronomy and physics eliminated many potential sites for the tribes, and their return shifted in much religious writing from an imminent, material occurrence to a more distant and perhaps metaphorical possibility. This is not to say, though, that Church members have completely abandoned the tribes as a source of inspiration. Indeed, the tribes prove excellent fodder for adventures, especially within young adult fiction. The novelist C. B. Andersen's 2002 work, *The Lost Tribe*, features a family that encounters an ancient civilization after being stranded (possibly in Russia) after a plane crash, and Tina Monson's 2005 work *The Legend of the Lamp* is the first in a trilogy of novels about siblings who discover a passage into the earth's core while on a historic-sites tour with their mother. In that book, the Hill Cumorah in upstate New York, rather than the North Pole, holds the entrance to the inner world.

In some ways, Latter-day Saints' engagements with the lost tribes theory are similar to those operant within other Christian traditions. In the absence of real information regarding the fate of the tribes, writers across religious perspectives have maintained the possibility that the tribes remain somewhere and will appear sometime. But because *The Book of Mormon*, unlike the Bible, explicitly insists that the tribes remain whole and intact, and because it is equally forceful in its denial of the possibility that they are in the Americas, it sparked a literary tradition more acutely concerned with their physical location and more certain that when they were discovered they would remember their history. The

Hebraic Indian theory may have offered *The Book of Mormon*'s earliest readers a context for understanding its historical premise, but its Lamanites are not the lost tribes, and European colonization of the Americas was not the apex of human history. Although they diverge significantly from other Christian accounts of the lost tribes, narratives by Latter-day Saints share with their mainline Christian counterparts an interest in how advancements in science might reveal theological truths. As religious writers worked to reconcile biblical and scientific accounts of the universe, the lost tribes moved into the space between those seemingly distinct worldviews, awaiting not only a divine command to reveal themselves but also a human intelligence sufficiently advanced to receive them.

5

Indian Removal and the Decline of American Hebraism

James Fenimore Cooper's late novel, *The Bee-Hunter; or, The Oak Openings* (1848), has fallen both out of print and off the critical radar. Set in the Territory of Michigan in the early days of the War of 1812, this novel tells the story of Benjamin Boden, a man whose exceptional moral character is surpassed only by his ability to observe the flight paths of bees. Boden's solitary life of honey harvesting is disrupted when local Native American populations begin choosing sides in the unfolding conflict. Further complication arises from Boden's budding relationship with Margery, the charming sister of a drunkard named Gershom Waring, who befriends the reluctant bee hunter and throws his life into disarray. Margery's nickname, conveniently, is Blossom, a reflection of her youth and beauty. Drawn to Blossom like, well, a bee to a flower, Boden risks everything to save the Waring family from the murderous plots of Scalping Peter—an accurately named, tribeless Native American whom the novel's white characters inexplicably trust. *The Bee-Hunter*'s subplot revolves around the kindly but oblivious Parson Amen, a Methodist preacher who has come to Michigan to convince the Potawatomi that they are the descendants of the ten lost tribes of Israel. At the intersection of these narrative lines, *The Bee-Hunter* configures the American frontier as a space hostile to both the Native peoples who challenge white settlement and the white Christians whose theological positions might buttress Native claims to sovereignty.

In Cooper's novel, bee hunting establishes a colonial geometry that both requires and produces the disappearance of Native peoples. Although scholars long have recognized the significance of sugar to the rise of American settler states, its sister sweetener has received far less attention.[1] As *The Bee-Hunter* shows, though, bees and their honey played an important role not only in emerging American economies but also in antebellum conceptions of frontier space. As this chapter's first section will demonstrate, *The Bee-Hunter*'s descriptions of the practice of tracking bees to their hives organizes the frontier landscape around the "vanishing point"—the point at which parallel lines seemingly converge beyond a horizon.

Honey gathering was more than a quaint occupation in Cooper's time; it was a trade that took white settlers first to the nation's rural edge and then deep into the territories. Documents of the colonial and early national eras frequently emphasize the link between honeybees and expansionism, continuing a long tradition of using bees as figures for various modes of social organization. This fact was not lost on Cooper, and indeed Boden is not the first bee hunter to appear in his works. *The Prairie* (1827) features Paul Hover, a young hunter pursuing his craft in a west newly opened to Anglo-Americans by the Louisiana Purchase. When a trapper asserts that bee hunting "pays well in the skirts of the settlements" but is "a doubtful trade, in the more open districts," Hover replies, "I have stretched out a few hundred miles farther west than common, to taste your honey."[2] As Boden will in Cooper's later novel, Hover follows the bee into the wilderness, paying little regard to the boundaries of existing nations.

Apart from a footnote explaining honey hunting—a real occupation still performed in a few parts of the United States—Cooper does not offer detailed descriptions of the practice in *The Prairie*. *The Bee-Hunter*, however, meticulously (though inaccurately) narrates the process. In this novel, the art of hive discovery depends upon Boden's carefully honed ability to track bees out of sight and calibrate their flight paths to a vanishing point. Through the alignment of bees and Native Americans in the text, Cooper suggests that a similar deductive process will allow an Anglo United States to obtain western lands. Bees and Native peoples alike exist in Cooper's text at the vanishing point, forever receding into the distance, only to be further chased by those laying claim to their dwellings. Bee hunting establishes an interpretive framework for the novel that situates indigenous peoples within an impossible geometry requiring their withdrawal from the landscape.

Boden's frontier geometry operates in direct opposition to the one touted by Parson Amen, who configures Native Americans as returning to rather than receding from sight. *The Bee-Hunter* is thus Cooper's most explicit response to the Hebraic Indian theory, as Amen is a forceful proponent of it. His expression of the theory is typical of its

144 | INDIAN REMOVAL AND THE DECLINE OF AMERICAN HEBRAISM

nineteenth-century versions, particularly those circulating among evangelical Christians. Drawing on biblical prophecies apparently linking the discovery of the lost tribes to the return of Christ, Amen holds that once Native Americans remember their true history, the stage will be set for millennium. Although God's action has placed the Kingdom of Israel out of sight, Amen contends, human faith in the tribes' continued existence and a corresponding willingness to look for them bear the potential to set an ancient prophecy in motion. The lost tribes' location operates as a unique (and as-yet-undiscovered) geographic site where human agency has the potential to combine with divine intent and fully synch sacred and profane time.

This conception of Native peoples poses a challenge to that other figure common in nineteenth-century writings: the vanishing Indian. There is a wealth of scholarship on the vanishing Indian, and for good reason; that figure is pervasive in the period. In his early study of the phenomenon, Brian W. Dippie defined the discourse as one that presents Native peoples as "a vanishing race . . . wasting away since the day the white man arrived, diminishing in vitality and numbers until, in some not too distant future, no red men will be left on the face of the earth."[3] It makes sense that Cooper would take up and disregard the question of Hebraic origins in his fiction, because his Native Americans are always the "last" of their kind, full of romantic sadness yet heroically resigned to their fates.[4] Deidre Dallas Hall has shown that Cooper first explored the potential links between indigenous and Jewish peoples in *The Last of the Mohicans* (1826), when he embedded signs of both identity positions in the body of the psalmist David Gamut.[5] "The Indianization of the pseudo-Jewish Gamut," Hall writes, "transforms the singing master, at least momentarily, into a budding frontiersman with a chance of survival in the harsh wilderness."[6] Gamut's dubious whiteness makes him a repulsive figure—he is ungainly at best—but it also offers him a way through the harsh realities of frontier race conflict. As Hall notes, though, by the time Cooper wrote *The Bee-Hunter*, he seems to have given up on the generative possibilities of hybridity. Reading Amen as a kind of revision of Gamut, Hall suggests that by "bringing Pastor Amen to uncooperative, incredulous Indians rather than to the anticipated crypto-Jews, Cooper disables any linkage between Indians and Jews completely, preventing the critical comparison of Native Other to European Other that enables imaginative 'whitening.'"[7] Indeed, the search for Israelites blinds the parson to what is right in front of him—the murderous intentions of Scalping Peter.

I find Hall's reading compelling but would further suggest that Cooper's situating of Amen against the backdrop of bee hunting allows the novel to present the brand of evangelism that the parson practices as an artifact destined, like the Native Americans Amen attempts to convert, to disappear in the face of an ascendant US nationalism. In beckoning indigenous peoples to return along a sightline and emerge in full view as Israelites, Parson Amen creates not only a racial but also a religious problem that the novel must solve if it is to succeed in its project of white nationalism. Although it bears all the trappings of a standard romance of indigenous decay, *The Bee-Hunter* also operates as a narrative of competing modes of American Protestantism. This chapter's second section shows that the vanishing perhaps most important to Cooper in 1848 is that of the enthusiastic Methodist. Set in the middle of the Second Great Awakening but written in its aftermath, the novel presents the Hebraic Indian theory as a potential disruption in a territory otherwise being put to order by the likes of Boden. The clear lines and accurate calculations that the bee hunter would impose upon the landscape are thrown into chaos by Amen's prophetic vision. Ultimately, it is bad geometry as much as bad theology that marks the parson's undoing: overly focused on a distant horizon, he has constructed a blind spot for Scalping Peter to occupy. Amen's inevitable destruction clears a frontier space to be filled by the right kind of Christianity—the practical, pious, and denominationally indeterminate sort embodied first by Margery and then by Boden and finally, most surprisingly, by Peter. Parson Amen begins as a comical but troubling proponent of the lost tribes theory, but in the end his alternative history fades away along with Cooper's Native populations, leaving the frontier to the bee hunter, his carefully drawn lines, and his hives.

Making a Beeline: Colonialism and the Vanishing Point

The honeybee is not indigenous to the Americas. There is archeological evidence that the inhabitants of Europe, Asia, and Africa have been harvesting honey for thousands of years, but the honeybee with which we are familiar is a recent addition to the western hemisphere, having arrived with settler colonists in the seventeenth century.[8] As Tammy Horn notes in her excellent history of American beekeeping, though Europeans who journeyed west often cited Numbers 14:8 in deeming America the "land of milk and honey," they had to fashion that land as such, importing cattle for the former and bees for the latter.[9] The first recorded English effort to ship beehives to North America occurred in 1609, but the *Sea Venture* that housed them blew off course and landed in Bermuda. The Virginia Company had more success about a decade later, when a 1621 vessel containing hives along with other supplies departed from England and landed safely. By the 1640s, there were town apiaries as far north as Massachusetts.[10]

Bees from England thrived in North America, probably because they were already accustomed to cold and shifting temperatures, especially after weeks at sea. The American landscape provided an excellent supply of food and shelter for bees: there were ample opportunities to feed on local flora, and new swarms could make homes in the hollow trees that were ubiquitous in the continent's vast forestlands. In these favorable conditions, the honeybee acclimated quickly and spread throughout the hemisphere. Honey became a popular sweetener not only for colonists but also among existing populations. Native Americans who had for generations been creating sweetener out of distilled maple sap adopted bee-tracking practices and traded honey with white settlers and each other. The honeybee thus had a sudden and lasting impact on both the physical and the social landscapes of the Americas.

As Horn and others have shown, the bee and its hive long have stood as potent symbols for human modes of social order and sovereignty. In seventeenth-century England, the beehive seemed a particularly apt example of a productive society, as a hard-working population organized around specific roles with a clear hierarchy held great appeal for supporters of the crown. Charles Butler's 1609 work, *The feminine monarchie, a paean to the late Queen Elizabeth I*, describes bees as living "under the government of one Monarch, of whom above al [sic] things they have principal care & respect, loving, reverencing and obeying her in al things."[11]

The queen was not the only appealing bee in the period: Horn notes that the drone—the male bee that performs no work in the hive and exists solely to mate a single time with an outside queen—stood as a sign for everything from beggars to sick people to, eventually, colonists.[12] The drone's forced exit from the hive at the beginning of winter (a sentence of death by exile) seemed a harsh but necessary warning to unproductive members of society. Like all signs, though, the beehive proved unstable as England devolved into religious war and extended its imperial reach. Just over a century after Butler's publication, Anglo-American colonists would deploy bee imagery as a word of caution to their English governors. In *The Christian Philosopher* (1721), Cotton Mather writes, of bees, "If they have no King, they pine, they die, they yield themselves a Prey to Robbers," but his description includes a caveat to those who might mistake the necessity of monarchy for a justification of totalitarianism. "Their King oppresses none, is a Benefactor to all," he explains, "so their Loyalty to him is inviolate."[13] Despite his error in identifying the sex of the queen bee, Mather's meaning is clear: a beehive prospers because its monarch operates from a position of benevolence rather than absolutism. The beloved queen of Butler's work becomes Mather's king, a ruler whose position is contingent upon resisting the temptation to oppress.

In the era of colonialism, the beehive evolved into a sign of white settlement in the Americas. The bee's European provenance and natural tendency to expand its population through migrating swarms made it a perfect analogy for the settler project. Correctly noting that the "chief cause of their swarm is the want of room," Mather suggests that the "king" bee joins a departing swarm "in view of a more flourishing state, and leaves his decaying and unpleasant kingdom, with the noisome old combs, to such successors as he has left alive."[14] This is not an accurate assessment of bee swarms, which occur in healthy hives that simply have exceeded their population capacity, but it is a useful window into the eighteenth-century colonial imagination. Inter- and intrahive conflict stem from overzealous leadership and a failure among bees to recognize each other as brethren. "Colonies are sometimes engaged in wars," he explains. "The king usually orders the battle, animating them with his voice, and like a general, for whose defence they unanimously expose themselves: They neither give nor take any quarter, and they distinguish one another by their smelling. Spurt any thing among them that may make them smell all alike, and their hostility ceaseth."[15] Read in light of the increasing discord at work within the Protestant colonies of Mather's day, this passage takes on a certain poignancy. The swarm that first marked departure from a "noisome old comb" has produced an all-out war. The benevolent king is now a bloodthirsty tyrant, and his bees deem themselves too distinct from each other to achieve peace. There is significant slippage in Mather's phrasing, as it becomes unclear whether the war being fought is between parent hive and new swarm, or several swarms following from the first. The bee colony thus becomes the English colonies, plagued not only by conflict with their original homeland but also by disagreement with each other.

Mather's description of the honeybee focuses on relations between colony and monarch, but bees increasingly operated as a sign of relations among white settlers and Native American nations. Most important for this project is the honeybee's emergence as a symbol for the spread of whiteness—and an ostensibly corresponding decline of indigeneity—across the American continents. While Mather used bees to highlight schism within English settlements, other writers of the period deemed the bee a sign of unified English dominion over the New World. In a 1720 article on bee-hunting techniques written for the Royal Society of London's Philosophical Transactions, for example, the Massachusetts jurist Paul Dudley notes that "the Aborigines (the Indians) have no word in their Language for a Bee . . . and therefore for many Years called a Bee by the name of English Man's Fly."[16] Here, the bee is definable to indigenous peoples only in terms of the colonist. The bee being foreign on the tongue as well as the landscape, to even speak of the honeybee is to reframe America as the domain of its new inhabitants. "The Indians therefore call them the white man's fly," Thomas Jefferson would later write in Notes on the State of Virginia, "and consider their approach as indicating the approach of the settlements of the whites."[17] The "English man's fly" of the colonies becomes the "white man's fly" of the United States. For Jefferson, the bee is a harbinger of territorial encroachment, warning Native peoples of what is to come but offering them no recourse to stop it. The westward spread of Anglo-Americans is a phenomenon as natural and unavoidable as the swarming of bees.

Read within this context, the bee hunting in Cooper's novel seems less a rustic vocation than a bellwether of US expansion. Although Michigan was a state by the time Cooper wrote The Bee-Hunter, in 1812 it was still a contested territory, even more in dispute because of the impending war. The novel opens by noting that Boden hunts his bees in the "then unpeopled forest of Michigan," which Cooper describes as "literally a wilderness" despite the large Potawatomi population inhabiting the area.[18] Cooper draws an explicit link between Michigan's physical geography and its racial makeup. "If a white man found his way into [the forest]," the narrator explains, "it was as an Indian trader, a hunter, or an adventurer in some other of the pursuits connected with border life and the habits of the savages" (11). Boden is one such adventurer, "the first to exercise his craft in that portion of the country" (12). Significantly, the pursuit of honey leads him outside of the incorporated United States and deeper into Native American lands. Describing the tools of Boden's trade, Cooper notes that the glass tumbler he uses to observe feeding bees "was his countryman in more senses than one. It was not only American, but it came from the part of Pennsylvania of which he was himself a native . . . [T]he glass was the best that Pittsburg could then fabricate" (16). Boden's glass marks him as a US citizen; his use of it takes him beyond the nation's edge. It also offers readers a sense of the terrain he has crossed in the search for honey. "Ben had bought [the glass] only the year before," Cooper writes, "on the very spot where it had been made" (16). In a single year, then, he has traversed the four hundred miles from western Pennsylvania to southern Michigan. Following the bees, Boden walks out ahead of the nation. If the bee is a harbinger of whiteness, then the bee hunter is a forerunner of the US border.

Cooper draws a clear link between bee hunting and US expansion in an early conversation between Boden and Pigeonswing, a member of the Ojibwe Nation (also referred to in the text as a Chippewa). When Boden describes himself as "plenty of Yankee," Pigeonswing objects, asserting that because the drunkard Waring is a "Yankee," Boden must be something else. "Mustn't say dat," he exclaims. "English; no Yankee. Him not a bit like you" (37). Pigeonswing hopes to capitalize on a schism within American whiteness, dividing Boden and Waring along the line separating "native" American whites from their English enemies. Boden, though, rejects Pigeonswing's equation: "My great father lives at Washington, as well as [Waring's]" (37). This assertion of mutual national feeling troubles the Ojibwe, who still insists that there are "[p]lenty Breetish in woods," but "Yankee no come yet" (37).

Pigeonswing's parsing of national identities is a bit of wishful thinking. The presence of white people in Michigan—English but not

Yankee—operates in his construction as a measure against rather than a marker of US expansion. If there are no Yankees in the woods yet, then Boden must be a harmless Englishman, visiting but not staying. The bee hunter, however, does not inhabit this fantasy. "I am an American," he asserts, "and mean to stand by my own people, come what will" (38). Here the hard truths of national and racial affinity enter Cooper's text. Although Boden shares a great deal with the Native American peoples around him, and he respects Pigeonswing far more than he does Waring, he will take up arms against the former in furtherance of the latter's interests if the conflict so demands. Boden's forays into the wilderness, then, are always potentially, if never explicitly, part of the larger project of extending the borders of the United States. Pigeonswing recognizes this truth: "T'ought you only peaceable bee-hunter, just now," he says with deep irony when Boden finally admits his sympathies (38). What begins as a conversation about Waring's drunken failings thus becomes a tense refinement of national loyalties, and Boden can no longer pretend that his position as a "peaceable bee-hunter" makes him anything less than an outlying operative of the nation-state. Today's bee hunter is tomorrow's soldier.

Cooper presents the practice of bee hunting itself as essential to the remapping of American space. From its outset, *The Bee-Hunter* evinces an interest in the geometry of bee hunting, and the novel offers several detailed descriptions of Boden's methods, focusing particularly on the tracking of bees' flight paths to a hive beyond the horizon. Eva Crane deems the novel "disappointing as a source of information" about actual bee-tracking practices, but it is clear that Cooper had at least passing familiarity with nonfiction accounts of honey gathering in North America.[19] Using a small piece of honeycomb as bait, Boden captures several bees in his Pennsylvania glass, allows them to eat their fill, and then watches closely as they depart for their hives. "The eye of Ben never left [the bee]," the narrator informs readers, "and when the insect darted off, as it soon did, in an air-line, he saw it for fifty yards after the others had lost sight of it. Ben took the range and was silent fully a minute while he did so" (20). A single bee does not provide sufficient data for hive discovery, of course, so Boden captures another and repeats the process. "To his disappointment," Cooper writes, "instead of flying in the same direction as the first taken, this little fellow went buzzing off fairly at a angle. It was consequently clear that there were two hives, and that they lay in very different directions" (21). A third bee breaks the tie, and when it flies off "directly in a line with the bee first taken," Boden notes its path and extrapolates the hive's location (21).

What Cooper presents as a kind of miraculous ability on Boden's part is actually a simplified and fantastical version of successful, mathematical honey-hunting practices. Dudley's essay describes a similar, though much more precise, method of tracking bees to their hives. The typical bee hunter, he explains, "carries with him his Pocket Compass, his Rule, and other Implements, with a Sheet of Paper, and sets down the Course" of each bee as it flies away from his bait.[20] Such "implements" allow the hunter to triangulate the hive's location using geometric projections. Dudley shows the bee hunter establishing different stations from which to observe beelines and extrapolating the location of the hive from an array of data points. Taking measurements and angles from at least three different bees, he is able to project the location of "bee trees" beyond his sightline. The process of real bee hunting, then, shares with Cooper's description of it an act of imaginative but accurate geometric calculation. The bee hunter cannot see the hive but knows that it must exist, and thus from the observable he predicts the unobservable.

Cooper discards the precise geometric operations of bee hunting and configures Boden's practice of it in terms of the vanishing point—the point at which parallel lines appear to meet at the horizon of a plane. In the visual arts, vanishing points are deployed to create an illusion of three-dimensional space on a two-dimensional plane. James Smith's 1815 work, *The Panorama of Science and Art*, defines them as the points "to which all lines inclined to the picture appear to converge, and in which those lines meet, when produced."[21] A drawing of a road going off into the distance, for example, will present its edges intersecting at the horizon, thereby forcing the viewer to imagine its continuation into an illusory distance. Importantly, as Smith notes, vanishing points "have no place in a finished picture; they are used to facilitate drawing in perspective."

The vanishing point is a paradox. It operates as a presence and an absence in perspective, offering a point of intersection to indicate infinite parallelism. Cooper's depiction of bee hunting relies on this paradox. Although Dudley's illustration shows intersecting lines merging at a distant

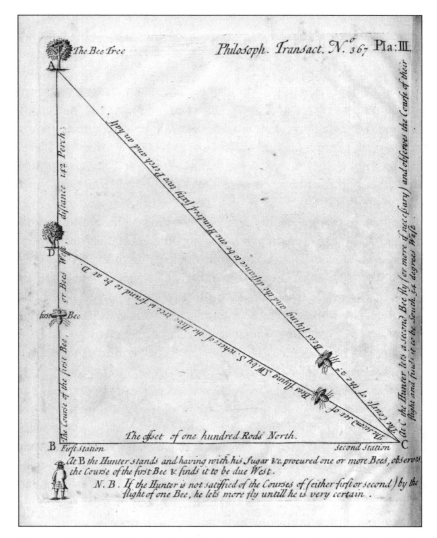

Figure 5.1. Diagram of a bee-hunting technique by Paul Dudley (1721). Source: Plate to "An account of a Method lately found out in New-England, for Discovering where the Bees Hive in the Woods, in order to get their Honey." Paul Dudley, *Philosophical Transaction of the Royal Society* 31, no. 367 (1721). Image ©The Royal Society.

point, forming a triangle in which the two known angles can be used to calculate the third, Cooper's narration highlights the fact that Boden's third bee flies "directly in a line with the bee first taken." Boden, in other words, is searching for the invisible point at which parallel lines converge. Two bees pursuing matching paths to a single point are required for the bee hunter to make his calculation, because their lines meet at a juncture just beyond the horizon. Situated in three-dimensional space, these beelines create a legible map for the hunter to follow. The hunter's success hinges on his ability to watch a bee disappear and calculate the point at which it will be seen again. Like the vanishing points of perspective drawing, the honey tree in Cooper's novel is always at once an end and a beginning. Discovery of the tree concludes one hunt but begins another, as Boden endlessly follows the honeybee across America.

The vanishing honeybee quickly becomes the vanishing Indian in *The Bee-Hunter*, as the novel explicitly associates the flight paths of bees with the movements of Native Americans. Following the successful honey hunt, when his guests take their leave, Boden notices that "neither of the Indians said anything to the other touching the path he was about to travel, but . . . each seemed ready to pursue his own way as if entirely independent" (49). These men move in solitary lines, and their movements can be tracked beyond the horizon. Watching the Potawatomi Elksfoot disappear from view, Boden notes that he "moved off in a south westerly direction, passing through the open glades and almost equally unobstructed groves, as steady in his movements as if led by an instinct" (49). The straight line of Elksfoot's travel and his instinctual maneuvering connects him directly to the bees. Earlier in the novel, Cooper's narrator informs readers, "Creatures which obey an instinct or such a reason as bees possess would never make a curvature in their flights without some strong motive for it" (23). If this link is too subtle, Cooper makes the point explicit when Boden turns to his companions and says, of the departing Elksfoot, "There he goes on a bee-line. . . . On a bee-line for the St. Joseph's River, where he will shortly be, among friends and neighbors, I do not doubt" (49). Here Boden's tracking of Native Americans outpaces his tracking of bees, as he does not even require a second line to determine Elksfoot's destination. Read in conjunction with Pigeonswing's observation that Boden might not be just a "peaceable bee-hunter" if the needs of his nation demand otherwise, the lining of Elksfoot and extrapolation of his destination take on a sinister cast. After all, Boden's hunts end only one way for his bees: discovery of the hive always results in its destruction.

Boden's prediction that Elksfoot is headed for the St. Joseph's River to meet up with "friends and neighbors" introduces a sense of foreboding into *The Bee-Hunter*, for although the Potawatomi people inhabited a great deal of land around that river in the 1812 of the novel's setting, by the 1848 of its writing they would be all but gone from the region. Like many Native American communities, the Potawatomi endured devastating land deals and forced migration at the hands of the federal government following passage of the Indian Removal Act. Over the course of the 1830s, the tribe signed several treaties ceding land to the United States, the results of which were disastrous. The land seizure culminated in the 1838 Trail of Death, when the army forced 859 of the remaining Potawatomi to march from Indiana to Kansas; forty people died along the way, mainly from exhaustion and exposure. In *The Bee-Hunter*, annihilation of the Potawatomi appears justified, as the tribe aligns with the British against the Americans in the war. Indeed, the tribe provides the novel with its villains. Cooper presents the defeat of the Potawatomi in miniature, when the Ojibwe Pigeonswing murders Elksfoot soon after they leave Boden's camp.

Pigeonswing is a historical anomaly in the text, as the Ojibwe in Michigan also aligned with the British in 1812. In Cooper's rendering, Pigeonswing's affinity for Boden overrides tribal alliance as well as self-interest. For my purposes, the significance of Elksfoot's murder lies in Cooper's presentation of it as the product of intersecting lines. When Boden notes that upon their departures from his cabin, the "Pottawattomie went on one path, and you went on another," Pigeonswing replies, "Path come together, somehow; and Pottawattamie lose he scalp" (117). Here, lines that should not converge "somehow" do. This geometry is not identical to the parallel flight paths of Boden's bees, but it operates within a similar, impossible geometric logic: lines that should never intersect traverse colonial space and meet at a vanishing point—out of sight, but nonetheless predictable. That meeting terminates both lines but establishes a single, new flight path for one subject (in this case, the Native person who sympathizes with white settlers). Taken as a whole, Cooper's linear imaginings draw a continent ripe for settler colonialism.

The bee hunter Boden advances across the continent, destroying hives as he goes and enjoying their spoils; colonial forces move in a similar fashion, forcibly relocating and annihilating indigenous communities on their way; and Native Americans move farther and farther beyond the horizon of the United States.

The white settler who watches the bee and the Native American disappear and then tracks them to their destinations asserts his power to move the national border even beyond what his eye can see and, in so doing, subverts Native claims to sovereignty. The Native Americans of Cooper's novel recognize this. At a council meeting to determine a course of action against the encroaching whites, Peter draws a link between Boden's threat to sovereignty and his bee hunting. "He knows how to talk with bees," Peter tells his fellow Native Americans. "Them little insects can fly into small places, and see things that Injins cannot see" (360). Although Peter expresses doubt over the wisdom of killing Boden, the Potawatomi Ungque has no such qualms. "It is a dangerous thing to know how to talk with bees," he asserts. "I would rather never taste honey again, than live among pale-faces that can talk with bees" (367).

Ungque's assertion lays bare the relationship between seemingly innocent trade practices and the ascendancy of an expanding United States. His solution to the problem of US expansion is simple: kill the bee hunter. Peter, though, offers a different picture of the potential future of the region: "When we get back all the land," he asserts, "we shall get the bees with it, and may then hold a council to say what is best to do with them" (360). For Peter, possession of the land and possession of the bees go hand in hand. The future council he imagines convened to discuss the status of the bees is not just a fantasy about controlling nature; it is a fantasy of national sovereignty. Control of the land means control over the life it contains. The future Peter presents is one in which the condition imposed upon Native Americans by the United States—existence in space without legal agency—will be transformed into full political life within rightfully inhabited territory. Once the Potawatomi and their allies secure their deserved status as self-governing sovereigns, they will control even the bees that once seemed to mark their undoing.

Of course, this is a Cooper novel, and so Peter's fantasy remains just that. The action of *The Bee-Hunter* concludes with Boden and the Warings escaping the wrath of the Potawatomi, along with Peter and Pigeonswing, and returning to the safety of Pennsylvania. The novel, though, does not conclude with its action; it contains a final chapter written in the plural first person and set in 1848. In this coda, the "we" voice of the narrator embarks on a journey from the Mohawk Valley in New York to Michigan, where Boden resettled following US victory in the war, offering readers a dissertation on how the region has changed since 1812 and updating them on the status of the bee hunter and his family. There is much to be written about this final chapter, but for this chapter's purposes, its most significant feature is its conversion of the frontier landscape into the national landscape, its insistence that the "literal wilderness" has been transformed into a site of meaningful, political, and white national life. The long walks and almost magical calculations that mapped the colonial landscape in the bulk of the novel have been replaced in this final chapter by the clear and straight line of the railroad. "Well could we remember the time when an entire day was required to pass between that point on the Mohawk where we got on the rails, and the little village of Utica," the narrator marvels. "On the present occasion, we flew over the space in less than three hours" (483). Similarly, the narrator notes that it takes only twenty hours to reach Buffalo, a journey that in previous decades "would have been a labor of more than a week" (484). The flight of bees has become the flight of high-speed travel, and with that transformation has come a vast and still expanding United States. "At Detroit we found a fine flourishing town," he explains, and notes that in that city "commenced our surprise at the rapid progress of western civilization" (491–92).

In this final chapter, Cooper completes the teleological narrative upon which the vanishing Indian myth depends. The colonial struggles of 1812 become the national triumphs of 1848. The narrator tells readers to remember that "at the period of our tale, the environs of Detroit excepted, the whole peninsula of Michigan lay in a state of nature" (492). Now, though, the bee hunter has become "what is deemed a rich man in Michigan," possessing "plenty of land, and that which is good" and "regard[ing] the United States, and not Michigan, as his country" (491). In skipping over the thirty years that have transpired between its penultimate and final chapters, *The Bee-Hunter* effaces the brutal violence that facilitated the United States' incorporation of Michigan. The straight line of national progress replaces the geometry of bee hunting.

Having tracked his bees to the vanishing point and driven his indigenous neighbors from view, the settler has become a citizen. In order to reach this conclusion, though, the novel first has terminated a subplot that threatened to undo its narrative from the inside. Long finished by the novel's close, the story of Parson Amen might be easily forgotten were it not so essential to Cooper's project. Wandering into the Michigan landscape with a tale of impending Native ascendancy that depends upon geometric projection at odds with Boden's vanishing points, Amen stands as a threat to be neutralized. His absence from *The Bee-Hunter*'s last pages marks a different kind of vanishing, but one that is essential to the novel's project—that of a religious perspective positing a theory of Native American history that runs counter to the project of white American exceptionalism.

Not Lost, but Losing: Reappearing Americans and Vanishing Methodists

From his first appearance in *The Bee-Hunter*, the Methodist Parson Amen disrupts the clean linearity of Boden's bee-hunting life by threatening to rewrite the story of the Michigan landscape. Traveling under the protection of Corporal Flint and with the aforementioned Peter as a guide, the itinerant Methodist Amen has come to the frontier to remind Native Americans of a past he believes they have forgotten and to set in motion a providential future that has nothing to do with the United States. When Boden expresses trepidation upon hearing the name "Scalping Peter," Amen reassures him, "Do not disturb yourself with names; they hurt no one, and will soon be forgotten. A descendant of Abraham, and of Isaac, and of Jacob is not placed in the wilderness by the hand of divine power for no purpose; since he is here, rely on it, it is for good" (181). To Boden's surprise at this answer, Amen replies, "Peter is a son of Israel, one of the lost children of the land of Judea, in common with many of his red brethren . . . though he may not know exactly of what tribe himself" (181–82). The tribeless Peter becomes a member of a very different tribe, and Amen is certain he knows which: "Turn to Genesis xlix and 14th, and there will you find all the authorities recorded. 'Zebulon shall dwell at the haven of the sea.' That refers to some other red brother, nearer to the coast, most clearly. 'Issachar is a strong ass crouching down between two burdens;' 'and bowed his shoulder to bear, and became a servant unto tribute.' That refers, most manifestly, to the black man of the Southern states" (182–83).

Here Amen draws on a long discursive tradition, with origins in some of the earliest colonial texts, which used biblical exegesis as the basis for proof of American Hebraism. Native Americans become the lost tribes through a scriptural analysis that creatively links descriptions of ancient cultures to contemporary peoples. Through this method, Amen deems Peter a descendant of Naphtali: "I turn to the 21st verse for the tribe of Peter," he explains. "'Naphthali [*sic*] is a hind let loose; he giveth goodly words.' Now, what can be plainer than this?" (184). Though the "plainness" of Amen's scriptural application is debatable, its consequences are not. The Peter of Amen's imagining is not a member of a dying civilization; he is an amnesiac poised to remember and exercise a divine right. Boden may deem the Native American a vanishing Indian, but Amen sees him as a returning Israelite.

It is clear that Cooper was familiar with a range of writings on the Hebraic Indian theory, because in addition to this exegetic reading, Amen draws on more contemporary, pseudo-ethnographic expressions of the theory in order to prove his claim. His assertion that the "very use of the word 'tribes' . . . is one proof of the truth of what I tell you," for example, is an argument straight out of James Adair's *History of the American Indians* (1775), which laid the groundwork for many nineteenth-century expositions of the Hebraic Indian theory (and which I examine in detail in this book's second chapter). Just as Adair argues, "As the Israelites were divided into tribes, and had chiefs over them, so the Indians divide themselves: each tribe forms a little community within the nation," so Amen asserts, "Who ever heard of the 'tribe' of New England, or of the 'tribe' of Virginia, or of the 'tribe' of the middle states? Even among the blacks there are no tribes" (210).[22] In a similar vein, Amen notes that "there is a very remarkable passage in the sixty-eighth Psalm . . . 'God shall wound the head of his enemies . . . and the hairy scalp of such a one as goeth on still in his wickedness.' Here," the parson insists, "is a very obvious allusion to a well-known and, what we think, a barbarous practice of the redman" (210).

Interpreted within a biblical frame, Scalping Peter's scalps and the wounded heads they leave behind take on religious significance. The practice, which the minister admits is "a horrid thing" to English eyes, receives "plain justification" in the scriptures and stands not as evidence of Native American cruelty but rather of divine wrath against the scalped subject. Scalping also seems, in this light, the residue of a forgotten Hebrew past still evident in an indigenous present. This example, it turns out, comes from the conclusion of the Reverend Ethan Smith's 1825 treatise on the Hebraic Indian, *View of the Hebrews*, a text Amen could not have read, but which Cooper seems to have (I also discuss Smith's work in more detail in the second chapter of this book). Describing the coming millennium, Smith writes that the "mountains and hills shall leap at the presence of the Lord, at the presence of the God of Jacob. And God will wound the head of his enemies, and the hairy scalp of them that oppose his march, when he shall again bring from Bashau and recover his banished again from the depth of the sea."[23] This is a crucial component of the Hebraic Indian theory: it does not merely offer explanation for indigenous cultural practices but always interprets those practices within a biblical framework focused on the imminent return of Christ. Even when Amen reads Native Americans ethnographically, the aim of his readings remains theological.

Amen's casting of indigenous Americans as lost Hebrews falls within the kind of millennialism typical of expositions of the theory in the early national period. Citing scriptural passages such as Jeremiah 3:18, which predicts a future day when "the house of Judah shall walk with the house of Israel, and they shall come together out of the land of the north to the land that I have given for an inheritance unto your fathers," writers such as Elias Boudinot (whose work I assess in this book's third chapter) proclaimed the discovery of indigenous peoples as the event that had set the millennium in motion.[24] These prophecies have distinct meanings in Jewish traditions, but within Christian millennialism they are imagined to predict a future in which the world's Jewish population will unite, embrace Christianity, and be redeemed. Read within the context first of European colonialism and then of US expansion, verses from Jeremiah and other prophetic texts seemed to suggest that Native Americans would depart from the continent and journey east to gather with the rest of their Jewish brethren. Thus, when he finally gets the chance to explain himself to the Potawatomi, Amen insists, "It will be the pleasure of the Great Spirit, one day, to restore you to the land of your fathers, and make you again, what you once were, a great and glorious people!" (277). The "land" in question here is not the Michigan wilderness—it is Jerusalem—and the "fathers" are not Potawatomi elders—they are Abraham, Isaac, and Jacob.

Amen's prophetic vision thus also imagines an America emptied of its indigenous inhabitants, but unlike the Vanishing Indian, whose departure from the Americas is a lamentable but permanent sacrifice made in the service of white supremacy, the Hebraic Indian will abandon the hemisphere only when the entire world is altered to fulfill millennial prophecy. Amen's Native Americans, in other words, are Israelites whose reentry into secular time will initiate their happy departure from American space. The Hebraic Indian's removal will be cause for rejoicing rather than remorse, as it will entail a return to what Amen deems their rightful homeland. "The Great Spirit . . . has brought my people hither," Amen tells Peter of white Americans, "and here they must remain to the end of time" (283). White occupation of the Americas is transformed from a brutal, human genocide to a plot point in a divine plan. For Amen, the end of time will arrive swiftly on the heels of his wonderful discovery, and it will mark not the destruction of indigenous nations but rather their unification with the rest of the chosen nation they have been all along.

Cooper first positions Margery against Amen's enthusiastic brand of prophetic Methodism, offering her more tempered and practical Christianity as the optimal model of frontier religion. A devout woman educated in New England, Margery is well positioned to argue the finer points of Amen's thesis. Even the parson admits, "You have read your Bible, Margery" (346). Despite its rationality, though, her careful questioning and logical reason cannot move Amen from his course. When Margery asks how he would explain the fact that "no red man keeps the Sabbath-day," Amen merely replies that "the Jews, even in civilized countries, do not keep the same Sabbath as the Christians" (228). All challenges to the Hebraic Indian theory can be met with explanation, and nothing on earth exists outside of this millennial narrative. "I can scarcely open a chapter, in the Old Testament," Amen explains, "that some passage does not strike me as going to prove this identity, between the red men and the Hebrews; and, were they all collected together, and published in a book, mankind would be astonished at their lucidity and weight" (210). Here, Cooper not only highlights the absolute control that the theory exercises over the parson's reading practices and cultural engagements; he also makes a bit of a joke. By 1812, several books outlining the lost tribes theory in precisely this manner already existed. Adair's was perhaps the most well known, but English texts on the subject had been available since 1650.[25] By *The Bee-Hunter*'s 1848 publication, there were even more (and more famous) expositions of the theory available— Boudinot's being probably the most familiar. None of these had particularly astonished "mankind," though they held sway in some evangelical circles. The future for which Amen waits, readers already know, never will come to pass. The book he would publish in 1812 already exists in several forms and will exist in even more by the 1848 publication of *The Bee-Hunter*. None of these books had the effect he predicts.

Cooper's decision to make a Methodist the spokesperson for the Hebraic Indian theory is telling. After all, none of the most prominent white proponents of the theory were Methodists. Thomas Thorowgood was an Anglican-turned-Presbyterian. James Adair's religious affiliation is unclear in his writings, but as he was a Protestant of Irish descent, it is likely that he, too, was Presbyterian—as was Elias Boudinot. The Reverend Ethan Smith was a Congregationalist. Like Cooper himself, Benjamin Rush was affiliated with the Episcopal Church (although Rush does not seem to have spoken publicly about the theory). Parson Amen's Methodism is thus more narrative device than historical reflection in *The Bee-Hunter*.

Although it is impossible to know precisely why Cooper chose Methodism as his vehicle for the theory, there are at least two reasons why such a choice makes sense. The first is that Methodism operates in the novel as a synecdoche for religious enthusiasm in general. Though he was a devout Christian, Cooper was suspicious of fervent religiosity. In his 1838 political essay, *The American Democrat*, he asserts, "The causes which led to the establishment of the principal American colonies, have left a deep impression on the character of the nation," and he further contends that some of that impression has been "for evil."[26] Rather than holding up Puritan settler colonists as paragons of Christian virtue, Cooper writes that "fanaticism was the fault of the age, at the time our ancestors took possession of the country, and its exaggerations have entailed on their descendants many opinions that are, at the best, of a very equivocal usefulness. . . . The nation," he proclaims, "is sectarian, rather than Christian."[27] A product of eighteenth-century revivalism and a burgeoning force in nineteenth-century American Christianity, Methodism would have been a ripe target for accusations of fanatical sectarianism. In depicting Amen as an itinerant and enthusiastic missionary, Cooper reframes the Hebraic Indian theory as a product of misguided awakening rather than a recurrent concern within orthodox Protestantism. In this way, it emerges as a threat to national and religious stability in the novel, even as it is voiced by a white Protestant American. Amen's Methodism, simply put, operates as shorthand for his irrationality.

Another explanation for Cooper's decision to characterize Amen as a Methodist is the sect's unique history as a religious structure that at times produced interracial and interclass alliances in the United States. As Claudia Stokes has shown in her extensive study of Methodism's impact on the discourse of sentimentality in the nineteenth century, "Methodism was distinguished by an anti-aristocratic belief in religious self-determination and a populist reconstitution of religious authority."[28] Rejecting the doctrine of predestination and embracing a practice of works, Methodism, Stokes writes, "enabled anyone—women, children, slaves—to assume moral and religious authority that had heretofore been available only to an educated male (and presumably white) elite."[29]

Methodism held radical social potential in this period, particularly for members of marginalized groups. Indeed, the most famous Native American to publicly adopt the Hebraic Indian theory, the Pequot William Apess, was a Methodist minister. This book's third chapter explores Apess's Methodism and his deployment of the theory in greater detail, but it is worth noting here that the cultural alignment of Methodism and racial difference would not have been lost on Cooper. The history of Methodism is not devoid of internal conflict around questions of race and identity, and Apess himself encountered white supremacy in his ministerial efforts.[30] Nonetheless, Methodism's rejection of traditional hierarchies and its insistence on the universal availability of grace made it appealing to a wide variety of people and even created the possibility for coalitions among them. Native Americans, free and enslaved black people, poor whites, young people, and women could discover common purpose and work together as equals. This is one reason why Methodism was the fastest-growing religious sect of the early republic and why, as Stokes further notes, "Methodism's influence spread well beyond its own sectarian borders, for, in elevating the religious authority of common people, it created a populist religious environment amenable to the emergence and acceptance of self-styled religious prophets."[31] Indeed, many of the earliest converts to Mormonism were poor, white Methodists living on the territorial and economic edge of the nation.

In the figure of Parson Amen, then, Cooper has placed not only the theory he would ridicule but also the religious sect that, at the time, most threatened to undermine traditional US Protestant hierarchies. The risk Amen poses in *The Bee-Hunter* is not merely one of religious enthusiasm or error; embedded, too, in his preaching is the threat of an American Christianity on the verge of betraying its investment in white respectability. Amen's willingness to make space for Native peoples in his millennial vision threatens to undermine the white nationalism at the core of Cooper's project.

Although Parson Amen is a likeable figure, he appears throughout Cooper's novel as a fool. On the heels of Amen's formulation of scalping as a divine exercise, for example, the narrator interjects, "We trust that no one of our readers will be disposed to deride Parson Amen's speculations on this interesting subject, although this may happen to be the first occasion on which he has ever heard the practice of taking scalps justified by scripture" (211). This passage is typical: over and over, Amen expounds on part of his theory, which the narrator or some other character immediately recasts as ludicrous. Boden himself reflects that the "idea that the American Indians were the descendants of the lost tribes of Israel was entirely new to him; nor did he know any thing to boast of, touching those tribes, even in their palmiest days" (184). Native Americans, too, appear as experts aiming to correct Amen's error. An "enlightened and educated red man," the narrator informs readers, "has quite recently told us in person, that he had been made the repository of some of these traditions, and that he had thus obtained enough of the history of his race to be satisfied that they were not derived from the lost tribes of Israel, though he declined communicating any more" (197). Thus there is little space within *The Bee-Hunter* for a reader to develop sympathy for the parson's beliefs, though there is plenty of room to develop sympathy for the parson himself.

The parson's commitment to the Hebraic Indian theory, readers know from his arrival in the text, will be his doom. From the moment of his introduction, Amen is depicted as the unsuspecting captive of Scalping Peter. The narrator informs us that having "been led, by the artful Peter, to expect great results to his theory from the assembly of chiefs which was to meet in the 'openings' . . . the credulous parson was, in one sense, going blindly on the path of destruction as any sinner it had ever been his duty to warn of his fate" (212). The prophecy to be fulfilled in the novel is not the one Amen anticipates; it is the narrator's. In a pivotal scene, the representatives of several tribes gather in the parson's absence to discuss his fate and the fates of the other whites Peter has lured into their midst. Here, rejection of the Hebraic Indian theory forms the basis for arguments in favor of violence against white settlers. "I am a Pottawattamie," one asserts. "My brothers know that tribe. It is not a tribe of Jews, but a tribe of Injins. It is a great tribe. It never was lost. It cannot be lost" (354). Another concurs, "It seems to me that all pale-faces get lost. They wander from their own hunting grounds into those of other people. It is not so with Injins. . . . Each tribe knows its own game. This is because they are not lost" (355). Peter offers a similar theory of global space that concludes with a call for vengeance. "What is the earth?" he asks. "It is one plain adjoining another; river after river; lake after lake; prairie touching prairie" (357). This linearity of the earth, to Peter, is proof of his American identity. "It would seem that the Great Spirit parceled out this rich possession into hunting-grounds for all," he argues. "We are not lost. We know where we are and we know where the Yankees have come to seek us. . . . If any are lost it is the Yankees. The Yankees are Jews; they are lost. The time is near when they will be found and when they will again turn their eyes toward the rising sun" (354).

Here, Peter stages a clever geographic reorienting, recasting the parson's call for indigenous peoples to look east toward the holy land into a call for whites to look away from the western frontier. Rejection of the Hebraic Indian theory by the Native American is not simply an assertion of a different lineage or even an alternative biblical hermeneutic; it is a wholesale rejection of white settler culture. This, in *The Bee-Hunter*, is what makes the Hebraic Indian theory dangerous. It is not just a theological mistake; it is a geographic error that opens the door to anticolonial violence.

The Bee-Hunter ultimately fulfills its narrator's prediction, when the parson discovers only too late that none of his potential converts ever has taken his theory seriously. Importantly, Cooper stages Amen's annihilation as a kind of parodic reworking of Boden's successful, linear navigation of the frontier. A "dark circle," the gathering of chiefs stands in contrast to the parallel lines of the bee hunter's commercial enterprise (266). This circle, which at first simply facilitates discussion of Amen's theory, ultimately morphs into a military formation from which he and Corporal Flint cannot escape. The council culminates with Crowsfeather's dramatic unveiling of Peter's true identity: the "tribeless chief has an Injin heart," Crowsfeather asserts. "Some thought he believed himself lost, and a Jew, and not an Injin. This is not so. Peter knows the path he is on. He knows that he is a redskin, and he looks on the Yankees as enemies" (390). Apprehending the situation correctly, Corporal Flint attempts one last stand: "We have fallen into a sort of ambush here, Parson Amen, if there were four on us we might form a square; but being only two, the best thing we can do will be to stand back to back, and for one to keep an eye on the right flank, while he nat'rally watches all in front, and for the other to keep an eye on the left flank, while he sees to the rear" (390–91). Flint's attempt to square the circle fails. As the parson prays for deliverance, Cooper writes, "So with the duty of offering up his petition, that he was utterly unconscious of what else had passed; nor had he heard one of the corporal's appeals for 'attention' and to be 'steady' and to march 'by the left flank'" (393). Their line, such as it is, collapses, and they are surrounded. By the time Amen comes to his senses, he and Flint are bound and awaiting execution. Searching for Israelites in Michigan, Amen finds only Native Americans, and he pays for that discovery with his life.

Once Amen is captured, Peter and the council interrogate him one final time about the Hebraic Indian theory. Cooper uses this scene both to reiterate a Native American rejection of "lostness" and to insert anti-Jewish rhetoric into the novel via its Native figures. "My brother has told too much for his own good," asserts the character Bear's Meat. "If the pale-faces killed their Great Spirit, they can have no Manitou, and must be in the hands of the Evil Spirit. This is the reason they want our hunting-grounds" (398). Here, again, the Hebraic Indian theory appears as far more than a historical error. The conflation of the Israelites with "Jews," and the attendant (anti-Jewish) association of Jewish people with the death of Christ serves as justification for Native resistance to white settlement. If white people are rapacious enough to murder their own messiah, Bear's Meat reasons, then naturally they will covet Native American lands. "It is time to begin to kill them," he asserts, referring to whites, "as they killed their Great Spirit. The Jews did this. My brother wishes us to think that red men are Jews! No; red men never harmed the Son of the Great Spirit" (398).

Bear's Meat inverts Amen's conflation of "Jews" with Native peoples and instead equates "Jews" with "pale-faces," assigning responsibility for the death of Jesus to white people. This in turn becomes grounds for the destruction of settlers, who must be killed "as they killed their Great Spirit." Thus the Hebraic Indian theory appears not only to insult Native populations by (however erroneously) inserting them into a history that includes the death of Jesus but also to provide them with a rationale for antiwhite violence. In a cruel twist, Bear's Meat adopts Christian accounts of the passion to make a case for Amen's execution: "This tradition is a wise tradition," he concludes. "It tells us that the red men have always lived on these hunting-grounds, and did not come from the rising sun. It tells us that pale-faces are not fit to live. They are too wicked. Let them die" (398). Adopting the story of Christ's passion but refusing to situate himself within it, Bear's Meat arrives at a fatal conclusion: people who would murder a god must be driven from the land.

Amen's departure from *The Bee-Hunter* is rendered in totalizing terms. His death takes place off-stage, as the chief Ungque is so moved by the parson's final prayer that he "bowed his head and moved away," and then "heard the single blow of the tomahawk which brained the victim" (401). Unlike many of the victims of violence in this frontier novel, Amen disappears without a trace: "In deference to his pursuits," Cooper explains, "his executioners dug him a grave, and buried him unmutilated on the spot where he had fallen" (401). Buried where he died, Amen leaves no record of his fate. Readers learn that "a veil like that of oblivion, dropped before the form of the missionary," and that "the pious persons who had sent him forth to preach to the heathen, never knew his fate; a disappearance that was so common to that class of devoted men, as to produce regret rather than surprise" (402).

There is no grand revelation in the end, for either Amen or the church he served. No transcendent truth emerges from this portion of the novel. Even Flint is left without a sign of the parson's fate, although he can guess it. "The corporal looked anxiously for the usual but revolting token of his late company's death," Cooper writes. "As has been said, however, the missionary was suffered to lie in his wild grave, without suffering a mutilation of his remains" (405). The decision to refrain from scalping Amen is a mark of respect on the part of his killers, but it also has the effect of eliminating from the narrative all material proof that he ever existed. Unlike Colonel Flint, who subsequently dies in a rather spectacular fashion—suspended and drawn between trees before Pigeonswing mercifully shoots him—Amen simply vanishes.

On the heels of Amen's annihilation, Cooper's novel explicitly repositions the Native American as a receding figure. As in many of Cooper's works, a Native voice articulates its own disappearance. "You are a pale face," Peter tells Boden near the novel's conclusion, "and I am an Injin. You are strong and I am weak. This is because the Son of the Great Spirit has talked with your people, and has not talked with mine. I see now why the pale faces overrun the earth and take the hunting grounds. They know most, and have been told to come here, and to tell what they know to the poor ignorant Injins. I hope my people will listen" (427). Peter speaks in religious as well as racial terms. His "pale faces" overrun the earth, not because they are a superior race but because they possess a theological truth that will outpace competing mythologies. Hope for the Native person, according to this formula, is assimilation not into whiteness (which the novel presents as impossible) but into an appropriate expression of Christianity. The unspoken corollary to this statement is that white Christians themselves must adhere to a correct understanding of their religion. This is where Parson Amen has failed. An incorrect reading of biblical history and a blind desire to see Israelites where there were only ever Americans made him a casualty of the frontier rather than its liberator. It is important to note, though, that Amen's death serves only the project of white expansionism. In the aftermath of the parson's murder, the Native Americans who made him their sacrifice still can assert only their own imminent disappearance. Like the whites around him, Peter mourns in advance the disappearance of Native Americans from the hemisphere and accepts the premise that he is "weak," while whites are "strong." Victory over Amen and his lost tribes theory simply wins Native Americans the right to disappear.

The Bee-Hunter's coda completes the story of Native American vanishing by converting "Scalping Peter" to Peter, not the Naphtali of Amen's imagining but a Christian whose new faith leads him to embrace his white neighbors. Although the 1848 narrator marvels at Boden's fine lands and family, he notes that Peter "was the great centre of interest with us" (496). This is the case because Peter is a man so changed as to be nearly unrecognizable. "There he was," Cooper writes, "living in the midst of the hated race, loving and beloved; wishing naught but blessings on all colors alike; looking back upon his traditions and superstitions with a sort of melancholy interest, as we all portray in our memories the scenes, legends, and feelings of an erring childhood" (496).

The future Amen predicted was half right: Peter has converted. But his conversion was not the result of a prophetic fulfillment, nor did it require a Jewish middle phase, nor has it resulted in the dawn of millennium. Peter has, more simply, vanished—or, at least, the scalping version of him has—into the ether of assimilation. Now he wears "the vestments of the whites" and regards his former self from a position of mourning as he embraces a kind of tepid multiculturalism by blessing "all colors alike." Gone is the man who wore the emblems of many tribes and spoke of vengeance against white intruders. "Was very foolish den," Peter says of his past. "Now all dem cloud blow away, and I see my Fadder dat is in Heaven. . . . When he got de force of de Holy Spirit, de heart of stone is changed to de heart of woman, and we all be ready to bless our enemy and die" (497). Conversion to Christianity operates in the end as the final annihilator of Native peoples: having accepted its tenets, Peter is ready to leave the world to his enemies. The return to favor Amen predicted is replaced by the steady progress of white Christianity in America, and in declaring himself "no Jew," the American is free at last to vanish.

6

The Hollow Earth and the End of Time

De Witt Clinton Chipman's 1896 novel, *Beyond the Verge: Home of Ten Lost Tribes of Israel*, opens in a hemisphere on the edge of genocide. "The origin of the Mound Builders and . . . Chickimecs [*sic*] . . . has no written history," its narrator explains. "Each claimed to have been always on the earth, coeval with each other, and to have been enemies from time immemorial."[1] Emerging from a long period of truce, the Chichimeca, "after years of preparation, [fall] upon the Mound Builders simultaneously with three grand armies" (16). In the ancient land that will come to be called America, the "brown-faced Mound Builders" have "been driven south of the Ohio, and west of the Mississippi" by the "black-eyed Chickimecs," whose leaders are "consulting about a crusade beyond these rivers" when the novel begins (15, 17). The Chichimec emperor, Oratonga, has achieved his goal of annihilation by "inflam[ing his people's] minds by an appeal to love of native land, and an appeal to their sensual appetites. . . . He told of the lovely valleys, winding streams of the 'sunny South . . .' and promised them concubines among the dark-eyed and beautiful Mound Builders" (17). His strategy has been effective. The Mound Builders are all but gone. "Such fearful slaughters were committed," Chipman writes, "that down into Indian language comes a tradition of 'the dark and bloody ground'" (17).

From its outset, then, *Beyond the Verge* draws a link between its fictional past and its reader's present. The "mounds" in question are a real feature of the North American landscape. As Chipman's readers would have known, earthen mounds built by American peoples before the era of European colonialism dot the continent from Virginia to Texas. The history of these mounds stood—among white people, anyway—as one of the nineteenth century's greatest archeological mysteries. Chipman's novel offers an explanation, albeit fictional, for the presence of these mounds: "There is scarcely a sacrificial, residential, monumental, historic, military, or inexplicable earth-work," the narrator explains, "but has some sad and pathetic memento of this dreadful tumult" (17). The war between the Mound Builders and the Chichimeca is drawing to a close when *Beyond the Verge*'s action begins. Its Mound Builders are a civilization on the brink of destruction, a population that, by the time a reader picks up the book in 1896, will be a "vanished race."

In its simultaneous evocation and destruction of the Mound Builders, *Beyond the Verge* situates itself within the general debates regarding the history of human life in the Americas and the more particular discussions of the material proof of that history's longevity. The mounds Chipman describes served both as real sites of what might be termed archeological interest throughout the eighteenth and nineteenth centuries and as imaginative spaces onto which white Americans projected fantasies of the continent's past as part of a strategy to secure its future for themselves. Beginning with Thomas Jefferson, who performed the first known excavation of a mound on his Monticello property, and continuing through the turn of the twentieth century, speculation about the identities of the Mound Builders typically served a political agenda that configured the Americas as the destined domain of white people and justified the removal of Native American populations. The key to America's future, in many white accounts of the mounds, lay beneath its soil. Even though some nineteenth-century studies asserted links between these ancient mounds and known Native American populations, Chipman's novel resists this historical narrative, conflating and reorganizing several (inaccurate) strains of Mound Builder discourse to present the mounds as the "sad and pathetic" remnants of a long-gone people rather than monuments to extant civilizations. Thus, despite the fact that the novel claims that the "chapters of [its] story are cabled with facts; supported by science; are in harmony with physical laws, [and] strengthened by discoveries from official reports by trusted men," its foundational history hinges on a rejection of empirical studies of the American past (5).

The first section of this chapter traces the development of Mound Builder discourse among white writers of this period to show how the emergent field of archeology deployed the Mound Builders as proof that Native Americans were not the rightful occupants of American land. *Beyond the Verge* affirms this reading of the mounds, rejecting the notion that they might have been constructed by the ancestors of Native Americans. Tellingly, though, the novel rejects the significance of Mound Builder history to the course of human events. What lies directly beneath the surface of America, in Chipman's novel, is merely a dead past. To discover the real truth of the planet's destiny, *Beyond the Verge* asserts, one must dig deeper.

Beyond the Verge has not experienced the kind of readerly renaissance that many equally odd novels of the period have, and its author, a patent attorney from Vermont who spent most of his adult life in Indiana, has not been added to the ranks of canonical late-century writers. Although *Beyond the Verge* was his lone novel, and he was by no means a professional author, Chipman is an interesting figure whose long life (1825–1910) meant that he witnessed some of the most important events of the nineteenth century. In 1864, while he was serving as collector of internal revenue for the eleventh district of Indiana, Chipman wrote to President Abraham Lincoln to inform him of the Pomeroy Circular— Senator Samuel Pomeroy's proposal that the Republican Party nominate Salmon P. Chase for president that year. Chipman enclosed the circular in his letter, along with a poem lauding Lincoln's achievements. The letter assures the president, "The slanderous and disgraceful charges contained in that circular, amounting to legal *scandalum magnatum* will be rejected by a Country which sees the administration exposing corruption, extravagance [*sic*] and rascality wherever found and pushing a victorious war all over the rebellious territory."[2] Chipman accounts for his loyalty to the president with a simple yet profound pronouncement: "When you issued the Emancipation Proclimation [*sic*], you did an act which history will chronicle and posterity recognise as the most imperishable monument of Liberty and Justice in the annals of time."

A civil servant, midwestern Republican, and one-time novelist, Chipman is the kind of author who disappears from public consciousness almost at the moment he emerges. He is worth a second look, though, because the one work he did produce encapsulates many of the questions and problems that haunted the postbellum United States. This chapter explores just one avenue of inquiry into a very complicated text: its engagement with the idea of American Hebraism.

Given its relative obscurity (and that of its author), a summary of *Beyond the Verge*'s plot is perhaps in order. Although the novel opens with an account of longstanding war between the Chichimeca and Mound

Builders, those populations are not the engine that drives its action. As they ponder their next military campaign, the Chichimeca encounter the ten lost tribes of Israel, who are trekking across the continent on their way to the North Pole, where they will enter a passage to the earth's interior. The tribes follow a "cloud by day . . . and [a] pillar of fire by night," and they carry with them "the Tabernacle, the Ark of Jehovah, with the Mercy seat, the Pot of Manna, Aaron's Rod, and the Ten Commandments" (27). Impressed with the tribes' leader, the high priest Melchisedec, and wary of their power, the emperor Oratonga grants them safe passage through his territory. A young Chichimec priest named Nardo falls in love with Rebecca, "a dark-eyed beauty, in the tribe of Simeon" (39). He joins her tribe, thus forging a link between Chichimec and Israelite history. The tribes take Nardo with them to the Pole, and then into the earth's habitable core.

This move "beyond the verge," it turns out, is not the last threshold for the faithful to cross, for every year a white ship arrives in the tribes' internal city. Melchisedec has constructed a mirror that assesses the spiritual status of anyone wishing to travel to the Happy Isle, a sacred island even deeper within the earth's interior. Only those whose purity is reflected in the mirror are permitted aboard the ship. In a cruel twist, the spiritually perfect Rebecca departs for the Happy Isle, while Nardo sees his sins reflected in the mirror and is forced to spend a year in repentance. Following a perilous journey to religious enlightenment— overcoming human treachery, the elements, and his own dangerous pride—Nardo faces the mirror again and joins his Rebecca in paradise.

What begins as a story of destruction and burial on the earth's surface, then, becomes one of a living present at its core. *Beyond the Verge* operates not only within the long tradition of Mound Builder literature but also (and in a more sustained manner) within the frame of hollow earth narratives. As I will demonstrate, it marshals both genres to reject the standard articulation of the Hebraic Indian theory and replace it with a new account of the location of the missing tribes and a reconfigured notion of American Hebraism. This chapter's second section examines the subgenre of nineteenth-century hollow earth fiction, focusing on how these works conjure self-sustaining and infinite worlds that hold the potential for perpetual utopian happiness. Situating *Beyond the Verge* within this tradition, the third section turns to the novel itself, arguing that Chipman borrows the ideas of natural self-sufficiency and continuous renewal that underpin this genre to construct a space resistant to spiritual in addition to material decline. *Beyond the Verge* is unique among hollow earth narratives in its explicit investment in Christian millennialism. Its fantasy of a separate space for the lost tribes, however, depends upon the same kind of scientific speculation that made other hollow earth narratives possible. Turning away from the "dead" space of earthen mounds, *Beyond the Verge* suggests that America's sacred destiny lies not in the bones below its surface but rather in a vibrant space beneath the entire world. For Chipman, that space was designed from the beginning to house those chosen by the divine and to safeguard them from corruption as they move toward their Christian future. American Hebraism is not a latent past that might emerge on the continent's surface in *Beyond the Verge*; it is instead the chosen path of the convert Nardo, who becomes a member of the tribes and follows them into the earth's living core.

Beneath the Surface: A Dead Past

The Chichimeca are undeniably brutal in their annihilation of their enemies, but in *Beyond the Verge* the Mound Builders appear to deserve their fate. They "were sun-worshippers and sacrificed human beings," Chipman writes. "At the height of their power they had one religion, but in time they degenerated into worshipers of the serpent, buffaloes, bears, elks, eagles, mastodons, and Koneta, or the Evil One." The division of this civilization into disparate religious sects has rendered it weak and diffuse, but even in its former days, the novel suggests, Mound Builder culture was not worth preserving. "This apostacy for the ancient faith is readily seen in their mounds," Chipman explains, "and these crumbling earth-works are all that is left to commemorate this vanished race" (16). All this once-mighty people has produced are "crumbling earth-works"; nothing of value remains.

Chipman's description of the Mound Builders' beliefs produces an odd temporality in the text. The presence of the mastodon lends a sense of longevity to the Mound Builders and suggests that their decline has been millennia in the making. At the same time, though, Chipman probably derived the name "Koneta" from "Wapakoneta," a town in

western Ohio that was inhabited by the Shawnee until their forced removal in 1831. These Mound Builders thus inhabit a past, but the precise
contours of that past remain vague. Chipman's list of religious practices
simultaneously conflates and flattens a range of white discourses circulating around indigenous American customs, evoking everything from
Aztec sacrificial practices to various North American nations' mythologies regarding animals to an unexplained reverence for "the Evil One."
What matters most here is that from the moment they appear in *Beyond
the Verge*, Chipman's Mound Builders are obsolete—within the narrative
itself and within American history.

The Mound Builders Chipman depicts in *Beyond the Verge* are most
certainly a fiction, but they are no more fictitious than those who popu-
late many of the era's accounts of the continent's mounds. Interest in the
mounds was widespread, because they appeared in so many parts of
North America and because they pointed to a history that remained inaccessible to white settler colonists even as they encroached upon Native
lands. As Andrew Lewis notes, "Pioneers to the early west, prepared to
settle a recently depeopled wilderness, instead encountered a landscape
that demonstrated ancient inhabitation."[3] Standing in the shadows of
the mounds, white settlers confronted proof of the long history of civilization in the Americas and, consequently, the flimsiness of their own
claims to the land. The mounds became sites of speculation, as whites
struggled to explain not only the structures' origins but also their significance within the context of US expansion.

Lewis explains that in some regions—particularly the Ohio Valley—a
budding national concern with antiquities merged with local treasure-
hunting traditions to produce a veritable run on these ancient structures. Thus, John Hay convincingly has argued that in the United States,
"The discipline of archaeology owes its origins to early nineteenth-
century fascination with the ancient population of the continent's past."[4]
If mound digging did not reveal literal treasure chests, it could yield
a variety of objects that might reveal exciting truths about the hemisphere—or at the very least could be sold to collectors. "The American
land was laden with mysteries, secrets, and possibilities," Lewis writes.
"It held objects with the economic potential to change a life" (75). With
little regard for those who built them, or for the Native populations who
might have an interest in preserving them, everyone from naturalists

to antiquities dealers to farmers dug into the mounds and extracted all manner of artifacts. As enticing as the material artifacts within the mounds were, though, the narratives that emerged out of the mounds proved equally crucial to writers seeking to situate themselves within the unfolding story of the American landscape.

One of the primary debates among whites concerned with the history of the mounds was whether those structures had been built by the ancestors of Native American populations or by a "lost civilization" that had been eradicated by the people who would become Native Americans. In *Notes on the State of Virginia*, which remains the most well-known early description of a mound dig, Thomas Jefferson writes that there was much conjecture in the region about the history of the mounds, and that his primary motivation for excavating one was to determine the correct theory. "That they were repositories of the dead, has been obvious to all, but on what particular occasion constructed, was matter of doubt," he writes. "There being one of these in my neighbourhood, I wished to satisfy myself whether any, and which of these opinions were just."[5]

The mound Jefferson dug into probably was destroyed when the Rivanna River flooded at the end of the nineteenth century; modern efforts to locate it have been unsuccessful.[6] Even when he encountered the mound, though, it already had been disturbed by white settlement. "It was of a spheroidical form, of about 40 feet diameter at the base," he notes, "and had been of about twelve feet altitude, though now reduced by the plough to seven and a half, having been under cultivation about a dozen years" (133–34). Despite this acknowledgment of the destructive impact of white agricultural practices on Native sites, though, Jefferson interprets the arrangement of the mound as evidence of indigenous disregard for the remains it contains. "I first dug superficially in several parts of it," he writes, "and came to collections of human bones, at different depths, from six inches to three feet below the surface. These were lying in the utmost confusion, some vertical, some oblique, some horizontal, and directed to every point of the compass. . . . Bones of the most distant parts were found together . . . so as, on the whole, to give the idea of bones emptied promiscuously from a bag or basket, and covered over with earth, without any attention to their order" (134). Jefferson's juxtaposition of the plough's uniform, external leveling of the area with the mound's apparent internal disarray is not an accident. Anglo-Americans frequently presented cultivation as the imposition of order on the American "wilderness" and, thus, as the proof that their claims to the land were more legitimate than those of indigenous populations. The "utmost confusion" Jefferson describes thus serves as a rhetorical analog for the plough, reconstituting Native space in the service of white interests.

Typical of the period, Jefferson's interest in the mound did not extend to include indigenous knowledge. In their study of the colonial impulses that underpinned early archeological practice, Ian McNiven and Lynette Russell note that "European explorers in the sixteenth and seventeenth centuries observed mounds used by Native Americans for various functions such as religious rituals and burials," but as disease and genocide decimated local populations, information that could have situated the mounds within a cultural context became scarce.[7] Even when such information was available, whites typically ignored it in favor of their own theories. *Notes* offers a poignant illustration of such indifference. The mounds, Jefferson writes, "are of considerable notoriety among the Indians; for a party passing, about thirty years ago, through the part of the country where this barrow is, went through the woods directly to it, without any instructions or enquiry, and having staid about it some time, with expressions which were construed to be those of sorrow, they returned to the high road, which they had left about half a dozen miles to pay this visit, and pursued their journey" (136–37).

The imagery is striking. The party is "passing through," suggesting transience, yet its members know "without any instructions or enquiry" where to find the mound, even though it takes them six miles off the road. Jefferson positions himself as a present actor throughout this section of *Notes*, but here he recedes into passive voice and out of the frame. He concludes his assessment with the kind of melancholy that typifies white accounts of the systematic destruction of indigenous populations, mourning in advance the disappearance of information about American origins. "It is to be lamented then," he writes, "that we have suffered so many of the Indian tribes already to extinguish, without our having previously collected and deposited in the records of literature, the general rudiments at least of the languages they spoke" (138). The tragedy here is not the deaths of indigenous peoples but rather the loss of records and evidence for whites to assess. Even as he presents his mound digging as an effort to uncover indigenous history, Jefferson relegates the mound, its builders, and even its living visitors to an inscrutable past that never will be uncovered. Native Americans may assign "notoriety" to the mounds, but those populations cannot serve as sources of information, because they merely are passing through his field of vision on their way into history.

Jefferson disingenuously asserts that he knows "of no such thing existing as an Indian monument," even as he attributes the construction of mounds to the ancestors of Native Americans. He was not alone in this view, and modern studies of the mounds have drawn a somewhat—though not entirely—similar conclusion. As Hay notes, "Today archaeologists generally recognize that mound-building was a trait associated with many different indigenous cultures over several eras" (117). There was, in other words, no singular "Mound Builder" culture; numerous American populations engaged in different forms of mound construction. Writers of the period in question, however, tended to lump Native peoples and histories together and treat the mounds as evidence of a singular civilization. And even those accepting the notion of Native American Mound Builders typically did so not out of support for Native claims of sovereignty or in the interest of recognizing the humanity of Native peoples or understanding the diversity of Native nations. Samuel Morton's infamous 1839 work, *Crania Americana*, stands as the starkest example of a study that gestures toward an accurate interpretation of the mounds' history while lending scientific credence to the racism undergirding the project of Indian Removal. Morton, a committed proponent of polygenesis (a theory I discuss in detail in the second chapter of this book), recorded measurements from 256 skulls and used those measurements to assert continuity between the Mound Builders and Native peoples. The "cranial remains discovered in the Mounds, from Peru to Wisconsin," he writes, "belong to the same race, and probably to the Toltecan family."[8] He further concludes that "the American Race differs essentially from all others" (260). This conclusion rightly has been discredited, not only because it is incorrect and racist but also because Morton acquired many of the skulls he studied, particularly those of indigenous people, through grave robbing.[9]

Crania Americana is an indefensible work that laid significant ground for future racial pseudo-science. But it still serves as a useful example of the ways in which religious, scientific, and national interests intertwine.

Like Jefferson's detailed accounts of his methods and discoveries, Morton's work, as Daniel Cole puts it, deploys "apparently meticulous numeric analysis to lend a veneer of validity to anti-Indian rhetoric that had been circulating for decades, thus giving racist views the imprimatur of elite science."[10] Morton's Mound Builders, like Jefferson's, are the ancestors of Native peoples. His conclusion, though, does not lead him toward recognition of Native rights, for his Mound Builders also are a fiction—a singular and unique race that will fade in the face of white supremacy.

Despite these early assertions of links between indigenous American peoples and the mounds, a competing narrative emerged in the nineteenth century, which attributed the mounds' construction to an extinct population. "Because the earthworks and the artifacts dug up from them provided only a faint portrait of their creators," Gordon Sayre explains, "and because the local native Indians' explanations of the mounds were rejected, stories about the Mound Builders drew heavily on the imagination of the writers."[11] Theories regarding the mounds were as plentiful and varied as the mounds themselves. Rejecting information available above ground, whites dug into the earth in search of American history, but they could not make complete sense of what they found there. Thus, as Lewis puts it, "origin stories blossomed" in the wake of early encounters with the mounds, and white Americans variously assigned Mound Builder status to "the Celts, the Druids, Scandinavian Vikings, the Phoenicians, and the Lost Tribes of Israel" (75).

It is perhaps clear from this list that many works depicting the mounds demonstrate an investment in constructing an American past that does not align with Native American history. Numerous populations emerged to fill what McNiven and Russell term a "constructed knowledge void," including the lost tribes of Israel (114). There were two political benefits to this kind of thinking. First, it allowed for a construction of American history that could potentially be "white," thus allowing writers to present Indian Removal as an act of reclamation rather than violation. Second, it presented Native Americans as the perpetrators of a genocide and thus configured federal policy as a kind of delayed justice. Read in this light, Indian Removal appeared as an act of retribution for a fallen civilization.

In its presentation of the Mound Builders as a once great but ultimately degraded and forgotten race, then, *Beyond the Verge* is not entirely unique. Throughout the eighteenth and nineteenth centuries, many writers depicted the mounds as the remnants of a single civilization, usually one that collapsed under the weight of war with the ancestors of Native Americans. Indeed, Andrew Jackson presented just such a picture of the Mound Builders in the service of his case for Indian Removal. In his Second Annual Address, delivered in December of 1830, he explains that

> to follow to the tomb the last of his race, and to tread on the graves of extinct nations, excite mancholly [sic] reflections. But true philanthropy reconciles the mind to these vicissitudes, as it does to the extinction of one generation to make room for another. In the monuments and fortresses of an unknown people, spread over the extensive regions of the west, we behold the memorials of a once powerful race, which was exterminated, or has disappeared, to make room for the existing savage tribes. Nor is there any thing in this, which, upon a comprehensive view of the general interests of the human race, is to be regretted.[12]

As Terry Barnhart has noted, Jackson's address marshals the picture of a lost Mound Builder race to present "a comforting argument—a fiction that rationalized the removal policy as a matter of utility."[13] Rather than appearing as the victims of a federal policy that violated the sovereignty of numerous indigenous nations, Native Americans inhabit this address as conquerors, indeed "exterminators," in their own right. Their fate is just that—fate—one turn of the wheel of history, which crushes some nations as it elevates others. The cost of genocide, for its perpetrators, is mere "mancholly," which "true philanthropy" will remedy in time. Chipman's novel adapts this picture of the Mound Builders for its setup. Its Mound Builders appear only in the narrative's margins, as a primitive civilization on its way to extinction in order to "make way" for the Chichimeca, who in turn one day will make way for whites.

Perhaps the most well-known literary example of the "lost race" theory is William Cullen Bryant's poem "The Prairies," the speaker of which ponders the continent's human past as he travels, solitary and on horseback, across an empty expanse. Bryant was, as Barnhart explains, a supporter of Jackson, and thus it is not a coincidence that his poem in many respects mirrors the Second Annual Address.[14] "Are they here—," the poem's speaker wonders as he rides. "The dead of other days? . . . Let the mighty mounds / That overlook the rivers, or that rise / In the dim forest crowded with old oaks, / Answer. A race, that long has passed away, / Built them."[15] Bryant's landscape has absorbed the Mound Builders. The poem's "old oaks" serve as a natural calendar: untrod for centuries, the prairie has yielded to forest. In Bryant's conjuring of them, the Mound Builders were agrarians, "a disciplined and populous race" that "[h]eaped, with long toil, the earth," which "nourished their harvest" and fed their herds. These Mound Builders kept bison in stalls and yoked them to ploughs, and they also inhabited "swarming cities." They were, in other words, not unlike the white settlers who were displacing Native Americans as Bryant composed "The Prairies" around 1832. In the poem, though, violent displacement comes at the hands of the "red man . . . The roaming hunter tribes, warlike and fierce."

Where Jackson imagined Native Americans hounding every Mound Builder to the grave—and whites returning the favor centuries later—Bryant leaves open the possibility that Mound Builder history has extended into the present. The poem imagines a "solitary fugitive, / Lurking in marsh and forest," rescued by his foes:

> Man's better nature triumphed then. Kind words
> Welcomed and soothed him; the rude conquerors
> Seated the captive with their chiefs; he chose
> A bride among their maidens, and at length
> Seemed to forget—yet ne'er forgot—the wife
> Of his first love, and her sweet little ones,
> Butchered, amid their shrieks, with all his race.

In Bryant's rendering, the disappearance of the Mound Builders is effected primarily through violence, with the butchering of children concretizing the destruction of that civilization's future.[16] But it also, importantly, is achieved through assimilation. The lone survivor chooses a bride and "seems to forget" what he lost. Bryant acknowledges that complete amnesia is impossible; the children's shrieks echo within the line, as its blank verse slips into irregularity. Nonetheless, the Mound Builder's absorption into this new society is contingent upon a reproductive futurism signified by the new bride. Chipman writes a similar kind of continuity into *Beyond the Verge*, when the priest Nardo leaves his home alone to join the lost tribes of Israel. Rebecca implores him to join the tribes, telling him she hopes he "will join the Tribe of Simeon, so we may journey northward the same tribe" (49). Nardo replies, "Fair Jewess your slightest wish would be imperative law to me" (49). As in Bryant's poem, *Beyond the Verge* positions the woman's body as a site of cultural futurism. Significantly, though, it is the Chichimec and not the Mound Builder who is imagined to inhabit the novel's millennial future.

What matters most about the Mound Builder controversy for this chapter is the fact that Chipman evokes it only to reject it. Although *Beyond the Verge* raises the specter of the Mound Builders, it does so to establish them as a foil for the lost tribes. In presenting the Mound Builders as the truly lost civilization, *Beyond the Verge* establishes a framework for considering the lost tribes of Israel merely as temporarily absent. Chipman's interest in the mounds clearly stemmed from the proximate location of some of them to his home. "Near Anderson, Indiana, the home of the author," he writes, "near the Anderson Mountains, on which the remains of the prehistoric race called the Mound Builders can be seen, is a high bluff, near these mouldering earth-works of an extinct people" (158). "It is only necessary to refer to them," Chipman informs readers almost immediately upon introducing this population, "so far as they relate to the lost Tribes of Israel" (16).

The novel opens with a gesture toward a sweeping saga of America's history that explains its most compelling human artifacts, but within a few pages it turns away from what lies beneath American soil to burrow more deeply into the earth. "The first event in the history of this book is about to open," Chipman writes, "and all that follows relates solely to the lost Tribes of Israel" (17). The novel thus acknowledges the Mound Builders' fraught status within American history, but it denies their importance to both the continent's past and the future of human civilization. To dig into American soil, *Beyond the Verge* suggests, is to engage too shallowly with the past. The truth of what came before and what is to come does not lie in burial mounds; it lives much farther down, beneath the crust and beyond the verge.

The Mound Builders are not the source of crucial American history in *Beyond the Verge*, but neither, it is important to note, are the Chichimeca. This is made clear when Oratonga beholds the miracle of manna, which sustains the lost tribes in America just as it sustained the biblical Israelites in the wilderness. Looking out over the plains at daybreak, Oratonga is confronted with a marvelous scene: "The sun which rises suddenly from the prairie threw its morning beams upon a wonderful scene. Instead of lighting up waving grass and blooming flowers it shone on a land of snowy whiteness. All over the rolling swells, down their sloping sides, across the level plain, for a long distance around the Israelitish camp, the ground was of that color except where the prairie-flowers lifted their lovely heads, and the contrast between their bright colors and the whiteness was enchanting" (92).

The Israelite's journey across America has the effect of blanketing the continent in "whiteness." The one brief description of manna offered in Exodus does read, "It was like coriander seed, white; and the taste of it was like wafers made with honey" (Exodus 16:31), but the "whiteness" of the manna is not nearly as important to the biblical account as it is to Chipman's. Indeed, the manna's whiteness is so insistent in this passage that it eradicates everything except those enchanting flowers. "The hush of nature hallowed the scene," Chipman writes. "No living thing disturbed its silent and glistening beauty. Not even a bird flew across its serene whiteness" (92). If Mound Builder literature of previous eras sought to recover a "white" American past, *Beyond the Verge* goes one step further, whitening the continent itself with manna from heaven. That whiteness overwhelms even the powerful Oratonga, who "in his inmost soul [thinks] to himself: 'The wonderful God of Israel!'" In this moment, Chipman presents the possibility of a new kind of American Hebraism, as Oratonga seems poised to make a religious conversion. Surrounded on all sides by heavenly whiteness, the indigenous emperor acknowledges the God of Israel.

It perhaps comes as no surprise that Chipman forecloses the possibility of a Chichimec-Israelite alliance in the very moment he raises it. Attracted as Oratonga is to the snowy feast before him, it turns out that he cannot eat the manna. Melchisedec warned him that "no heathen could eat, but could handle, the manna," but Oratonga (understandably) endeavors to sample it (94). "It looked exceedingly inviting," Chipman writes, "and as he turned it over in his hand, forgetful of what Melchisedec had said, he put some towards his mouth. Suddenly he smelled a nauseating stench. He lowered his hand and a disgusting worm was in his grasp which immediately putrified [*sic*]" (94). Divine bread literally turns to fetid earth in the hands of an indigenous American. Despite the recognition he had felt in "his inmost soul" for the Israelites' deity just moments before, Oratonga is prohibited from breaking holy bread with them.

The manna scene concretizes what *Beyond the Verge* has signaled since its opening: neither the Mound Builders nor the Chichimeca are the bearers of divine favor in the Americas, and their mutual destiny is to rot beneath the surface of the earth. "Three weeks after the transaction concerning the manna," Chipman explains, "the Israelites broke camp, and started after the cloud, and it was the last that Oratonga ever saw of the cloud or that wonderful people" (95). This is also the last the reader hears of Oratonga and his people; like the Mound Builders before them, the Chichimeca slide into historical irrelevance as the Israelites make their way out of America and into the verge. Unlike the Mound Builders, however, the Chichimeca remain as a trace in Chipman's narrative in the figure of the priest Nardo, who joins the Israelites on their journey to the earth's core. In what follows, this chapter will explore how Chipman reconfigures the dead, earthen history of Native America into a living and present Christianity preparing to erupt from the planet's center and reclaim its surface.

Into the Earth: A Living Present

The theory that the earth might be hollow, and that its interior could sustain life, was nothing new when Chipman composed *Beyond the Verge*. Much like the mounds on the American surface, the earth's core had been the subject of scientific, religious, and literary speculation for centuries. Chipman offers readers a veritable catalogue of "proofs" in support of his fiction's premise, many of which draw on works by respectable scientists and theologians. Perhaps the most influential of these was Sir Edmond Halley's work, *An Account of the Cause of the Change of the Variation of the Magnetic Needle, With an Hypothesis of the Structure of the Internal Parts of the Earth*, a serious study first published in 1692.

Halley's aim in this treatise was to explain why compasses experienced variant readings, particularly near the earth's poles. This *Account* stands as a slight revision of earlier work Halley had produced, in which he had argued that the earth operated like a giant magnet with four poles. "But after all," he writes, "though that Discourse was favorably received . . . yet I found two difficulties not easie to surmount, the one was that no Magnet I had ever seen or heard of, had more than two opposite Poles; whereas the Earth had visibly four. . . . And secondly, it was plain that those Poles were not, at least all of them, fixt in the Earth, but shifted from place to place, as appeared by the great changes in the Needles [sic] direction within this last Century."[17] Inviting readers to compare compass readings taken over time in a variety of locations, he writes, "I am assured, that it will be thereby evident, that the Direction of the Needle is in no place fixt and constant" (566). But how could the earth's magnetic poles be moving? And why isn't that movement visible? "These difficulties," Halley says, "had wholly made me despond, and I had long since given over an inquiry I had so little hopes of" (564). Fortunately, he explains, "When in accidental discourse, and least expecting it, I stumbled on the following hypothesis" (564).[18] That hypothesis, of course, is that the earth is composed of more than one sphere, and that two of its four poles lie within its interior, moving independently of the poles on the surface.

Extrapolating from a significant error in Sir Isaac Newton's *Principia* (1687), which miscalculated the density of the moon and thus posited a very dense moon revolving around a relatively light earth, Halley writes, "If the Moon be more solid than the Earth as 9 to 5, why may we not reasonably suppose the Moon, being a small Body and a Secondary Planet, to be solid Earth, Water, Stone, and this Globe to consist of the same Materials, only four ninths thereof to be Cavity?" (574–75). That "cavity," Halley suggests, is not a single empty chamber but a series of concentric spheres. The earth is like a giant nesting doll in his account, with each layer perhaps containing space that could support life.

Halley's status as a respected scientist lent some credibility to his hollow earth theory. In a fascinating analysis of the official portrait painted of an eighty-year-old Halley by the Swedish artist Michael Dahl—a portrait that depicts Halley holding a diagram of the earth represented by concentric spheres—Peter Sinnema explains that by "the time he posed for Dahl, Halley occupied a rank of distinction among practical philosophers of the early Enlightenment."[19] In addition to identifying his

eponymous comet, Halley's credits include "authorship of the first catalogue of stars in the southern hemisphere, the laying of actuarial foun-
dations for life insurance and annuities . . . investiture into the Savilian
professorship of geometry, and some sixteen years' service as Astrono-
mer Royal."[20]

Although Halley's theory did not gain traction in scientific circles,
it remained a salient feature in certain corners of public discourse regarding the composition of the earth. As Sinnema recognizes, Halley
himself probably remained committed to his theory despite its improbability, and others followed suit, because the notion of a hollow earth
fell neatly in line with a popular theological position in the period. In
his history of hollow earth theories, David Standish explains that, like
many Christians in this era, Halley subscribed to a "notion of an 'abundant Providence,' the idea that creation must be as copious as possible
because that would logically be part of the Creator's plan."[21] The earth,
this logic suggests, must have been designed to maximize the life it can
sustain. In Halley's words, "Almighty Wisdom [would] yield as great a
Surface for the use of living Creatures as can consist with the conve-
nience and security of the whole." He reminds readers, "We ourselves, in
Cities where we are pressed for room, commonly build many Stories one
over the other, and thereby accommodate a much greater multitude of
inhabitants" (575). Human behavior follows divine logic here, stacking
lives "one over the other" in the interest of proliferation. The earth is like
a great city, encasing its inhabitants in layers upon layers.

The theological, in addition to scientific, implications of Halley's theory made it appealing to religious thinkers such as Cotton Mather, who
integrated it into *The Christian Philosopher* (1720). Citing both Newton's
error and Halley's account of the earth's variable magnetism, Mather
writes, "We may reckon the external parts of our globe as a shell, the internal as a nucleus, or an inner globe included within ours; and between
these a fluid medium . . . Mr. Halley allows there may be inhabitants of
the lower story, and many ways of producing light for them."[22] Sinnema
suggests that Mather's endorsement "might be viewed as a late 'scientific' defense of [Halley's] 'Account'—after which the hollow-earth idea
was increasingly relegated to the purview of utopian novelists and fringe
enthusiasts" (435). I do not disagree, but I do wish to highlight the fact
that Mather's interest in Halley's theory is as religious as it is scientific.

Indeed, the two lines of reasoning are inseparable for Mather, so even to give them distinct labels is to obscure their mutual operation within his work.

That inseparability also is a feature of *Beyond the Verge*. Scientific possibility lays the groundwork in Mather as well as Chipman for religious ecstasy. "The diameter of the earth being about eight thousand English miles, how easy it is to allow five hundred miles for the thickness of the shell!" Mather exclaims, "and another five hundred miles for a medium capable of a vast atmosphere, for the globe contained within it!" (117). The revelation within the passage is mathematical and theological. Mather resists imagining to what specific end such an atmosphere might exist: "But it is time to stop," he writes before offering some truly excellent puns: "We are got beyond human penetration; we have dug as far as it is fit any conjecture should carry us" (117).

Mather was not wrong about the limits of human penetration: the most significant data about the earth's core would not be collected until the twentieth century—once seismographic technology could produce precise data in the aftermath of phenomena such as earthquakes and nuclear detonations—and even today there remain many unanswered questions about the core's composition and temperature. But solving the mystery of the earth's interior is not the aim of *The Christian Philosopher*. "You must acknowledge," Mather concludes, "that human reason is too feeble, too narrow a thing to comprehend the infinite God" (117). For Mather, the mystery itself is enough to prove his thesis. The earth must be hollow, not only because its magnetic field defies prevailing scientific assumptions but also because in housing a wondrous secret, the planet mirrors the workings of the divine.

Mather may have been content to stop short of conjecture, but others were not, and over the course of the eighteenth and nineteenth centuries, numerous writers experimented with representations of the earth's core and its potential inhabitants. The most obvious influence on Chipman's thinking is the work of John Cleves Symmes. In 1818, Symmes, an army veteran and sometime trader, printed a "Circular" announcing, "I declare the earth is hollow, and habitable within; containing a number of solid concentric spheres, one within the other, and that it is open at the poles 12 or 16 degrees; I pledge my life in support of this truth, and am ready to explore the hollow, if the world will support and aid me in the undertaking."[23] Chipman certainly developed the idea of a polar "verge," as well as the notion of an earth comprised of concentric spheres, from Symmes. As Hester Blum notes, the "verge is a spatial concept Symmes repeatedly invoked to describe the circumpolar regions; for him, the verge is the indeterminate, transitional space between the external and internal worlds—a polar version of the littoral."[24]

Blum usefully traces the echoes of Symmes's theory through the nineteenth century, and I do not wish to replicate her analysis here. It is important, though, that Chipman's novel borrows heavily from the literature that grew out of Symmes's work. Symmes did not publish his theory in book form, but some of his proponents did; the most well known of these is James McBride's *Symmes's Theory of Concentric Spheres* (1826). That work makes prodigious use of the idea of a verge, including positing a scenario in which a traveler could "arrive at the coast of Siberia, without going far into the concavity of the sphere, and without knowing that he had been within the verge."[25] McBride argues that the region around the verge might be quite cold, but that once the verge is traversed, the climate will improve. In Chipman's novel, the tribes cross into the verge "without fully and completely understanding the matter," because the space of the verge is liminal—at once illuminated but not sunlit, temperate but not warmed by the usual air currents (114). *Beyond the Verge* even includes a reprinting of an article entitled "Symmes' Hole Up to Date," which was published in several newspapers around the country in 1894. That article, a call for volunteers to travel to the verge, asks, "Who shall defy the ice-bound North and enter that 'open sea' so long sought for and greet their long-lost cousins who migrated from Babylon 3,000 years ago?" (79).[26] It thus is not difficult to trace a line from Symmes to Chipman, and it is easy to see how Symmes's insistence on a hollow earth opened up space for those who believed him to imagine its spheres as a home for the lost tribes.

Although it held interest for a dedicated minority of scientifically oriented writers through a few centuries, over time, the hollow earth theory was relegated to the realm of speculative fiction. In this, it is not unique. Victoria Nelson's work suggests that Western "culture has a long history of pushing discredited religion and science alike off their former pedestals and recycling them in works of the imagination."[27] In the case of the hollow earth theory, she argues, "After the scientific revolution of the seventeenth century followed by the first polar expeditions, the *mundus subterraneus* could no longer be accepted as a real physical location and was transformed . . . into a fictive transcendental-psychological locus."[28] Sinnema, too, makes a compelling case for reading Halley's "self-styled 'Extravagant' hypothesis as the originary moment of a literary sub-genre—the hollow earth fantasy or romance—that flourished in England and America in his wake" (426).

Though scientifically untenable, the idea of a hollow earth never fully receded from fictional discourse, because it still stands as a site of tempting possibility. As Elizabeth Hope Chang's wide-ranging study of hollow earth fictions demonstrates, this subgenre is "wholly transatlantic," and it "bring[s] together adventure fiction and utopian fantasy with a pronounced attention to the operations of closed, near-planetary ecosystems."[29] Examining works as diverse as Jules Verne's *Journey to the Center of the Earth* and L. Frank Baum's *Dorothy and the Wizard of Oz* (1908), Chang demonstrates how, despite their many differences in plotlines and politics, these fictions share a concern with "explicating and historicizing the phenomena of a self-sustaining ecology" (389). The hollow earth, in other words, often appears as an earthly space that defies earthly limits, resistant to human interference and impervious to the forces—human and natural—that threaten to corrupt its resources.

Beyond the Verge shares an interest in utopia and sustainability with other hollow earth writings. The self-sustenance with which it is most concerned, however, is religious. Borrowing the genre's concern with environmental equilibrium, Chipman marshals the hollow earth in the service of presenting a space immune to spiritual decline. In this, the novel is unique among hollow earth fictions. It forecloses the possibility of a true adventure plot by asserting from the outset that its characters are destined for eternal safety, and, although it presents in great detail the natural workings of the inner world, the interiors with which it is most concerned are human.

Beyond the Verge: A Perfect Future

Chipman's novel shares many features with other hollow earth fictions produced in the nineteenth century. It details a long and potentially perilous journey, depicts great acts of human heroism, and couches its (in retrospect) preposterous narrative in the language of scientific rationalism. Unlike most hollow earth novels, though, *Beyond the Verge* is primarily concerned with solving a theological problem. A work of Christian fiction deeply entwined with late-century science, *Beyond the Verge* offers a useful case study in efforts to reconcile empiricism with revealed religion, as well as a picture of how some millennialist Protestants managed the tension caused by the ever-shrinking territory of the unknown earth and the corresponding deferral of the end of days. For such Christians, the lost tribes do not operate as a metaphor in the scriptures; their return to civilization from wherever they are hidden is an essential precursor to the return of Christ. Thus the contracting of earthly space resulting from exploration has the effect of expanding earthly time within the millennial frame: every square inch of territory that does not reveal the tribes prolongs the wait for the Second Coming.

By the 1890s, the revelatory promise of the Hebraic Indian theory seemed to have failed, as Native American people simply were not unveiled as the lost tribes of Israel. Running out of room on the earth's surface, Chipman shifts his readers' attention below ground, where a physical and spiritual paradise awaits the tribes. My primary concern here is with how Chipman deploys scientific reasoning to posit a link between the inner world's material and spiritual climates. Chipman's lost tribes are not the beneficiaries of some kind of divine magic—rather, the laws of matter have been designed to shield them from physical harm and religious corruption. Drawing on longstanding tropes within hollow earth science and science fiction, Chipman constructs a space of religious perfection as well as natural equilibrium.

Upon entering the action of *Beyond the Verge*—and thus, upon replacing both the Mound Builders and the Chichimeca as the engines driving the novel's plot—the lost tribes situate their journey to the earth's core within the frame of biblical prophecy. When Orotonga quite reasonably asks why the tribes "travel northward, where all is ice, frost, and eternal snow," Melchisedec responds by citing prophecies referencing the future unification of Israel and the return of its remnant from "northern" regions. This reply includes several verses from Jeremiah, predicting, "Behold, I will bring them from the North country, and gather them from the coasts of the earth . . . a great company shall return thither" (33, ellipses original). In this moment, Chipman takes a familiar refrain within the discourse of the Hebraic Indian theory and reconfigures it to suit his narrative. Where in some earlier writings the "North country" was imagined to be the Pole itself, or some other space just beyond the mapped world, here it operates as the gateway into a world below. When the tribes reappear "from the North," they will do so only because the opening to their destined home is located at the Pole. Rejecting the possibility that the tribes one day will be discovered upon the face of the earth, Chipman reorients biblical prophecy to allow for continuous deferral of their return. Rather than moving toward a hostile environment, Melchisedec suggests, the tribes are walking toward an ordained space where they will not be subject to the kind of punishing climate Orotonga imagines. The "land where we are traveling is northward," he asserts, "where violence shall cease, where there shall be neither sun nor moon, nor stars, but there shall be everlasting light" (35). In the land set aside for the tribes, the material contingencies of life on the earth's surface will be effaced by divine love.

Importantly, Melchisidec's account of the "everlasting light" awaiting the Israelites is simultaneously spiritual and material. "While we follow the cloud and pillar," he says, "it shall lead us to a land described by Isaiah": "The sun shall no more be thy light by day; neither for brightness shall the moon give light unto thee: but the Lord shall be unto thee an everlasting light, and thy god thy glory. Thy sun shall no more go down: neither shall the moon withdraw itself: for the Lord shall be thine everlasting light, and the days of thy mourning shall be ended" (34–35). This prophecy, which appears in Isaiah 60:19, is on its face metaphorical. There is no literal blotting out of the sun in Isaiah, and the light of the Lord appears to be internal to the believer. This rendering of the verse in the King James Bible underscores its own status as a rhetorical flourish with a sunrise pun: in the absence of the sun, "the days of thy mourning shall be ended." For those basking in the eternal light of God, there is need for neither mourning nor morning. Chipman, though, concretizes this prophecy and draws on existing conventions within speculative fiction to produce a world that is at once sunless and luminous. Describing the surprisingly well-lit interior of the earth's core, he writes, "Bible readers will remember that there was a light spoken of before the sun was made, and that was electricity, which, as will presently appear, is in all bodies, and is everywhere present wherever matter is to be found" (115).

Here, Chipman makes reference to a quirk in the first book of Genesis, in which God says "let there be light" and divides the light from the darkness in the third and fourth verses but then later makes "two great lights; the greater light to rule the day, and the lesser light to rule the night" in the sixteenth verse. In the space between the initial creation of light and the explicit creation of the sun, Chipman finds luminous electricity, a divine light source perfect for sustaining the tribes.

Chipman did not invent the notion that the hollow earth could be illuminated by a prevalent yet benign electricity. He may have borrowed the idea from Jules Verne, whose *Journey to the Center of the Earth* (first published in 1862 and released in English in 1871–72) depicts an inner atmosphere lit by "a ray of remarkable intensity" that is "not the sun, for its light [gives] no heat."[30] Chipman attributes the production of this magnificent electricity to the flow of water between the earth's surface and its core. The oceans, his narrator explains, circulate not only upon the earth but also into and through its interior, hydrating the inner world and producing the cycles needed to sustain life therein. The sun, Chipman writes, "in the daytime warms the oceans over the equator of each hemisphere":

> Currents of heated water are created on the surface of the oceans, and flow along, while cold water from the inner world pours out at the verges, and at the submarine outlets in vast quantities, which at certain hours sensibly lessens the quantity of water in the inner world, pouring over the huge waterfalls therein, that lessens the friction, that reduces the quantity of electricity, for the electric sun, the light sensibly lessens with the receding water, thus producing a twilight, which is called night in the inner world, but at opposite time of the day from the outer world. (116)

This passage is emblematic of the lengthy and frequent interventions of earth science information that interrupt the novel's plot. In addition to answering an important material question—namely, how a space devoid of sunlight could support life of any kind—this passage foregrounds the cyclical nature of life inside Chipman's earth. The waters rush and ebb, and the light follows suit. This pattern mirrors the surface of the earth's tides as well as its predictable cycling of night and day, and thus the inner world is amenable to human as well as other kinds of life. The hollow earth, in other words, always was designed to house the tribes. No miraculous intervention is required once they arrive, because the planet was built from the start to contain life within it.

In addition to the favorable climate and familiar cycles of day and night, the Israelites living just beyond the verge enjoy living conditions far easier than those at the surface: the core's animal populations are diverse and plentiful, and, as they are unaccustomed to interaction with humans, many are friendly enough for easy hunting. (The core does house some particularly unpleasant wild hogs, but the Israelites manage to best them.) Food is easy to obtain and requires neither labor nor environmental considerations. Before they even realize that they have crossed the threshold into the earth's interior, the Israelites notice that "the climate was growing warmer and warmer . . . [V]egetable life and trees and grasses became larger and more plentiful" (114). The inner world is "full of game, apples, plums, grapes, and peaches," with "numerous small streams . . . fertile valleys and beautiful rolling hills," and where "deer, wolves, rabbits, prairie-chickens, quails, turkeys, and song-birds [are] abundant" (134). At one point, the tribes discover a 240-square-mile apple orchard, which, although it is tended by no one, "astonished the Hebrews, [as] apples by countless bushels lay on the side-hills, and were piled up many feet deep in the hollows and ravines, while the trees were many of them loaded down with fruit" (135).

These descriptions of the Israelites' new dwelling place are reminiscent of colonial-era texts depicting the Americas as a paradise on earth. Andrew Marvell's poem "Bermudas," written around 1654, offers a typical (if fraught) example of such a fantasy. In the poem, religious refugees from England sing about the colony that awaits them as they approach it in a "small boat":

> He gave us this eternal spring
> Which here enamels everything,
> And sends the fowls to us in care,
> On daily visits through the air.
> He hangs in shades the orange bright,
> Like golden lamps in a green night;
> And does in the pomegranates close
> Jewels more rich than Ormus shows.

> He makes the figs our mouths to meet
> And throws the melons at our feet,
> But apples plants of such a price,
> No tree could ever bear them twice.

As scholars of Marvell's work long have noted, the specific fruits he names in this poem create a typological link between his English Protestants and the biblical Exodus—figs and pomegranates evoke Holy Land geography, even as the "apples" may serve as a reminder of Eden.[31] Chipman performs a similar sleight of hand in *Beyond the Verge*, filling his hollow earth with American produce and game meats. Unlike Marvell's colonists, the Israelites reach this land of plenty. Once they penetrate the planet's surface, all their needs are met through the workings of a self-sufficient ecosystem.

The space immediately beyond the verge is friendly to human life and ideal for human concealment. But Chipman's inner world has more than one layer: concentric spheres like the ones Halley postulated in 1692. The farther one descends into Chipman's earth, the friendlier the material and spiritual climates become. Describing the conditions of the Happy Isle—the hollow earth's innermost and most sacred space— Chipman writes, "The falling waters of all the world into this profound abyss created the incomputable mass of electricity already referred to, which, rising on high, collected in a great globe, or sun of electricity, above the island, and gave light and heat sufficient to make this center of earth the most delightful climate ever known or dreamed about" (148). The "climate" to which Chipman refers is meteorological and biological: "The amount of electricity was such," he writes, "that the air over the Happy Isle looked like diamond dust, and it toned up all animal and vegetable life, so that flowers, and men and women, looked radiant and bright beyond the power of description" (154). And this radiance is not skin deep. Free of corruption and exposed to this wondrous electricity, the isle's water "is as clear as crystal, and cures all diseases," and "where the thundering waters pour into the gulf, a mist rises towards the heavens, and the whole sky is surrounded by brilliant rainbows, presenting a spectacle of enchanting and indescribable splendor" (154–55).

If the Hebrews inside the verge are living in approximation to paradise, those who cross over into the Happy Isle completely reclaim a prelapsarian state. "The people walk with God and live in paradistic pleasures," the narrator explains. "Every tree and shrub produces bud, blossom, flower, and fruit like Paradise before the fall at Eden. Indeed, some of the Rabbis say the inner world was Paradise, and at the fall Adam and Eve were driven out of the inner world, on to the bleak outer world of thistles and thorns" (155). Here Chipman effects a clever inversion, in which to rise is to fall, and to descend is to remedy humankind's most terrible, formative descent.

It will perhaps come as no surprise that Chipman's inner world is not merely a climatic paradise, and that its exceptional weather and natural conditions have been designed to produce—or, it might be more precise to say, reproduce—human perfection. Material and spiritual climates merge within Chipman's earth, with the former serving as both the site and the concrete manifestation of the latter. The residents of the Happy Isle "spend their time in studying science, religion, the philosophy of life, the structure and essence of matters, and intellectual and spiritual development" (157). There is no distinction between the sacred and the profane within the earth; the contemplation of science and the essence of matter is the contemplation of religion. "Under the instructions of their wisest men," Chipman writes, "they have obtained such a knowledge in chemistry and the laws of nature that they can produce any food they want, and they are independent of the slavish labor imposed upon men on the outer world" (155). Where those on the surface toil, and those immediately beneath the surface work, the residents of the Happy Isle enjoy a life in which production does not require labor.

Like many novels of the era that conjure a world of infinite and equally shared resources, *Beyond the Verge* attempts to write the violence of consumption out of human life. "[A]ll calls for animal food is [*sic*] met by chemical process," the novel explains, "but the wonderful food-supply of nature is such on the Happy Isle, that the bloody spectacle of the butcher's shop and the taking of animal life is never seen" (157). Freed from the contingencies of the earth's surface, the residents of the Happy Isle do not simply inhabit a paradise—they overcome death itself, in all of its forms: "None ever die on the Happy Isle as they die on the exterior world; they simply go to sleep and lie on the side of Mount Zion, awaiting the call of the Resurrection trumpet at the Millennium. . . . None ever go to sleep under 420 years, and they spend their time in studying science, religion, the philosophy of life, the structure and essence of matter, and intellectual and spiritual development" (157).

The specter of a mountainside littered with the inert yet undead bodies of geriatric Israelites is not meant to terrify the reader. In fact, it is the most urgent promise of *Beyond the Verge*: an exterior space that is safer than any interior on the surface. One can sleep until the millennium on the side of Mount Zion; there is no need for privacy or comfort, because the earth itself has been divinely ordered to accommodate its most perfect inhabitants. Inside its hollow core, the earth is transformed from a space where one needs shelter into shelter itself. Having been chosen by God, and having in turn chosen to follow divine commands, those welcomed into the earth's interior are treated to the most delightful climate ever known as they await the end of the earth itself.

In moving the tribes into the center of the earth, Chipman solves the problem of their continued absence and preserves the possibility of their eventual return as an intact people. In isolating the tribes so completely, though, his narrative creates a problem for its own millennialist project: namely, the continued Hebraism of the tribes. The future revelation *Beyond the Verge* imagines is Christian, and thus the question of how the tribes will embrace Christianity if they are locked inside the planet alone is a potential stuck-point within its plot. Chipman's solution is Nardo, the Chichimec tagalong. Early in the work, as he and Rebecca profess their love for one another, Nardo confesses to her "what no other person has ever been told," revealing, "Through our land there came, years ago, an Israelite, who said Abraham was his father and Christ his Saviour, and he taught such a beautiful theory, that I was deeply impressed" (44).

The novel never explains the presence of this man in the Americas, nor does it attempt to reconcile the disparate timelines his entry into the text produces. Readers simply must accept the fact that a Christian Israelite arrived in North America ahead of the lost tribes of Israel and converted Nardo. "I am in the sunlight and under the care and marvelous protection and peace of God," he tells Rebecca. "I love all I see, feel, smell, hear, touch or comprehend, for God made them" (47). Impressed by his ecstasy, Rebecca replies, "Brave Chickimec, I have never heard an experience like yours. It has around it the halo of heaven, you have tasted of the unseen manna from the gardens of God" (47). She does not immediately embrace Christianity, but Rebecca's response to Nardo suggests that his testimony has affected her deeply. "I tacitly acquiesce in what [the tribes] teach and believe," she tells Nardo. "Still the Christ you acknowledge is such a worker of wonders and miracles, that I confess I am sometimes staggered . . . [I]t seems to me a faith like yours should belong to the Hebrew nation" (47). In this moment, Chipman introduces the possibility of Hebrew Christianity into *Beyond the Verge*. A Christian future travels with the tribes in the body of Nardo, a marvelous secret destined to unfold beyond the reach of human corruption.

Depicting Nardo as an indigenous American who has converted through the teachings of a Christian Israelite, *Beyond the Verge* brings the Hebraic Indian theory full circle. Although the novel rejects the notion that Native peoples are the direct descendants of the lost tribes or any other Hebraic population, it raises the possibility of a different kind of American Hebraism. "The man whose preaching converted me was a Hebrew," Nardo tells Rebecca, "and so if not by actual physical at least by spiritual adoption, I am a Hebrew" (48–49). Though Nardo's identity claim differs from the kinds of pronouncements James Adair, Elias Boudinot, and even William Apess had made about indigenous American peoples, it nonetheless operates as a powerful assertion of national and religious belonging. Nardo is a Hebrew, because he chooses to be a Hebrew; that choice forecloses neither the possibility of being a Native American nor the possibility of being a Christian. Rebecca assents to his claim, replying, "Brave and wise Chickimec, our people have always adopted those whom we call heathens . . . and I am sure you would be thrice welcome" (49). There is a poignancy to that word "thrice," as Nardo is a man with three identities, proclaiming belief in a three-person God.

This, *Beyond the Verge* suggests, is the true expression of American Hebraism. Its indigenous peoples cannot trace an ancestral line to biblical lands, but they can join those who do, and they simultaneously can bear with them the potential for the conversion of those people. Thus even as it rejects the Hebraic Indian theory's most basic tenets, *Beyond the Verge* retains its central fantasy, constructing a world in which an indigenous American, through his adoption of both Hebrew and Christian identities, will one day carry out the promise of millennium.

Coda

DNA and the Recovery of History

The Hebraic Indian theory structured discussions of American origins from the earliest moments of European arrival in the western hemisphere through the establishment of the United States. For three centuries, the theory emerged periodically as a central concern for those interested in deciphering the continents' human history; and for three centuries it also diminished in the face of competing ideas. By the middle of the nineteenth century, though, this boom-and-bust cycle had ceased. Following the publication of *The Book of Mormon* in 1830, the theory's popularity declined among other Christian sects. It is possible that the Church of Jesus Christ of Latter-day Saints' full embrace of the Hebraic Indian theory rendered it unpalatable to other Christians, but it is equally possible that the theory's failure to produce the gathering of Israel accounts for its ultimate rejection by most US Protestants. Historical contingencies, too, might explain reduced interest in the theory: as the United States ramped up its efforts to remove Native populations from its borders and then collapsed into civil war at midcentury, the question of human origins faded into the background of national concern.

As it receded from the religious and political landscapes, the Hebraic Indian theory also began to fall out of scientific discourse. These developments are not entirely distinct; as the theory's religious urgency subsided in the face of Indian Removal and the Civil War, and as its prophetic power weakened over time, so, too, did the need for its verification. The theory appears as little more than a footnote in late-nineteenth-century discussions of Native American origins, and by the twentieth century it is nearly gone—gone, that is, until it emerges anew with the sequencing of the human genome. A largely dormant discourse for over a century, the Hebraic Indian theory was reinvigorated by the discourse of DNA at the end of the twentieth century, and, this coda will suggest, its influence reverberates through these new endeavors to trace the history of human life on earth.

The study of human genetics has developed rapidly since 1953, when Francis Crick and James Watson published their discovery of the molecular structure of DNA: the double helix. Crick and Watson's work built on that of other scientists, most notably Rosalind Franklin and Maurice Wilkins, who pioneered the use of x-ray diffraction to produce the image of DNA that would allow Watson and Crick to determine its shape. Twenty years later, the biochemist Fred Sanger developed a technique for mapping the order of nucleobases in long sections of DNA, which set the stage for the sequencing of the human genome.[1] In the last decade, that sequencing has become both more efficient and less expensive. In the updated 2017 introduction to his study of human genomics, *The Journey of Man*, the geneticist Spencer Wells writes that when he initially wrote his book in 2002, "the first human genome had only recently been sequenced—the culmination of over a decade of concerted work by an international consortium of scientists. The cost of doing so totaled more than $3 billion. . . . Starting in around 2007, though, new methods of sequencing DNA—termed 'next generation sequencing'— made it economically feasible to expand our study of human genetic variation exponentially."[2] These methods had such a drastic impact on the field that by 2016, Wells notes, it became "possible to sequence an entire human genome in a few days at a cost of roughly $1,000."[3]

The ability to map DNA quickly and at a low cost has made it possible for private companies to offer a range of genetic tests, which in turn has generated a surge in genetic data collection, as millions of people have submitted genetic material for testing.[4] The notion that information about human history in general and individual lineage in particular can be discerned from the pattern of nucleobases inside each of us undergirds this new industry. Where the human past once seemed the domain of historians and archeologists, it now has entered the world of genomic science.

Though DNA testing often is described as an objective, material process concerned with the empirical study of nucleotides within human cells, it is inseparable from broader conversations about human history, race, and religion. As Priscilla Wald puts it, "Retelling the story of human migrations is in fact the chief aim of population genomics," and thus the field of human DNA research cannot be entirely distinguished from earlier discourses regarding the origin of human life.[5] At the heart of efforts to sequence the human genome lies a set of questions bearing sacred and secular weight: Where did we come from? How did we get here? Who was here first? Whose history matters? And where does history reside? Is it in the stories we tell or the records we keep? Is it in our bodies? Is it in the ground? These questions are at once ephemeral and material; they reverberate in religious and cultural discourses in myriad ways, and they often form the basis for governmental policies that determine the course of individual lives. This has been perhaps most pressingly the case in efforts to sequence the DNA of Native American populations. In the most comprehensive study of the cultural phenomenon of "Native American DNA" written to date, Kim TallBear notes that scientific attempts to answer questions about migrations to the Americas are deeply embedded within the history of colonialism and the emergence of whiteness as a racial category. "Native American DNA could not have emerged as an object of scientific research and genealogical desire," she reminds readers, "until individuals and groups emerged as 'Native American' in the course of colonial history."[6]

Colonial history not only shapes the design and interpretation of DNA ancestry tests but also creates the desire for such tests. The idea that Native and indigenous American populations are discrete, and that their "origin story" can be told apart from the stories of other peoples, is itself a product of a historically bound, colonial imagination. The continents and hemispheres we currently experience as distinct, in geography and history, were not always so. The drive to trace migration into the western hemisphere from the eastern hemisphere itself presumes both a temporal and a spatial relationship between the continents that only has been possible for a relatively brief period of human history.

Genomic efforts to isolate and describe DNA markers in Native American populations are not that far removed from early modern and Enlightenment efforts to faithfully describe cultural practices that promised to reveal the hemisphere's history even as they were imagined to be disappearing. If a colonialist perspective undergirds the hope of discovering "New World" origins in DNA studies, so too does an urgent sense of impending loss. As TallBear puts it, "It is the arrival of the settler in 1492 and many subsequent settlements that frame the search for Native American DNA before it is 'too late,' before the genetic signatures of the 'founding populations' in the Americas are lost forever in a sea of genetic admixture."[7] For both the scientists collecting DNA samples and the consumers seeking information about their own genomes, the possibility of recovering a "lost" lineage always is in play. The notion of "mixing," TallBear usefully reminds us, "is predicated on the notion of purity." Genetic markers associated with indigenous and Native American populations often appear in popular discussions of DNA as traces of the past preserved in the bodies of those who carry them. TallBear writes, "Standing where they do—almost never identifying as indigenous people themselves—scientists who study Native American migrations turn and look back over their shoulders with a desire to know the 'origins' of those who were first encountered when European settlers landed on the shores of these American continents." The discourse surrounding that search for origins often contributes to the ongoing erasure of actual Native American peoples through the creation of a pernicious synecdoche in which "Native" genes perform the work of Native American vanishing through admixture. It also links the study of Native American DNA to the search for the lost tribes of Israel.

The hope that the lost tribes and other Hebraic groups might be discovered somewhere in the human genome hovers at the margins of origins-oriented genetic mapping, and sometimes it even moves to the center. This has been true of genetic studies conducted beyond the western hemisphere, as well as of those in the Americas. Perhaps the most prominent efforts to locate "Jewish" origins in the DNA of different populations have been conducted by the British historian Tudor Parfitt. The most famous of these is Parfitt's study of the Lemba people, who mainly live in Zimbabwe and South Africa. Oral histories among the Lemba describe an ancient migration from Judea led by a figure named Buba, and Parfitt observed what he believed to be customs related to Judaism within that population.[8] In 1996, Parfitt began Y-chromosome DNA testing of Lemba men, hoping to determine whether they shared genetic material with people known to originate in what currently is called the Middle East. Specifically, he was looking for genetic markers associated with a group often referred to as the "kohanim" (and sometimes as "Cohen Jews"), a subset of the Jewish population with a family tradition of Priestly (i.e. Levite) descent following the male line. The testing Parfitt organized revealed the presence of such markers among some Lemba men. "As a result of these and other studies," Parfitt writes, "it is now widely believed that the Lemba are of Jewish origin, and that this has a scientific basis."[9]

This assertion is not without controversy, as Parfitt's correlation of certain genes with "Jewishness" is debatable. For my purposes here, the most telling aspect of Parfitt's work with DNA testing is that it has been accompanied by ethnographic descriptions of the Lemba people that, frankly, could have been written by Thomas Thorowgood or James Adair. A 1999 *New York Times* article by Nicholas Wade—himself the author of a hotly contested book about race and genetics—opens its description of Parfitt's DNA study by noting that the Lemba "practice circumcision, keep one day a week holy and avoid eating pork or piglike animals, such as the hippopotamus."[10] Written 350 years after Thorowgood's *Iewes in America*, Wade's article about "Jewish" ancestry begins by identifying the same old cultural markers: circumcision, a sabbath, and dietary restrictions. These practices, his piece suggests, have been preserved in Lemba culture just as "Priestly" DNA has been preserved in their chromosomes. (It doesn't seem to matter to Wade that a hippopotamus is not a pig.) Now, though, these observations of cultural similarity are accompanied by a new kind of "scientific" proof. If ethnography and biblical exegesis are not sufficient standards of evidence in the twentieth century, then DNA promises to fill in the gaps. Where explorations above and below ground have failed to locate the lost tribes, genomic science will succeed.

In the specific context of the Americas, DNA testing among Native American populations has had the most potentially unsettling consequences for the Church of Jesus Christ of Latter-day Saints, because its main scripture, *The Book of Mormon*, asserts a Hebraic ancestry for indigenous Americans. In 2002, the anthropologist Thomas Murphy—a member of the Church—examined the genetic information available about Native American populations at that time and concluded, "While DNA shows that ultimately all human populations are closely related, to date no intimate genetic link has been found between ancient Israelites and indigenous Americans, much less within the time frame suggested by the Book of Mormon."[11]

Murphy would build on this argument in subsequent publications and eventually team up with former Latter-day Saint Simon Southerton, who produced perhaps the most scathing rebuke of the Church using genetic studies. His book, *Losing a Lost Tribe: Native Americans, DNA, and the Mormon Church*, aims to debunk *The Book of Mormon*'s narrative history through molecular biology. Explaining his interest in the topic, Southerton writes, "I encountered research into molecular genealogy that compelled me to compare what I thought I knew religiously with what I knew from my training in science. . . . [F]or fellow Mormons who believe American Indians and Polynesians are largely descended from ancient Israelites, the recent findings of science may compel them, as I was compelled, to re-evaluate their thinking."[12] The "recent findings" to which Southerton refers are the genomic studies that Murphy assessed, which found genetic similarities among indigenous American and Asian populations, rather than with groups associated with the Middle East. "The DNA evidence supports the morphological evidence," he writes, "of a close relationship between Native Americans and Mongoloid peoples from Asia," further arguing that the "reason for this is that human morphology is largely predetermined by DNA."[13]

Although Southerton treats DNA as a neutral commodity that can be objectively described, his work is freighted with the kind of racialist assumptions that Wald has identified in both scientific and popular accounts of genetic research. "The stories about ancestry that emerge from population genomics can be incomplete and misleading," she notes. "Yet they inform many of the assumptions through which researchers constitute self-identified race and ethnicity as proxies. . . . Genomic stories have thus reconstituted the biological basis of race as a central question in scientific research and public discussion at the moment when, according to population geneticists, cultural and reproductive intermingling are recombining genomic profiles at unprecedented rates, hence the threatened 'disappearance' of some genetic markers."[14]

Southerton's tautology—that DNA proves morphology, which in turn points to DNA—is not uncommon in the popular rhetoric of population genomics, and the field bears an uneasy relationship to the history of racial science. "The scientific and public accounts of genomic medicine and human migration," Wald warns, "risk infusing the genomic creation story with the authority of science and the history of racism."[15] But as I hope this book has demonstrated, there always also is a third player at work in the endeavor to recover the history of human migration: religion. If the quest for human origin stories never can be separated from the history of racism in the aftermath of colonialism, neither can it be untangled from the complex web of creation stories that has underpinned centuries of cultural contact.

Though Southerton certainly is concerned with making genetic science accessible for a popular audience, his book mainly is organized around a stark critique of the Church of Jesus Christ of Latter-day Saints, and it marshals the language of science to undercut a theology. "It seems among the obstacles facing the Church," he writes, "the real stumbling block is not . . . the fact that there is no evidence for a Hebrew influence in Mesoamerica, or the preponderance of Asian DNA among living Native Americans and Polynesians. The real challenge comes from a failure to confront the evidence and state what it means for the church."[16]

Since the publication of his book and Murphy's articles, the Church has addressed questions of how DNA research relates to its foundational narrative. In a 2006 essay for the *FARMS Review*, the journal of the Foundation for Ancient Research and Mormon Studies at Brigham Young University, David G. Stewart (a medical doctor who is not a geneticist) addressed the work of Murphy and Southerton directly. Although he does note the existence of "research demonstrating considerable homology between modern Native American, Mongolian, and southern Siberian DNA, as well as a seeming lack of homology between modern Jewish and Native American DNA," Stewart asserts that "closer examination demonstrates that modern DNA evidence does not discredit traditional Latter-day Saint beliefs and that the views of critics are based on nonfactual assumptions and unsupportable misinterpretations of genetic data."[17]

Stewart's rejoinder to Murphy and Southerton hinges on a notion of genetic variation among "Hebrew" and "Jewish" populations. "Mitochondrial DNA studies have had little success in linking different Jewish groups," he asserts, "leading geneticists to discount mtDNA as a reliable means of ascertaining 'Jewish' roots."[18] DNA studies that focus on maternal lines (as mtDNA studies do), Stewart argues, will produce deceptive results. "Joseph's wife Asenath, daughter of Potipherah, priest of On," he writes, "is the ancestral mother of the tribes of Ephraim and Manasseh (Genesis 46:20). While her genealogy is unknown, there is no reason to believe that her mitochondrial lineage or that of her descendants, including the Lehites [Hebraic people who migrate to the

Americas in *The Book of Mormon*], would have matched that of the tribe of Judah. The presence of mtDNA types in Native Americans that do not match those found in modern Jewish groups is fully consistent with both Book of Mormon and Bible accounts."[19]

In this line of reasoning, biblical genealogy augments DNA study, and scientific research is brought into line with religious reasoning. Stewart concludes his rejoinder with a savvy note about the limits of scientific knowledge in any historical moment. "It is fascinating to consider," he writes, "not only how frequently science has changed its pronouncements, but also the societal amnesia that leads each new theory to be proclaimed as fact as definitively as those it supplanted." Even as he deploys the language of empirical science in the service of his religious argument, Stewart warns readers that secular reason always is in flux: "The real test of our insight as scientists and of our discernment as Christians," he concludes, "is not in our acknowledgment of past findings that are already widely accepted, but in our ability to correctly identify present truths." This is perhaps not bad advice, even for those who do not accept his broader claims about American origins. But it is advice that demonstrates the deep intertwining of the secular and the religious in the field of human genomics. The search for DNA strands never is completely divorced from the search for a genesis.

Because genetic testing that runs counter to *The Book of Mormon*'s historical claims has the potential to undermine its theological authority, the Church has approached the question of Native American DNA directly. The Church's official website, churchofjesuschrist.org, hosts a page entitled "Book of Mormon and DNA Studies" (which, incidentally, makes no mention of Murphy or Southerton). "Although the primary purpose of the Book of Mormon is more spiritual than historical," the site asserts, "some people have wondered whether the migrations it describes are compatible with scientific studies of ancient America. The discussion has centered on the field of population genetics and developments in DNA science. Some have contended that the migrations mentioned in the Book of Mormon did not occur because the majority of DNA identified to date in modern native peoples most closely resembles that of eastern Asian populations."[20] In response to the suggestion that there is no conclusive evidence of a Middle Eastern origin for indigenous American populations, the site notes that "the Book of Mormon . . . does not claim that the peoples it describes were either the predominant or the exclusive inhabitants of the lands they occupied. In fact, cultural and demographic clues in its text hint at the presence of other groups." As I discuss in this book's fourth chapter, that is true: the book leaves open the possibility of other peoples and other migrations. What is more, the site's writers contend, "Nothing is known about the DNA that Lehi, Sariah, Ishmael, and others brought to the Americas. Even if geneticists had a database of the DNA that now exists among all modern American Indian groups, it would be impossible to know exactly what to search for." If genomic studies do not align with *The Book of Mormon*'s narrative, in other words, that is the case because the information required for such alignment has been lost forever. For skeptics such as Southerton, this might seem a convenient loophole in the Church's main narrative. For believers, though, it is an explanation that allows theology and genomics to coexist.

The Church of Jesus Christ of Latter-day Saints attempts to solve the theological problem DNA poses to its scriptural record by highlighting parts of *The Book of Mormon* that imply other migrations to the Americas and by noting that no genetic material from populations described in the book is available for comparison, but for some believers these explanations ring hollow. There have been efforts among some Church members to find a genetic link between the Hebrew peoples described as migrating to the Americas in *The Book of Mormon* and contemporary Native Americans. The FIRM Foundation, for example, is an organization that describes itself as being "dedicated to showing forth evidence for the Book of Mormon in order to provide Church members with well-researched information enabling them to powerfully and respectfully defend its historicity and thus its truthfulness—with the ultimate goal of bringing people unto Christ."[21] Perhaps the most important phrase in this mission statement is "well-informed," by which is meant scientific as well as scriptural research. In its list of goals, the organization promises "to conduct research in a multiplicity of scientific and scholarly fields of endeavor which may provide secular support for the historicity of the Book of Mormon—including, but not limited to such disciplines as genetics, archaeology, climatology, anthropology, history, religion, geography, linguistics, mythology, meteorology, astronomy, metallurgy, architecture, ancient texts, Jewish customs, zoology, agronomy, oceanography, geophysics, etc."

In many respects, FIRM Foundation participates in a long tradition of combining secular and religious reasoning to affirm a story of American origins. Like many of the writers considered in this study, this organization combines investigatory methods and pushes at the boundaries of what constitutes "scientific" or "secular" evidence. "Jewish customs," for example, is not a scholarly field, per se, but it sits in this list alongside natural science disciplines such as genetics and climatology, as well as other scholarly fields (history, linguistics, anthropology) and fields more specifically concerned with topics related to *The Book of Mormon*, such as religion and the study of mythology and ancient texts. On the one hand, this list might seem an epistemological hodgepodge; on the other, though, it might seem an ideal realization of academic interdisciplinarity. For members of FIRM Foundation, the truth of *The Book of Mormon* is inseparable from its historical claims, and those claims, the organization asserts, are about North America. It is thus no surprise that "genetics" is the first discipline to appear on this list, as the foundation asserts wholeheartedly that Native Americans share a genetic link to ancient Hebraic peoples.

The primary genetic argument made by FIRM Foundation is that the presence of what is termed "haplogroup X" in the DNA of a small percentage of Native Americans proves a link between indigenous American and Middle Eastern populations. A haplogroup, to put it very simply, is a cluster of gene variants inherited together from a single parent. "Haplogroup X" is an umbrella term for a set of related variant clusters that are found in humans inhabiting a variety of regions on earth. It is relatively rare, but it has wide geographic range. One of the haplogroup X variants has been identified in the mitochondrial DNA of several different populations, including a small minority of Native Americans and Europeans, and some inhabitants of the Middle East, Siberia, and North Africa. The identification of this haplogroup, and the fact that it does not tend to appear in Asian populations outside of a small region of Siberia, has formed the basis for arguments favoring a Hebraic origin for Native Americans. A new annotated edition of *The Book of Mormon* assembled by FIRM Foundation members makes this argument plainly. "It is significant," the edition's editors write, "that DNA studies have shown that some of the Native American Nations have mtDNA lineages traced to both Egypt and the regions of northern Israel."[22] This position is much stronger than that taken by the Church itself, which mainly has argued that there is no clear way of testing *The Book of Mormon*'s veracity using DNA technology. For the members of FIRM Foundation, DNA and the presence of a haplogroup in both North America and the Middle East offer conclusive proof that the book's history is true.

My aim is not to take a position on the proper interpretation of DNA science—that truly would be outside the scope of my expertise. What I wish to point out, though, is that these debates over the origins of human life in the western hemisphere, though they deploy new empirical methods and different kinds of data, are not entirely divorced from the centuries of debates that have preceded them. Just as the search for the lost tribes of Israel stretched first across and then into the globe, the search for Hebraic Americans today has migrated from the body's surface—its morphology, its enactment of cultural practices, its movement in space—into the cells of those who might bear the promise of scriptural prophecies. In this way, DNA joins a long line of empirical methodologies that believers hope will reveal a sacred truth.

Even beyond the study of "Native American DNA" and efforts to locate a Hebraic trace within it, the popular discourse of human genomics frequently blurs distinctions between the secular and the sacred. Wells's *Journey of Man*, for example, opens its discussion of genetics and human history with an epigraph from Genesis: "So God created man in his own image, in the image of God created he him; male and female he created them. And God blessed them, and God said unto them, Be fruitful and multiply."[23] The study of DNA, Wells suggests, is the study of creation, and his scientific endeavor is organized around the Genesis myth. He gives the name "Eve" to "the female ancestor of everyone alive today, who lived in Africa around 150,000 years ago," and he suggests that genetic evidence of this singular ancestor raises the question "of where Eve actually lived—Where in Africa was the Garden of Eden?"[24] It is not good for Eve to be alone, so Wells introduces "Adam" into his discussion of male genetic lines. Acknowledging the limits of current DNA testing models in the recovery of a universal human lineage, for example, Wells writes, "We hit a barrier when we trace back into the past beyond a few thousand generations—there is simply no more variation to tell us about these questions of very deep history. Once we reach this point, there is nothing more that human genetic variation can tell us about our ancestors. We all coalesce into a single genetic entity—'Adam' in the case of the Y-chromosome, 'Eve' in the case of [mitochondrial DNA]—that existed for an unknowable period of time in the past."[25] The DNA sequencing projects Wells describes in his book are complex, and they have emerged out of decades of empirical study and scientific experimentation. Nonetheless, the journey undertaken in his book is to a mythical garden in a sacred text. Wells's methodology is new, but his conclusions are old. Looking for the past in a string of nucleotides, Wells ends where he began: in Genesis.

A sacred past serves as the structuring metaphor for Wells's DNA study, but popular genomics is equally invested in human destiny. Wells concludes by asserting that genetic mapping is a moral imperative. "Each of us is carrying a unique chapter, locked away inside our genome," he asserts, "and we owe it to ourselves and to our descendants to discover what it is."[26] Although Wells does not explicitly state what "our descendants" stand to gain from our genomic information, his conclusion suggests that DNA information is needed to secure humanity's future. "One responsibility that we neglect at our peril," he writes, "is self-discovery."[27]

Written in 2002, *Journey of Man* does not precisely outline the "peril" in question; the book merely ends on this suggestive note. A 2016 episode of the PBS series NOVA, entitled "Great Human Odyssey," however, renders the danger at which Wells hints in more concrete terms. Combining information about recent archeological and genomic studies with dramatic reenactments of historical migrations, "Great Human Odyssey" contends that human beings' superior adaptability has allowed the species to flourish in diverse environments for millennia. But that adaptability, the show suggests, may fail in the face of climate change. In the opening sequence, Donald Johanson—the paleoanthropologist who discovered the fossil remains known as "Lucy"—asserts, "Globally, everyone is *Homo sapiens*, if we're united by our past, united by our present, we're certainly united by our future."[28] The idea that a common destiny awaits all humans is both scientific and teleological in the program, as depictions of contemporary cultures presumed to share survival techniques with "our ancestors" are juxtaposed with analyses of "ancient DNA" to show how humans historically have adapted to extreme environments to survive. "Our powerful mind got us this far, but what lies ahead?" the narrator asks ominously, as shots of geneticists working in labs fill the screen. "Will we continue to evolve, or will the *Homo sapien* line die out with us?" The answer to this question, the episode's conclusion suggests, lies in the past. "We are the single most adaptable creature," Johanson asserts in the end. "We can sit on top of a rocket and shoot ourselves into space. We are incredibly adaptable. That is, hopefully, our salvation." In the story of evolution, in the trajectory of human genomics, lies the hope not only of human survival but also of human salvation. Indeed, the two are one and the same.

Although DNA testing is a new development in the study of human biology, the rhetoric of genetic ancestry—whether produced by geneticists or churches or critics of churches—fits (at times uncomfortably, at times perhaps too comfortably) into a longstanding discourse about the origins and dispersal of human life on the globe. With its emphasis on the recovery of "lost" histories and "vanishing" lineages, contemporary population genomics is not all that different from earlier attempts to trace the origins of the western hemisphere's earliest people. The notion that empirical information, impassively collected and faithfully recorded as data, will produce a revelation regarding human origins has structured four hundred years of discussions about American populations and their roots. The genealogical thread traced in this book is rhetorical rather than genetic, but it traces back from DNA testing to colonial imaginings of the edges of the known world. In the case of the Hebraic Indian theory, to unveil a biblical past for Native peoples is to inaugurate a glorious Christian destiny. In the recovery and restoration of lost tribes lies the hope of the future.

As method after method has failed to produce such discovery, new avenues of inquiry have opened. If ethnography fails to find Hebraic peoples in North America, perhaps geography will locate them at the North Pole. That failing, geology may lead the way into the earth, or perhaps astronomers will locate them on a distant planet. And if the universe fails to deliver them, perhaps they will be found deep inside us all, churning within our mitochondria, replicating themselves until the time of their return is revealed. In the absence of a complete scriptural record, and without the capacity to either see the full panorama of the universe or comprehend the full range of human history, those concerned with population origins will have to content themselves with collecting data, looking over their shoulders, and waiting for answers.

ACKNOWLEDGMENTS

This book was hard to write. I'd like to begin by acknowledging that fact. That I was able to complete it is a testament to the support, personal as well as institutional, I received throughout the writing process. This is a book about steadfast belief in a proposition that may be impossible. I am indebted to the people who believed I could write it during the periods when I found such belief impossible.

The University of Vermont has been my academic home for many years, and I have been fortunate to find friends as well as colleagues on its campus. I am thankful to the Department of English for its long-standing support of my work. I am grateful to Dean William Falls of the College of Arts and Sciences, as well as to my department chair, Daniel Fogel, for securing the funding and time needed for me to complete this project. My colleague Val Rohy is always my first and best reader, and this book would not exist had she not been willing to talk to me about it all the time for seven years. Jen Sisk is my favorite half of the two-headed monster. And, truly, I never would accomplish anything were it not for Holly Brevent. For the simple but crucial gift of friendship at work, I thank Eve Alexandra, Emily Beam, Jean Bessette, Isaac Cates, Kathy Floyd, Lisa Holmes, Jinny Huh, Deb Noel, Holly Painter, Nicole Phelps, and Chris Vaccaro.

This project owes much to the intellectual and moral support I have received from far-flung colleagues. I am indebted to Claudia Stokes, not only for her friendship but also for her willingness to receive, again and again, screen shots of old books bearing the caption, "Is this Hebrew?" Jared Hickman was one of the first people to talk to me about this project, and his generosity and good humor have sustained it through the years (as have the insights of Leslie). When I told Caroline Levander I didn't think I could finish this book, she insisted that I could. Many thanks to Bob Levine, whose mentorship has been a great gift to me. I owe a lot to my perennial conference compatriots: AnaMaria Seglie

Clawson, Lindsay DiCuirci, Ashley Reed, Jillian Sayre, Sarah Sillin, and Susanna Compton Underland. I also would like to thank the members of the Book of Mormon Studies Association—especially Joseph Spencer—for engaging with my work and encouraging it. Badia Ahad is the kind of friend every professor needs. So is Molly Robey, who has put up with me for nearly two decades.

It is a true pleasure to thank the editorial team at NYU Press, whose hard work made this book much better than it otherwise would have been. Thank you especially to Jennifer Hammer, for smart and challenging feedback, and to the anonymous reviewers who produced the most meticulous reader reports I've ever seen. This is a better book for their generosity. I also wish to thank the North American Religions series editors—Tracy Fessenden, Laura Levitt, and David Harrington Watt—for their enthusiasm about this project and their ideas for its improvement. I will be forever grateful to Tracy, whose unwavering belief in my work has made so many things possible. Although these and other readers offered important feedback at different stages of the project, any errors contained within these pages are mine alone.

I couldn't have written this book without a lot of help close to home. I drafted much of it at Nest Coffee and Bakery in beautiful downtown Essex Junction, Vermont, and I am indebted to the staff there for their kindness (and exceptional coffee). I'm also lucky to live near the Brownell Library, a fantastic public institution, where I did quite a bit of revising. My friends have endured the version of me that was writing this book for many years, and I'm lucky to have them. Thanks particularly to Liz Adams and Jill Hoppenjans, Rachel Bracken, Mark and Alicia Cernosia, Larissa Hebert, Carrie Lutz, Andy Kolovos, Susanne and Pete MacArthur, Jess and Tim Proctor, Kim Roy, and Sue Wilson. Thanks also to Linda Atkins, who kept me sane in the final stages of writing. I could not work at all if I did not have access to high-quality childcare, and I am grateful to the State of Vermont for its Act 166 preschool subsidy, which makes such care more affordable. I'm deeply thankful for Essex Hollow Playschool and its hard-working staff. Thank you to the teachers there who have had such a positive impact on my daughter: Lisa Allen, Riley Allen, Stacey DiVenere, Kimberly Dolan, Liza Driscoll, Stacie Freeman, Brittany Line, Kalie Magnant, Melissa Paquette, Kerrie Theye, and Cindy Tomko.

My family has been a wellspring of support for me, and I want to say thank you to the great clan of Fentons—especially to Mike and Joanne Fenton. Thanks also to Hank and Jamie Ellis, and to Nancy Lord, for taking an interest in my work. Thank you, Brigid and Mary Beebe, for absolutely everything. And thanks to Daniel Blankenship and David Viau for being the World's Best Guncles. Joey Ellis and Teluse Fenton did not live to see me complete this book, but I couldn't have written it without them, my dear old pals. Thank you, Danny Ellis, for all the squirrels. Jen Ellis and Helen Vesta Fenton have made space in their lives to accommodate my work, and their presence in my life makes the work worth it. I can't thank them enough.

NOTES

INTRODUCTION

1 Donald Jackson, ed., *Letters of the Lewis and Clark Expedition with Related Documents, 1783–1854* (Urbana: University of Illinois Press, 1978), 50.

2 Jackson, ed., *Letters of the Lewis and Clark Expedition*, 158.

3 Edward Winslow, preface to *The Glorious Progress of the Gospel amongst the Indians in New England* (London, 1649), [iv–v]. The pages of Winslow's book are unnumbered. To aid readers in locating my citations within the text, I cite those unnumbered pages using roman numerals, added by me and thus indicated with brackets, with the book's title page serving as the first in the sequence.

4 Winslow, preface, [vi].

5 Winslow, preface, [vi–vii].

6 Richard Popkin is probably the most well-known scholar of this phenomenon to use the phrase, which appears in his work "The Rise and Fall of the Jewish Indian Theory," in Yosef Kaplan, Henry Méchoulan, and Richard Popkin, eds., *Menassah ben Israel and His World* (Leiden, the Netherlands: Brill, 1989), 63–82. Richard Cogley refers to the theory as the "lost tribes theory," which I think is more accurate but does not cover theories of Hebraic origins in the Americas that are not linked to the lost tribes (see "'Some Other Kinde of Being and Condition': The Controversy in Mid-Seventeenth-Century England over the Peopling of Ancient America," *Journal of the History of Ideas* 68.1 [January 2007]: 35–56). Because this study examines theories of the lost tribes as well as other types of biblical origins for humanity in the Americas, I've opted for the broadest possible term that encapsulates the phenomenon in question.

7 In his study of Christian Hebraism in America, Shalom Goldman reminds readers that it is important to distinguish between the use of Hebrew by Jewish people and interest in the language and Jewish culture by Christians in the colonial period and its aftermath. His work stands as a necessary "corrective to the prevailing notion that Christian study of the Hebrew language and Hebrew texts in both Europe and America implied sympathetic interest in Jews, be they individual Jews or members of an established Jewish community. To the contrary, some Christian Hebraists, though they demonstrated the 'Christian truth' through their study of Hebrew, were most vocal and active in their anti-Judaism" (*God's Sacred Tongue: Hebrew and the American Imagination* [Chapel Hill: University of North Carolina Press, 2004], 3). Many of the figures I examine in this book operate in a similar

vein to those Goldman describes; although they are deeply invested in the Hebrew language and some Jewish writings, for the most part the Christian writers who appear in this book have little interest in—and in some cases deep animosity toward—actual Jewish people or contemporary expressions of Judaism.

8 Scott Eric Lyons, "Introduction," *The World, the Text, and the Indian: Global Dimensions of Native American Literature* (Albany: SUNY Press, 2017), 1–16, 4.

9 Lyons, "Introduction," 4.

10 It is worth noting that the word "America" is no less fraught than any other in this study, and neither is the phrase "western hemisphere." Certainly, neither exists in the absence of colonial history. However, in the absence of a better alternative, I will use both. Because this study does not explore the theory in reference to Canadian populations, I do not use the phrase "First Nations."

11 Zvi Ben-Dor Benite, *The Ten Lost Tribes: A World History* (New York: Oxford University Press, 2009), 4.

12 Here, too, the math is not precise, as many lost tribes theories contend that half of the Levites joined the tribes of Judah and Benjamin, and thus are not lost. Still, the phrase "ten lost tribes of Israel" is a bit more melodious than "the roughly nine-point-five lost tribes of Israel."

13 All biblical citations in this book refer to the King James version unless otherwise indicated.

14 As Tudor Parfitt explains, the "elements of the Ten Tribes exiled to Assyria may be presumed to have been absorbed into the Assyrian population, as had many others who fell prey to the Assyrian policy of forced assimilation and ethnic cleansing. There is some Assyriological evidence that individuals with Hebrew names were still to be found in Assyrian army units in the seventh century but there is no other clear evidence of the existence of the exiles. . . . [I]t would appear that this is the point at which the history of the Lost Tribes of Israel stops and the history of the myth of the Lost Tribes starts" (*The Lost Tribes of Israel: The History of a Myth* [London: Weidenfeld & Nicholson, 2002], 3–4).

15 Benite, *The Ten Lost Tribes*, 8.

16 Klaus-Peter Adam and Mark Leuchter, eds., *Soundings in Kings: Perspectives and Methods in Contemporary Scholarship* (Minneapolis, MN: Fortress Press, 2010), 7.

17 Benite, *The Ten Lost Tribes*, 2–3.

18 Stanford Lyman, "The Lost Tribes of Israel as a Problem in History and Sociology," *International Journal of Politics, Culture, and Society* 12.1 (Fall 1998): 7–42, 7.

19 Parfitt, *The Lost Tribes of Israel*, 24.

20 Lyman, "The Lost Tribes of Israel," 31.

21 Useful studies of the epistemological shifts produced by European colonialism include Joyce Appleby, *Shores of Knowledge: New World Discoveries and the Scientific Imagination* (New York: Norton, 2013); Anthony Grafton, *New Worlds, Ancient Texts: The Power of Tradition and the Shock of Discovery* (New York: Belknap, 1992); David Livingstone, *Adam's Ancestors: Race, Religion, and the Politics of Human Origins* (Baltimore, MD: Johns Hopkins University Press, 2008).

22 Livingstone, *Adam's Ancestors*, 17.

23 I will discuss the Noah story in more detail in the first chapter of this book. For a useful overview of its importance in the early modern era, see Don Cameron Allen, *The Legend of Noah: Renaissance Rationalism in Art, Science, and Letters* (Urbana-Champagne: University of Illinois Press, 1963).

24 Livingstone, *Adam's Ancestors*, 6.

25 John Sutton Lutz, "Introduction: Myth Understandings; or First Contact, Over and Over Again," *Myth and Memory: Stories of Indigenous-European Contact* (Vancouver: University of British Columbia Press, 2007) 1–14, 3.

26 Lutz, "Introduction," 2. This was, of course, also true for American populations, who frequently integrated Europeans into their existing mythologies. As Lutz notes, some indigenous cultures "had prophets who had foretold the arrival of these unusual visitors," and others were simply accustomed to periodically encountering outsiders (2). Colonial encounters are complex negotiations that take place both in specific moments and over long periods of time. They take place in a sometime shocking moment of the present, but they are shaped by long histories that project a variety of futures.

27 One of the most comprehensive studies of early theories regarding the Americas' human origins is Lee Eldridge Huddleston's *Origins of the American Indians: European Concepts, 1492–1729* (Austin: University of Texas Press, 1967).

28 This book has been deeply influenced by much recent work on US religious and literary cultures, and it would be impossible to provide a comprehensive list of all the excellent scholarship that has been produced in the past two decades. Still, some representative works that have influenced my thinking about religion and American literature include Joanna Brooks, *American Lazarus: Religion and the Rise of African-American and Native American Literatures* (New York: Oxford University Press, 2003); Tracy Fessenden, *Culture and Redemption: Religion, the Secular, and American Literature* (Princeton, NJ: Princeton University Press, 2006); Dawn Coleman, *Preaching and the Rise of the American Novel* (Columbus: Ohio State University Press, 2013); Claudia Stokes, *The Altar at Home: Sentimental Literature and Nineteenth-Century American Religion* (Philadelphia: University of Pennsylvania Press, 2014); Kevin Pelletier, *Apocalyptic Sentimentalism: Love and Fear in US Antebellum Literature* (Athens: University of Georgia Press, 2015); and Abram van Engen, *Sympathetic Puritans: Calvinist Fellow Feeling in Early New England* (New York: Oxford University Press, 2015).

29 Important here is the work of Sarah Rivett, which has demonstrated the important epistemological links between theological and scientific thinking that characterized the sixteenth and seventeenth centuries in Europe. As she puts it, "Continuity between science and religion can be especially difficult to perceive from a twenty-first-century perspective because we have generally accepted these categories as opposites, organized according to a kind of binary logic. In the early modern period, the opposite was true. Theologians and natural philosophers shared a commitment to pursue knowledge of God as the highest attainable form

of truth" (*The Science of the Soul in Colonial New England* [Chapel Hill: University of North Carolina Press, 2011], 6).

30 Stephanie Kirk and Sarah Rivett, "Introduction," *Religious Transformations in the Early Modern Americas,* ed. Kirk and Rivett (Philadelphia: University of Pennsylvania Press, 2014): 1–22, 1.

31 For an excellent account of how racism combined with the drive for capital to produce colonial brutality in the Americas, see Gerald Horne, *The Apocalypse of Settler Colonialism: The Roots of Slavery, White Supremacy, and Capitalism in Seventeenth-Century North America and the Caribbean* (New York: Monthly Review Press, 2018). Horne contends, "As the religious conflicts that animated the seventeenth century began to recede—Christian vs. Muslim, Catholic vs. Protestantism—as the filthy wealth generated by slavery and dispossession accelerated, capitalism and profit became the new god, with its curia in the basilicas of Wall Street" (10). Although I'm not certain that these conflicts have receded as much as Horne suggests, his sense that capitalism is infused with a kind of sacred urgency and that it is the heir of religious machinations in settler colonial states is worth noting.

32 For a history of Anglo-settler colonialism in the aftermath of US independence, see James Belich, *Replenishing the Earth: The Settler Revolution and the Rise of the Anglo-World, 1783–1939* (Oxford: Oxford University Press, 2009).

33 Nicholas Guyatt, *Providence and the Invention of the United States, 1607–1876* (New York: Cambridge University Press, 2007), 14.

34 Guyatt, *Providence and the Invention of the United States,* 177. Guyatt offers an in-depth discussion of the competing answers to this question in his book, especially pages 173–213.

CHAPTER 1. PROOF POSITIVE

1 Thorowgood's use of the terms "Jews" and "Judaical" to refer to the lost tribes (i.e., the Kingdom of Israel described in the Bible as being conquered and exiled by the Assyrian empire around 722 BCE) is anachronistic. The "lost tribes" depicted in 2 Kings are not "Jewish" people, as their exile predates the formation of the religion now known as Judaism. The history of actual Judaism(s) and Jewish peoples is beyond the scope of this study, which will focus almost entirely on white Christian writings that contain many errors about both "Jewish" and Native American cultural practices. Though it is inaccurate, Thorowgood's terminology is typical of Christian writing on this topic through the nineteenth century. I do not wish to replicate his error, and so I must be clear that this book is not a study of "Judaism," nor does it assess actual indigenous American cultures. It is, rather, a study of Christian perceptions of "Jewishness" and settler-colonial notions of Native American life. Like most religious traditions, Judaism has a complex and contested history. A useful study of the rich and varied history of Judaism can be found in Martin Goodman, *A History of Judaism* (Princeton, NJ: Princeton University Press, 2018).

2 A useful account of early European imaginings of the western hemisphere and the history of its peoples can be found in Joan-Pau Rubiés, "Hugo Grotius's Dissertation on the Origin of the American Peoples and the Use of Comparative Methods," *Journal of the History of Ideas* 52.2 (1991): 221–44.

3 Cogley, "'Some Other Kind of Being and Condition.'"

4 Richard Cogley, "The Ancestry of the American Indians: Thomas Thorowgood's *Iewes in America* (1650) and *Jews in America* (1660)," *English Literary Renaissance* 35.2 (2005): 304–30, 306.

5 Richard Popkin, "The Rise and Fall of the Jewish Indian Theory," 67.

6 In particular, Menasseh ben Israel used the Hebraic Indian theory as the foundation for his argument—made to Oliver Cromwell—that Jewish people should be readmitted to England (from which they had been expelled in the thirteenth century). Menasseh was a significant figure in the development of the Hebraic Indian theory in Europe. His work falls beyond the scope of this book, but more information on him can be found in the collection *Menasseh ben Israel and His World*, ed. Kaplan, Méchoulan, and Popkin. For more on Menassah's impact in the period, see Grant Underwood, "The Hope of Israel in Early Modern Ethnography and Eschatology," in *Hebrew and the Bible in America: The First Two Centuries*, ed. Shalom Goldman (Hanover, NH: University Press of New England, 1993), 91–101.

7 Cogley, "The Ancestry of the American Indians," 309.

8 John Dury, "An Epistolicall Discourse of Mr. John Dury, to Mr. Thorowgood. Concerning His Conjecture That the Americans Are Descended from the Israelites," in *Iewes in America; or, Probabilities That the Americans Are of That Race*, by Thomas Thorowgood (London, 1650), [xxxii]. Although the text proper of *Iewes in America* has standard page numbers, the prefatory material—including the dedication, Thorowgood's preface, and Dury's letter—are unnumbered. To aid readers in locating my citations within the text, I will refer to those unnumbered pages using roman numerals, added by me and thus indicated with brackets, with the book's title page serving as the first in the sequence.

9 Dury, "An Epistolicall Discourse," [xxvii].

10 Dury, "An Epistolicall Discourse," [xxviii].

11 Dury, "An Epistolicall Discourse," [xxviii].

12 Cogley, "The Ancestry of the American Indians," 309. "Marrano" is a name sometimes given to Jewish converts to Christianity in Spain and Portugal during this era. Though nominally Christian, many Marranos converted to escape persecution and continued to practice Judaism in secret. The word bears a derogatory connotation and reflects the anti-Jewish sentiment often found among Christians in the period, but in the context of Dury's work, it is meant to highlight Antonio de Montezinos's proximity to Judaism and, thus, his ostensible ability to recognize members of the lost tribes.

13 Dury, "Epistolicall Discourse," [xxviii].

14 Thomas Thorowgood, *Iewes in America; or, Probabilities That the Americans Are of That Race* (London, 1650), 1. All subsequent references to this work will be to this edition and appear parenthetically in the text.

15 Anders Hald, *A History of Probability and Statistics and Their Application before 1750* (New York: Wiley, 1990), 28.

16 Hald, *A History of Probability and Statistics*, 28.

17 Perhaps the most influential early study of the history of probability is Ian Hacking's *Emergence of Probability* (Cambridge: Cambridge University Press, 1975). Other useful engagements with this topic include Barbara Shapiro, *Probability and Certainty in Seventeenth-Century England* (Princeton, NJ: Princeton University Press, 1983); Lorraine Datson, *Classical Probability in the Enlightenment* (Princeton, NJ: Princeton University Press, 1988); and Ian Hacking, *The Taming of Chance* (Cambridge: Cambridge University Press, 1990).

18 For more on early efforts to predict gambling outcomes, particularly in dice throwing, see Hald, *A History of Probability and Statistics*, 13.

19 For a full account of the Pascal-Fermat correspondence, see Keith Devlin, *The Unfinished Game: Pascal, Fermat, and the Seventeenth-Century Letter That Made the World Modern* (New York: Basic Books, 2008).

20 Daston, *Classical Probability*, xi. Although Pascal and Fermat's correspondence ultimately would have a significant impact on the field of mathematics, probability was relatively slow to enter the quantitative field, and numerical probability remained on the edge of the discipline until the eighteenth century. Still, these early developments both reflected and contributed to wider shifts in European thinking about the role of likelihood and possibility within rational decision making.

21 For a full discussion of Graunt's calculations, see Hald, *Classical Probability*, 81–104.

22 Ian Hacking, "Introduction 2006: The Archaeology of Probable Reasoning," in *The Emergence of Probability: A Philosophical Study of Early Ideas about Probability, Induction, and Statistical Inference*, 2nd edition (Cambridge: Cambridge University Press, 2006), n.p.

23 Hacking, "Introduction 2006."

24 Shapiro, *Probability and Certainty*, 37.

25 As Hacking puts it, "What happened to signs, in becoming evidence, is largely responsible for our concept of probability. . . . [T]he concept of internal evidence of things is primarily a legacy of what I shall call the low sciences, alchemy, geology, astrology, and in particular medicine. By default those could deal only in *opinion*. They could achieve no demonstration and so had to resort to some other mode of proof. . . . New modes of argument arose, perforce, among the students of opinion" (Hacking, *The Emergence of Probability*, 35).

26 Shapiro, *Probability and Certainty*, 77.

27 Shapiro, *Probability and Certainty*, 119.

28 Daston, *Classical Probability*, 14.

29 Peter Martyr d'Anghiera, *De Novo Orbe; or, The Historie of the West Indies Containyng the Actes and Adventures of the Spanyardes, Which Have Conquered and*

Peopled Those Countries, Inriched with Varietie of Pleasant Relation of the Manners, Ceremonies, Lawes, Governments, and Warres of the Indians, trans. R. Eden (London, 1612), 10.

30 Barry Isaac, "Aztec Cannibalism: Nahua versus Spanish and Mestizo Accounts in the Valley of Mexico," *Ancient Mesoamerica* 16.1 (2005): 1–10, 8.

31 Isaac, "Aztec Cannibalism," 8.

32 Hamon L'Estrange, *Americans No Iewes; or, Improbabilities That the Americans Are of That Race* (London, 1651), [iii].

33 L'Estrange, *Americans No Iewes*, 11.

34 L'Estrange, *Americans No Iewes*, 14.

35 L'Estrange, *Americans No Iewes*, 19.

36 L'Estrange, *Americans No Iewes*, 74.

37 Thomas Thorowgood, *Jews in America; or, Probabilities, That Those Indians Are Judaical, Made More Probable by Some Additionals to the Former Conjecture* (London, 1660), 25. All subsequent references to this work will be to this edition and appear parenthetically in the text. Readers should note that this work contains several different sections, each with its own discrete numbering. When needed, I make note of these sections in order to aid readers in locating cited portions of the text. In addition to this, it is important to note that pages are misnumbered throughout the text. Where a page number is repeated in the text, I will indicate the second and following instances using letters (a, b, etc.).

38 This is an example of the repeated numbering I described in note 37. The page number should be 12.

39 Richard Cogley, "John Eliot and the Origins of the American Indians," *Early American Literature* 21.3 (1986): 210–25, 211.

40 Cogley, "John Eliot," 212.

41 Cogley, "John Eliot," 216.

42 John Eliot, Letter to Edward Winslow, in *The Light Appearing More and More towards the Perfect Day; or, A Farther Discovery of the Present State of the Indians in New-England concerning the Progress of the Gospel among Them. Manifest in Letters from Such as Preacht to Them There* (London, 1651), 14–15.

43 A very useful explanation of Pascal's Wager and its print history can be found in Justine Crump, "'Il Faut Parier': Pascal's Wager and Fielding's *Amelia*," *Modern Language Review* 95 (2000): 311–23, esp. 312–15.

44 Ian Hacking, "The Logic of Pascal's Wager," *American Philosophical Quarterly* 9.2 (1972): 186–92, 186.

45 Crump, "'Il Faut Parier,'" 313.

46 For more on Pascal's Wager, see Jeff Jordan, *Pascal's Wager: Pragmatic Arguments and Belief in God* (New York: Oxford University Press, 2006).

47 For more on Williams's banishment, see Nan Goodman, "Banishment, Jurisdiction, and Identity in Seventeenth-Century New England: The Case of Roger Williams," *Early American Studies* 7.1 (2008): 109–39.

48 Thorowgood, *Iewes*, 81.

49 Roger Williams, "To My Deare and Wellbeloved Friends and Countrey-men, in Old and New England," preface to *A Key into the Language of America* (London, 1643), [v]. As with Thorowgood's texts, I will indicate the unnumbered pages of Williams's prefatory materials with bracketed roman numerals, assigning the first to his title page. It is worth noting that it was not "granted on all hands" in this period that indigenous American populations sprang "from Adam and Noah." Numerous theories of American descent emerged coincidently with the Hebraic Indian theory, and some of those theories held that the western hemisphere was populated by a separate creation. I will discuss this kind of theory, often termed "polygenesis," in more detail in the second chapter of this book.

50 Williams, "To My Deare," [vi].

51 Williams, "To My Deare," [vii].

52 Williams, "To My Deare," [vii].

53 Thorowgood, *Iewes*, 3.

54 Williams, "To My Deare," [viii–ix].

55 Williams, "To My Deare," [ix].

56 Williams, "To My Deare," [x].

57 John Eliot, "The Learned Conjectures of the Reverend Mr. John Eliot Touching the Americans of New and Notable Consideration, Written to Mr. Thorowgood," in *Jews in America*, by Thomas Thorowgood (London, 1660), 2. All references to this work will be to this edition and appear parenthetically in the text.

58 The foundation study of the Noah story's impact on European thought is Don Cameron Allen's *Legend of Noah: Renaissance Rationalism in Art, Science, and Letters* (Urbana-Champagne: University of Illinois Press, 1963).

59 Benjamin Braude, "The Sons of Noah and the Construction of Ethnic and Geographical Identities in the Medieval and Early Modern Period," *William and Mary Quarterly* 54.1 (1997): 103–42.

60 Braude, "The Sons of Noah," 108.

61 Braude, "The Sons of Noah," 108.

62 James VanderKam, "The Apocryphon of Eber: A New Translation and Introduction," in *Old Testament Pseudepigrapha: More Noncanonical Scriptures*, vol. 1, ed. Richard Bauckham, James R. Davila, and Alexander Panayotov (Grand Rapids, MI: Eerdman's, 2013): 47–52, 47.

63 VanderKam, "The Apocryphon of Eber," 48.

CHAPTER 2. "A COMPLETE INDIAN SYSTEM"

1 In current practice, participant observation ethnography involves a researcher developing a relationship with a group for the purposes of sociological or anthropological study. Adair was not an ethnographer in this sense, not only because the field as it is did not then exist but also because his aim initially was not to study the cultures with which he had contact, but to trade with them. Still, it is useful to think about Adair's *History* within the context of emerging anthropological study, because to do so sheds light on the significance of his

methods. In his work on Adair's relationship to what would become the field of anthropology, Charles Hudson notes that "Adair was not a participant-observer in the modern sense," because he did keep himself at some distance from those he was observing and, unlike many other white traders, did not fully engage in many indigenous cultural practices ("James Adair as Anthropologist," *Ethnohistory* 24.4 [1977]: 311–28, 319). However, Hudson also suggests that "because of [his] sustained first-hand experience with Indian life, Adair's *History* has a modern flavor" (321). It is a work that illustrates a budding interest in the systematic study of cultures and the use value of conclusions that might be derived from such study.

2 James Adair, *A History of the American Indians*, ed. Kathryn E. Holland Braund (Tuscaloosa: University of Alabama Press, 2005), 289. All subsequent reference to this work, including references to Braund's editorial remarks, will be to this edition and appear parenthetically within the text.

3 As Braund notes, even today "historians, ethnohistorians, and anthropologists regard Adair's *History of the American Indians* as one of the most valuable primary accounts of the southeastern Indians" (xi).

4 Cogley, "The Ancestry of the American Indians," 304.

5 For an in-depth analysis of secularism's complex and culturally contingent relationship to religion, see Talal Asad's *Formations of the Secular: Christianity, Islam, Modernity* (Stanford, CA: Stanford University Press, 2003). Perhaps the most influential study of the history of secularism in Western thought is Charles Taylor's *Secular Age* (Cambridge, MA: Belknap Press of Harvard University Press, 2007). Taylor's work has been the subject of critique, revision, and expansion since its publication—see, for example, *Varieties of Secularism in a Secular Age*, ed. Michael Warner, Jonathan VanAnterpen, and Craig Calhoun (Cambridge, MA: Harvard University Press, 2013). Other recent, important works on the subject of secularism in nineteenth-century American literature include Tracy Fessenden, *Culture and Redemption: Religion, the Secular, and American Literature* (Princeton, NJ: Princeton University Press, 2007); and John Lardas Modern, *Secularism in Antebellum America* (Chicago: University of Chicago Press, 2011). More general work dealing with the secular's relationship to criticism includes Vincent Pecora, *Secularization and Cultural Criticism: Religion, Nation, and Modernity* (Chicago: Chicago University Press, 2006); Michael Kaufman, "The Religious, the Secular, and Literary Studies: Rethinking the Secularization Narrative in Histories of the Profession," *New Literary History* 38.4 (2007): 607–28.

6 Guy Collins, *Faithful Doubt: The Wisdom of Uncertainty* (Eugene, OR: Cascade Books, 2014), 50.

7 Henry Home, Lord Kames, *Sketches of the History of Man Considerably Enlarged by the Last Additions and Corrections of the Author*, 3 vols., ed. James A. Harris (Indianapolis: Liberty Fund, 2007), vol. 1: n. 4. All subsequent references to this work will be from this edition and appear parenthetically within the text.

8 A useful introduction to this vein of inquiry is William Lehmann's *Henry Home, Lord Kames, and the Scottish Enlightenment: A Study in National Character and in the History of Ideas* (The Hague, Holland: Martinus Nijhoff, 1971).

9 Livingstone, *Adam's Ancestors*, 6.

10 Livingstone, *Adam's Ancestors*, 8.

11 As Livingstone notes, Montesquieu makes the grand claim that "the empire of climate is the first, the most powerful, of all climates," in his *Spirit of the Laws* (qtd. in Livingstone, *Adam's Ancestors*, 55). Buffon, in his *Histoire Naturel*, similarly argued that "those marks which distinguish men who inhabit different regions of the earth, are not original, but purely superficial" (qtd. in Livingstone, *Adam's Ancestors*, 56).

12 All references to the Bible in this chapter are to the King James version.

13 It is perhaps worth noting that just two paragraphs later Kames asserts that the "Esquimaux are a different race from the rest of the Americans," citing their similarities to people inhabiting Greenland (*Sketches*, 557).

14 I, too, suffer from a deficiency in Hebrew and so would like to thank Claudia Stokes for examining Adair's text and verifying that his definitions of Hebrew words are accurate (though he often puts those definitions to dubious use).

15 Hudson, "James Adair as Anthropologist," 315.

16 The most significant attempt to link Joseph Smith to Ethan Smith may be found in David Persuitte's *Joseph Smith and the Origins of the Book of Mormon* (Jefferson, NC: MacFarland, 2000).

17 See, for example, Larry Morgan, "Oliver Cowdery's Vermont Years and the Origins of Mormonism," *BYU Studies* 39.1 (2000): 107–29.

18 Ethan Smith, *View of the Hebrews* (Poultney, VT: Smith & Shute, 1823), iii. All subsequent references to this work will be to this edition and appear parenthetically within the text.

19 Robert Lowth, *Isaiah: A New Translation; With a Preliminary Dissertation and Notes, Critical, Philological, and Explanatory* (London, 1778), 44. Smith phrases the verse as "Ho! to the land shadowing with wings," but in Lowth's translation the line is rendered as, "Ho! to the land of the winged cymbal." Smith probably adapted the phrase "shadowing with wings" from Boudinot's *Star in the West*, which makes a similar claim about the inaccuracy of the "Woe!" in the King James Bible and offers some extended commentary on the phrase "the shadow of wings" (*A Star in the West* [Trenton, NJ, 1816], 224). Boudinot's main source for the translation of Isaiah is George Stanley Faber's *Dissertation on the Prophecies relative to the Great Period of 1,200 Years, the Papal and Mahomedan Apostasies, the Reign of Antichrist, and the Restoration of the Jews*, 2 vols. (London, 1807). Boudinot also cites Lowth throughout his text, though, so he clearly read both men's work.

20 For a detailed biography of Noah, see Jonathan Sarna's *Jacksonian Jew: The Two Worlds of Manuel Mordecai Noah* (New York: Holmes and Meier, 1981). For an account of Ararat's fraught relationship to early US politics, see Eran Shalev, "'Re-

vive, Renew, and Reestablish': Mordecai Noah's Ararat and the Limits of Biblical Imagination in the Early American Republic," *American Jewish Archives Journal* 62.1 (2010): 1–20.

21 Manuel Mordecai Noah, *The Select Writings of Mordecai Noah*, ed. Michael Schuldiner and Daniel J. Kleinfeld (Westport, CT: Greenwood, 1999), 112. All subsequent references to this work will be from this edition and appear parenthetically within the text.

22 Noah, *Discourse on the Evidences That the American Indians Being the Descendants of the Lost Tribes of Israel* (New York: James Van Norden, 1837), 10. All subsequent references to this work will be from this edition and appear parenthetically within the text.

23 John Henry Logan, *A History of the Upper Country of South Carolina, from the Earliest Persons to the Close of the War of Independence*, 2 vols. (Charleston, SC: S.G. Courtenay, 1859), 1:345. All subsequent references to this work will be from this edition and appear parenthetically within the text.

24 Livingston Farrand, *Basis of American History, 1500–1900* (New York: Harper & Brothers, 1904), 277, 285.

CHAPTER 3. ELIAS BOUDINOT, WILLIAM APESS, AND THE ACCIDENTS OF HISTORY

1 William Apess, *On Our Own Ground: The Complete Writings of William Apess, a Pequot*, ed. Barry O'Connell (Amherst: University of Massachusetts Press, 1992), 52. All subsequent references to this work will be from this edition and appear parenthetically within the text.

2 I discuss Boudinot's engagement with the Hebraic Indian theory in a different register in "Nephites and Israelites: *The Book of Mormon* and the Hebraic Indian Theory," in *Americanist Approaches to* The Book of Mormon, ed. Jared Hickman and Elizabeth Fenton (New York: Oxford University Press, 2019), 277–97.

3 Sandra Gustafson, "Nations of Israelites: Prophecy and Cultural Autonomy in the Writings of William Apess," *Religion & Literature* 26.1 (1994): 31–53, 34.

4 Rochelle Raineri Zuck, "William Apess, the 'Lost Tribes,' and Indigenous Survivance," *Studies in American Indian Literatures: The Journal of the Association for the Study of American Indian Literatures* 25.1 (2013): 1–26, 2–3.

5 Richard Popkin, "*The Age of Reason* versus *The Age of Revelation*: Two Critics of Tom Paine: David Levi and Elias Boudinot," in *Deism, Masonry, and the Enlightenment: Essays Honoring Alfred Owen Aldridge* (Newark: University of Delaware Press, 1987): 158–70, 165. Popkin was correct when he wrote his piece that Boudinot had received almost no attention from historians and other critics. Since then, though, some scholarship has taken notice of Boudinot and begun to unpack his legacy. See, for example, Jonathan Den Hartog, "Elias Boudinot, Presbyterians, and the Quest for a 'Righteous Republic,'" in *Faith and the Founders of the American Republic*, ed. Daniel L. Dreisbach and Mark David Hall (New York: Oxford University Press, 2014), 253–76.

6 Elias Boudinot, *The Second Advent; or, The Coming of the Messiah in Glory, Shown to Be a Scripture Doctrine, and Taught by Divine Revelation from the Beginning of the World* (Trenton, NJ: Fenton, Hutchinson, and Dunham, 1815), 2.

7 Boudinot, *The Second Advent*, 151–52.

8 Boudinot, *The Second Advent*, 345.

9 Elias Boudinot, *A Star in the West; or, A Humble Attempt to Discover the Long Lost Ten Tribes of Israel, Preparatory to Their Return to Their Beloved City, Jerusalem* (Trenton, NJ: Fenton, Hutchinson, and Dunham, 1816), 25. All subsequent references to this book will be to this edition and appear parenthetically in the text.

10 *Portico Review* 5 (1818): 246.

11 *Eclectic Review* 2.2 (August 1829): 117.

12 Michael Witmore, *Culture of Accidents: Unexpected Knowledges in Early Modern England* (Redwood City, CA: Stanford University Press, 2002). Other useful critical assessments of the idea of the "accident" include Ross Hamilton's *Accident: A Philosophical and Literary History* (Chicago: University of Chicago Press, 2007) and Jason Puskar's *Accident Society: Fiction, Collectivity, and the Production of Chance* (Redwood City, CA: Stanford University Press, 2012).

13 Qtd. in Witmore, *Culture of Accidents*, 28. As Witmore notes, though, Aristotle goes on in the *Metaphysics* to give accidents a fairly comprehensive treatment.

14 Witmore, *Culture of Accidents*, 5.

15 Witmore, *Culture of Accidents*, 10.

16 John Calvin, *Institutes of the Christian Religion*, vol. 1, trans. Henry Beveridge (Edinburgh: Calvin Translation Society, 1845), 232–33.

17 Jeffrey Makala, "'Spiritual Machinery': The American Bible Society and the Mechanisms of Large-Scale Printing in the Nineteenth Century," *Printing History* 25 (2019): 45–66, 48.

18 John Fea provided me with this information about ABS bibles and the apocrypha, and I am deeply grateful to him. For more on the ABS and its history, see Fea's *Bible Cause: A History of the American Bible Society* (New York: Oxford University Press, 2016).

19 Zvi Ben-Dor Benite, *The Ten Lost Tribes: A World History* (New York: Oxford University Press, 2013), 60–61.

20 Benite, *The Ten Lost Tribes*, 61.

21 Benite, *The Ten Lost Tribes*, 142–43.

22 Benite, *The Ten Lost Tribes*, 148.

23 The Bering Strait is about fifty-five miles wide at its narrowest point.

24 Fenton, "Nephrites and Israelites," 285–86.

25 In the preface to the 1829 edition, Apess, speaking of himself in the third person, writes that the book "was written under many disadvantages, and the bare acknowledgement of his entire want of a common education, will, he hopes, be a sufficient apology for any inaccuracies that may occur."

26 Carolyn Haynes, "A Mark for Them All to . . . Hiss At: The Formation of Methodist and Pequot Identity in the Conversion Narrative of William Apess," *Early American Literature* 31.1 (1996): 25–44, 25.

27 As Drew Lopenzina notes in his recent biography, the renewed interest in Apess at the close of the twentieth century owes much to O'Connell's publication of *On Our Own Ground* in 1992. "This has facilitated a conversation on Apess that has brought him not only to the attention of scholars but into the classroom as well, where his writings serve a vital role in establishing Native presence and intellectual engagement in a period dominated by white males and a very small handful of plucky women writers" (*Through an Indian's Looking-Glass: A Cultural Biography of William Apess* [Amherst: University of Massachusetts Press, 2017], 3). Other useful, early studies of Apess's life and work include Hilary E. Wyss, *Writing Indians: Literacy, Christianity, and Native Community in Early America* (Amherst: University of Massachusetts Press, 2000), 154–67; and Lisa Brooks, *The Common Pot: The Recovery of Native Space in the Northeast* (Minneapolis: University of Minnesota Press, 2008), 163–218.

28 Mark Rifkin, "Shadows of Mashantucket: William Apess and the Representation of Pequot Place," *American Literature* 84.4 (2012): 691–714, 691.

29 Arnold Krupat, *The Voice in the Margin: Native American Literature and the Canon* (Berkeley: University of California Press, 1989), 148.

30 Haynes, "A Mark for Them All," 27.

31 Haynes, "A Mark for Them All," 26.

32 As Mark Miller has shown, the Methodist reform movements taking root in New York, especially among African Americans, further allowed Apess to situate his racial politics within a Christian framework. For more on this, see his "'Mouth for God': Temperate Labor, Race, and Methodist Reform in William Apess's *Son of the Forest*," *Journal of the Early Republic* 30 (Summer 2010): 226–51.

33 Laura Donaldson, "Making a Joyful Noise: William Apess and the Search for Postcolonial Methodism," *interventions* 7.2 (2005): 180–98, 188.

34 Mark Rifkin makes this point quite powerfully in *Beyond Settler Time: Temporal Sovereignty and Indigenous Self-Determination* (Durham, NC: Duke University Press, 2017), 20–25.

35 Rifkin, *Beyond Settler Time*, 2.

36 Rifkin, *Beyond Settler Time*, 5. Joanne Barker makes a similar point, noting that "the belief is that if Native cultures and identities can be fixed in a specific time and place, they can be measured for degrees of deviation and loss from that place to another. This logic makes a flawed assumption, however, that Native culture and identity—or any other for that matter—*can be* frozen in time as if they were then whole and pure to be measured against another time" (*Native Acts: Law, Recognition, and Cultural Ancestry* [Durham, NC: Duke University Press, 2011], 193).

37 Rifkin, *Beyond Settler Time*, 33. Other studies of temporality and settler colonialism that inform this study include Philip J. Deloria, *Indians in Unexpected*

Places (Lawrence: University Press of Kansas, 2004); and Jared Hickman, "600 B.C.E.–1830 C.E.: The Book of Mormon and the Lived Eschatology of Settler Colonialism," in *Timelines of American Literature*, ed. Cody Marrs and Christopher Hager (Baltimore, MD: Johns Hopkins University Press, 2019), 67–84.

38 I have avoided resorting to bodily metaphors when discussing the appendix, but it is worth noting that the textual appendage was named before the vermiform organ.

39 Gérard Genette, *Paratexts: Thresholds of Interpretation*, trans. Jane E. Lewin (Cambridge: Cambridge University Press, 1997), 1–2.

40 See Spivak's preface to Jacques Derrida's *Of Grammatology*, trans. Gayatri Spivak, ed. Judith Butler (Baltimore, MD: Johns Hopkins University Press, 2016), xxviii.

41 Apess also is making a claim of monogenesis, a concept I describe in more detail in chapter 2 of this book.

42 Roumiana Velikova, "'Philip, King of the Pequots': The History of an Error," *Early American Literature* 37.2 (2002): 311–35, 312.

43 Velikova, "'Philip, King of the Pequots,'" 314.

44 Significantly, although Apess slightly revises Boudinot here, in *A Star in the West* Boudinot himself is revising someone else's document. Immediately preceding his assertion that the biblical "Pekod" have become American Pequots is a citation from William Robertson's *History of America*, which describes the assault on the Pequot people by English colonists. Boudinot and Apess both quote Robertson's assertion that the English "stained their laurels by the use they made of their victory," but they also both omit Robertson's succeeding assertion that the whites' "vigorous efforts in this decisive campaign filled all the surrounding tribes of Indians with such a high opinion of their valor as secured a long tranquility" (see *The Historical Works of William Robertson*, vol. 4 [Edinburgh: Doig & Stirling, 1813], 493).

45 Eric Wolfe, "Mourning, Melancholia, and Rhetorical Sovereignty in William Apess's Eulogy on King Philip," *Studies in American Indian Literatures* 20.4 (2008): 1–23, 5.

46 Wolfe, "Mourning," 3.

CHAPTER 4. *THE BOOK OF MORMON*'S NEW AMERICAN PAST

1 For an account of Smith's early life and discovery of the plates, see Terryl Givens's *By the Hand of Mormon: The American Scripture That Launched a New World Religion* (New York: Oxford University Press, 2002). Although *The Book of Mormon*'s title frequently is printed in plain text, I italicize it because I am treating it as a lengthy work of prose, rather than a sacred text.

2 The earliest edition of the book resembled contemporary bibles in appearance as well as content. Paul Gutjahr has noted that Smith "was intimately involved in *The Book of Mormon*'s production process, and he carefully signaled through every aspect of the process that this was no ordinary book." Like the most popular bibles of the era, *The Book of Mormon* was bound "in brown leather with twin

gold bars impressed on the spine at regular intervals . . . [and] a black label im-
printed with gold letters on the spine bearing the volume's name" ("The Golden
Bible in the Bible's Golden Age: The Book of Mormon and Antebellum Print
Culture," *American Transcendental Quarterly* 12.4 [December 1998]: 275–93, 278).
For a more in-depth account of *The Book of Mormon*'s structure and plot, see
John Christopher Thomas, *A Pentecostal Reads the Book of Mormon: A Literary
and Theological Introduction* (Cleveland, TN: CPT Press, 2016).

3 Alexander Campbell, *Delusions: An Analysis of the Book of Mormon; With an
Examination of Its Internal and External Evidences, and a Refutation of Its Pre-
tences to Divine Authority* (Boston: Benjamin H. Greene, 1832), 15; Daniel Kidder,
*Mormonism and the Mormons: A Historical View of the Rise and Progress of the
Sect Self-styled Latter-Day Saints* (New York: Carlton & Phillips, 1842), 290–91.
For more on early anti-Mormonism in the United States, see J. Spencer Fluhman's
*"A Peculiar People": Anti-Mormonism and the Making of Religion in Nineteenth-
Century America* (Chapel Hill: University of North Carolina Press, 2012).

4 Eber D. Howe, *Mormonism Unvailed; or, A Faithful Account of That Singular
Imposition and Delusion, from Its Rise to the Present Time: With Sketches of the
Characters of Its Propagators* (Painseville, OH: Self-published, 1834), 37.

5 Howe, *Mormonism Unvailed*, 37.

6 I further discuss *The Book of Mormon*'s use of the Hebraic Indian theory in
"Nephites and Israelites."

7 The most sustained, recent effort to discredit the book on these grounds is
David Persuitte's *Joseph Smith and the Origins of* The Book of Mormon (Jefferson, NC: MacFarland, 2000), which deems Ethan Smith's 1825 text, *View of the
Hebrews,* to be the source text for *The Book of Mormon*. Persuitte offers side-by-
side comparisons of the texts' thematic and linguistic similarities. In asserting such close ties between these two works, Persuitte may have inadvertently
contributed to the fairly widespread misconception that *The Book of Mormon*
tells the story of the lost tribes of Israel, which is found among both nonbeliev-
ers and some Latter-day Saints. This error about the book's focus is almost as
old as the book itself. In 1833, for example, an article written by Constantine
Samuel Rafinesque appeared in the *Atlantic Journal and Friend of Knowledge,*
excoriating what he called "the singular but absurd opinion that American
tribes are descended from the Hebrews or the ten lost tribes. In the same article,
he complains that "a new Religion or sect has been founded upon this belief!"
(1 [1833]: 98). Even serious scholars of the lost tribes theory have incorrectly
echoed Rafinesque's error. In a recent piece about this very topic (which is, incidentally, where I found the reference to Rafinesque), Zvi Ben-Dor Benite writes,
"Whereas others turned to science to prove the Jewish Indian theory, Joseph
Smith appealed to supernatural revelation: a prophecy declaring that the 10 lost
tribes had indeed found their way to the Americas" ("Mormon Scripture and
the Lost Tribes of Israel," Bible Odyssey, https://www.bibleodyssey.org, accessed
May 8, 2019). Benite's work on the history of the lost tribes is exemplary, and his

scholarship is not anti-Mormon, so the appearance of this misconception in his work speaks to its pervasiveness.

8 In August 2018, President Russell M. Nelson announced official changes to the terminology that should be used when referring to the Church of Jesus Christ of Latter-day Saints and its members. The new guidelines include the following statement: "While the term 'Mormon Church' has long been publicly applied to the Church as a nickname, it is not an authorized title, and the Church discourages its use. Thus, please avoid using the abbreviation 'LDS' or the nickname 'Mormon' as substitutes for the name of the Church. . . . When referring to Church members, the terms 'members of The Church of Jesus Christ of Latter-day Saints' or 'Latter-day Saints' are preferred. We ask that the term 'Mormons' not be used." I will follow the Church's terminology guidelines as closely as possible in this chapter. Because Joseph Smith Jr. did not receive a revelation regarding the Church's name until 1838, there is a brief period (1830–1838) during which it would be anachronistic to refer to it as the Church of Jesus Christ of Latter-day Saints. When describing texts or events from that period, I simply will use phrases such as "the Church" and "Church members." I have retained the adjective "Mormon" when referring to "anti-Mormonism." The Church's new style guide is available at https://www.mormonnewsroom.org.

9 See, for example, Givens, *By the Hand of Mormon*, 161–62.

10 Elizabeth Fenton, "Open Canons: Sacred History and American History in *The Book of Mormon*," *J19: The Journal of Nineteenth-Century Americanists* 1.2 (2013): 339–61.

11 As Grant Underwood explains, the book depicts "several migrations from the Kingdom of Judah to the Western Hemisphere around 600 B.C." Early Church members imagined the ten lost tribes as "sequestered somewhere in the frozen 'north countries,'" distinct from America's "Jewish Indians" and still missing in the nineteenth century (*The Millenarian World of Early Mormonism* [Urbana: University of Illinois Press, 1999], 66).

12 R. Clayton Brough, *The Lost Tribes: History, Doctrine, Prophecies and Theories about Israel's Lost Ten Tribes* (Bountiful, UT: Horizon, 2005). This study is indebted to Brough not only for his cogent summary of different approaches Church members have taken to the story of the lost tribes but also for his archival research and bibliography, which includes the literary works analyzed here.

13 Brough, *The Lost Tribes*, 73.

14 Brough, *The Lost Tribes*, 74.

15 *The Book of Mormon: The Earliest Text*, ed. Royal Skousen (New Haven, CT: Yale University Press, 2009), 3. All references to *The Book of Mormon* will be to this edition and appear parenthetically within the text. In the interest of making it easy for readers to locate my quotations of the text in different editions of *The Book of Mormon*, I have opted to use the chapter and verse format for my citations, rather than page numbers.

16 David Holland, *Sacred Borders: Continuing Revelation and Canonical Restraint in Early America* (New York: Oxford University Press, 2011), 147.

17 "Visions, 3 April 1836 [D&C 110]," 193, The Joseph Smith Papers, http://www.josephsmithpapers.org. I would like to note that research on this and other topics related to the early Church would be nearly impossible were it not for the Joseph Smith Papers project.

18 To see this revelation in its original, handwritten form, see *Revelation I*, 116, The Joseph Smith Papers, http://www.josephsmithpapers.org.

19 "Doctrine and Covenants, 1835," 248, The Joseph Smith Papers, http://www.josephsmithpapers.org.

20 Brough, *The Lost Tribes*, 48.

21 Claudia Stokes, *The Altar at Home: Sentimental Literature and Nineteenth-Century Religion* (Philadelphia: University of Pennsylvania Press, 2014), 168.

22 For an excellent account of Snow's poetics, see Edward Whitley, *American Bards: Walt Whitman and Other Unlikely Candidates for National Poet* (Chapel Hill: University of North Carolina Press, 2010), 67–112.

23 Eliza Snow, "Address to Earth," *Latter-Day Saints' Millennial Star* 12.17 (September 1851): 272.

24 "The Prophecy of Enoch," *Latter-Day Saints' Millennial Star* 1.5 (September 1840): 109–13, 113.

25 Matthew Dalton, *The Period of God's Work on This Planet; or, How Science Agrees with Our Beloved Redeemer: A Key to This Earth* (Willard, UT, 1906), 10.

26 Dalton, *The Period of God's Work on This Planet*, 33.

27 Dalton, *The Period of God's Work on This Planet*, 33.

28 Dalton, *The Period of God's Work on This Planet*, 34.

29 Dalton, *The Period of God's Work on This Planet*, 34.

30 Orson Pratt, "Discourse by Elder Orson Pratt, Delivered in the New Tabernacle, Salt Lake City, Sunday Morning, April 1875," reported by David W. Evans, *Journal of Discourses by President Brigham Young, His Counselors, and the Twelve Apostles* (Liverpool: Joseph F. Smith, 1877), 16–29, 26. I should note that the *Journal of Discourses* is an imperfect source, because it is a collection of reports of sermons and speeches, and thus this sermon was not written down by Pratt himself. But whether or not Pratt actually spoke these particular words in this particular way, the record suggests that he did, which is what matters most for this project.

31 O. J. S. Lindelof, *A Trip to the North Pole; or, The Discovery of the Ten Tribes, as Found in the Arctic Ocean* (Salt Lake City, UT: Tribune Printing, 1903), 198. All references to this source will be to this edition and appear parenthetically within the text.

32 *Evening and Morning Star* 1.2 (July 1832): 23, available at http://contentdm.lib.byu.edu.

33 I would not have found this piece in the *Evening and Morning Star* were it not for a website produced and managed by Dale R. Broadhurst, and I am grateful for the work he has done on this subject: http://www.olivercowdery.com.

34 There are two different versions of this book, both published in 1886. The one I am citing contains five chapters and is about forty-one pages long. The other version, titled *The Inner World: A New Theory, Setting Forth That the Earth Is a Hollow Sphere Containing an Internal Habitable and Inhabited Region*, contains only the first three chapters and does not delve in detail into the question of the lost tribes. I am deeply grateful to the UVM Interlibrary Loan office for helping me sort through confusion around this text and find a copy of the longer version.

35 Frederick Culmer, *The Inner World: A New Theory, Based on Scientific and Theological Facts, Showing That the Earth Is a Hollow Sphere, Containing an Internal and Inhabited Region* (Salt Lake City, UT, 1886), 5. Further references to this source will appear parenthetically within the text.

36 "Le Trou de Symmes," trans. George Hamlin, *Parry's Literary Journal* 1 (1885): 57–59. *Parry's* (and thus Culmer) misattributes the original work to the Parisian journal *Revue de Deux Mondes*. The French piece actually appeared in *La Revue Britannique* 5 (1882): 619–22.

37 "Le Trou de Symmes," 58, italics original.

38 "Le Trou de Symmes," 58.

39 "Le Trou de Symmes," 59.

40 George Reynolds, *Are We of Israel?* (Salt Lake City, UT: J.H. Parry, 1883).

CHAPTER 5. INDIAN REMOVAL AND THE DECLINE OF AMERICAN HEBRAISM

1 Perhaps the most famous study of sugar and colonialism is Sidney Wilfred Mintz's *Sweetness and Power: The Place of Sugar in Modern History* (New York: Penguin, 1986). More recent, useful studies include Keith A. Sandiford's *Cultural Politics of Sugar: Caribbean Slavery and Narratives of Colonialism* (Cambridge: Cambridge University Press, 2000) and D. Pal S. Ahluwalia, Bill Ashcroft, and Roger Knight's collection, *White and Deadly: Sugar and Colonialism* (Hauppauge, NY: Nova Science Publishers, 1999).

2 James Fenimore Cooper, *James Fenimore Cooper: The Leatherstocking Tales*. Vol. I, *The Pioneers, The Last of the Mohicans, The Prairie* (New York: Library of America, 2013), 913.

3 Brian W. Dippie, *The Vanishing American: White Attitudes and U.S. Indian Policy* (Middletown, CT: Wesleyan University Press, 1985), xi. Dippie aptly shows that rhetoric regarding the vanishing American was often more performative than descriptive, because federal and state policies took as their starting point a belief that it was only a matter of time before Native Americans disappeared.

4 Critics have long recognized the importance of the "Vanishing American" to Cooper's fiction. Laura Romero's important work on the topic ("Vanishing Americans: Gender, Empire, and New Historicism," *American Literature* 63.3 [September 1991]: 385–404) reads depictions of indigenous decline within the dual contexts of nineteenth-century education and nation building to show how the ostensible distinctions between macro- and micro-politics in fact are entwined and mutu-

ally reinforcing in Cooper's fiction as well as other cultural productions of the antebellum era. To give just a few recent examples of scholarship on this topic: John Hay has connected Cooper's depictions of indigenous decline to contemporary interests in human extinction in general ("Narratives of Extinction: James Fenimore Cooper and the Last Man," *Literature in the Early American Republic: Annual Studies on Cooper and His Contemporaries* 6 [2014]: 245–68); Sarah Klotz has noted how the erroneous notion that indigenous populations left no trace of themselves on the landscape facilitated a discourse of their erasure ("The Red Man Has Left No Mark Here: Graves and Land Claim in the Cooperian Tradition," *ESQ* 60.3 [2014]: 331–69); and Stephen Germic has usefully linked the complex status of indigenous land claims to rhetorics denying their very existence in the works of Cooper's daughter, Susan ("Land Claims, Natives, and Nativism: Susan Fenimore Cooper's Fealty to Place," *American Literature* 79.3 [2007]: 475–500).

5 Diedre Dallas Hall, "Remarkable Particulars: David Gamut and the Alchemy of Race in *The Last of the Mohicans*," *ESQ* 58.1 (2012): 36–70. As Hall puts it, "From Gamut's first appearance, 'remarkable particulars' of both Jew and Indian begin to accumulate around the mysterious stranger, enabling the text to establish a rhythm of cultural flux by Indianizing its pseudo-Jewish singing master and Judaizing its Indians" (45). Thus the novel raises the specter of simultaneous Jewish and Indian identities, though it does not directly depict a "Jewish Indian."

6 Hall, "Remarkable Particulars," 62.

7 Hall, "Remarkable Particulars," 60.

8 E. Eva Crane, *The Archaeology of Beekeeping* (London: Duckworth, 1983). See especially ch. 2. The Americas are home to some native bees, but those species do not produce honey.

9 Tammy Horn, *Bees in America: How the Honey Bee Shaped a Nation* (Lexington: University Press of Kentucky, 2006), 3.

10 Horn, *Bees in America*, 20–23.

11 Qtd. in Crane, *The World History of Beekeeping and Honey Hunting* (Taylor & Francis, 1999), 592.

12 Horn, *Bees in America*, 22.

13 Cotton Mather, *The Christian Philosopher: A Collection of the Best Discoveries in Nature, with Religious Improvements* (J. M'Kown, printer, 1815), 162–63.

14 Mather, *The Christian Philosopher*, 163.

15 Mather, *The Christian Philosopher*, 163.

16 Paul Dudley, "An Account of a Method Lately Found Out in New-England, for Discovering Where the Bees Hive in the Woods, in Order to Get Their Honey," *Philosophical Transactions* 31 (1720–21): 150.

17 Thomas Jefferson, *Notes on the State of Virginia* (J. Stockdale, 1787), 121.

18 Cooper, *The Oak-openings; or, The Bee-hunter* (D. Appleton, 1873), 11. The first edition of this novel was titled *The Bee-Hunter; or, The Oak Openings*, but subsequent editions reversed the title. Although I am citing a later edition of the text

throughout this chapter, and all parenthetical references will be to this edition, I will refer to the novel by its original title.

19 Crane, *Archaeology*, 34.

20 Dudley, "An Account of a Method," 148. Dudley notes that some people find honey simply by observing bees in the wild and tracking several of them to the hive.

21 James Smith, *The Panorama of Science and Art: Embracing the Sciences of Aerostation, Agriculture and Gardening, Architecture, Astronomy, Chemistry . . . the Arts of Building, Brewing, Bleaching . . . the Methods of Working in Wood and Metal . . . and a Miscellaneous Selection of Interesting and Useful Processes and Experiments*, vol. 2 (Nuttall, Fisher, 1815), 710–11.

22 James Adair, *The History of the American Indians* (E. & C. Dilly, 1775), 15.

23 Ethan Smith, *View of the Hebrews; or, The Tribes of Israel in America . . .* (Smith & Shute, 1825), 269.

24 Boudinot, *A Star in the West*, 76.

25 The earliest English-language work on the subject was Thorowgood's *Iewes in America*. I discuss Thorowgood's contributions to the theory at length in the first chapter of this book.

26 James Fenimore Cooper, *The American Democrat; or, Hints on the Social and Civic Relations of the United States* (Cooperstown, NY: H. & E. Phinney, 1838), 188.

27 Cooper, *The American Democrat*, 188–89.

28 Claudia Stokes, *The Altar at Home: Sentimental Literature and Nineteenth-Century American Religion* (Philadelphia: University of Pennsylvania Press, 2014), 26.

29 Stokes, *The Altar at Home*, 26. For a comprehensive account of Methodism's impact on the early republic, see Dee. E. Andrews, *The Methodists and Revolutionary America, 1760–1800: The Shaping of an Evangelical Culture* (Princeton, NJ: Princeton University Press, 2000).

30 For a fuller account of Apess's Methodism, see Laura Donaldson, "Making a Joyful Noise: William Apess and the Search for Postcolonial Methodism," *interventions* 7.2 (2005): 180–98.

31 Stokes, *The Altar at Home*, 27.

CHAPTER 6. THE HOLLOW EARTH AND THE END OF TIME

1 De Witt Clinton Chipman, *Beyond the Verge: Home of Ten Lost Tribes of Israel* (Boston: James H. Earle, 1896), 15. All subsequent references to this book will be to this edition and appear parenthetically within the text. The name "Chickimecs," which Clinton uses throughout the opening chapters of his novel, is a mishearing and misspelling of "Chichimeca," a name applied to several indigenous populations—including the Aztecs—that arrived in central Mexico in the twelfth and thirteenth centuries. I will retain Clinton's term in citations but use the proper designation in my own descriptions.

2 Abraham Lincoln, *Abraham Lincoln Papers: Series 1. General Correspondence. 1833 to 1916: De Witt C. Chipman to Abraham Lincoln, Monday, Pomeroy Circular. 1864.*

Manuscript/Mixed Material, available at the Library of Congress's website, https://www.loc.gov.

3 Andrew Lewis, *A Democracy of Facts: Natural History in the Early Republic* (Philadelphia: University of Pennsylvania Press, 2011), 72.

4 John Hay, *Postapocalyptic Fantasies in Antebellum American Literature* (Cambridge: Cambridge University Press, 2017), 118. The field we now call archeology has a long and complex history with no precise point of origin. As Paul Bahn notes, "People have always been aware that others came long before them," and ancient records contain accounts of excavations similar in motive and method to nineteenth-century archeological practices. According to Bahn, the "earliest known 'archaeological' probings are usually reckoned to be those of Nabonidus [r. 555–539 BCE], last native king of Babylon," who "excavated a temple floor down to a foundation stone laid 3200 years earlier" ("The Archaeology of Archaeology: Pre-Modern Views of the Past," in *The History of Archaeology: An Introduction*, ed. Bahn [New York: Routledge, 2014], 1). The removal of artifacts from the earth is thus itself an ancient practice. Over the course of millennia, different cultures have extracted artifacts from the ground for a variety of purposes, and it is impossible to separate a nation's interest in archeological discovery at any given moment from its particular historical context.

5 Thomas Jefferson, *Notes on the State of Virginia* (Boston: H. Sprague, 1802), 133.

6 For more information on the mound Jefferson excavated, as well as the Virginia mounds more generally, see Debra Gold, *The Bioarchaeology of Virginia Burial Mounds* (Tuscaloosa: University of Alabama Press, 2004).

7 Ian J. McNiven and Lynette Russell, *Appropriated Pasts: Indigenous Peoples and the Colonial Culture of Archaeology* (Lanham, MD: AltaMira Press, 2005), 114.

8 Samuel Morton, *Crania Americana; or, A Comparative View of the Skulls of Various Aboriginal Nations of North and South America* (Philadelphia: John Penington, 1839), 260.

9 Although the ugly racism of Morton's work, and the unethical methods through which he obtained research skulls, are not in question, there has been debate over the soundness of his data. The most famous modern examination of Morton's work is Stephen Jay Gould's *Mismeasure of Man* (New York: Norton, 1981). Gould contended that Morton's racism had caused him not only to design a racially charged study but also to inaccurately measure the skulls at his disposal. However, in 2011 a team of anthropologists led by Jason Lewis remeasured Morton's skull collection (which is owned by the University of Pennsylvania) and determined that, although the premise and conclusions of the original study certainly aimed at promoting white supremacy, Morton did not manipulate his data. (See Jason Lewis et al., "The Mismeasure of Science: Stephen Jay Gould versus Samuel George Morton on Skulls and Bias," *PLOS Biology* 9.6 [June 2011]], available at https://doi.org.) My purpose here is not to present Morton as an exemplary scientist but merely to note that his work continues to generate controversy.

10 Daniel Cole, "*Kairos* and Quantification: Data, Interpretation, and the Problem of *Crania Americana*," *Rhetoric Review* 34.1 (2015): 19–37, 23.

11 Gordon Sayer, "The Mound Builders and the Imagination of American Antiquity in Jefferson, Bartram, and Chateaubriand," *Early American Literature* 33.1 (1998): 225–26.

12 Andrew Jackson, Second Annual Message, December 7, 1830, *Messages of Andrew Jackson: With a Short Sketch of His Life* (Concord, NH: Brown and White, 1837), 114.

13 Terry A. Barnhart, *American Antiquities: Revisiting the Origins of American Archaeology* (Lincoln: University of Nebraska Press, 2015), 249.

14 See Barnhart, *American Antiquities*, 249–50. For an account of the particular influence Mound Builder literature may have had on both Bryant and early Mormonism, see Curtis Dahl, "Mound-Builders, Mormons, and William Cullen Bryant," *New England Quarterly* 34.2 (June 1961): 178–90.

15 William Cullen Bryant, *Poems by William Cullen Bryant: Collected and Arranged by the Author*, vol. 2 (New York: Appleton, 1854), 23–30, 25.

16 Andrew Galloway argues, quite compellingly, that Bryant's poem attempts to construct a "Middle Ages" for North America through his presentations of antiquities in this poem. He also offers a more sustained analysis of the poem's engagement with questions of miscegenation and race than this chapter can, in "William Cullen Bryant's American Antiquities: Medievalism, Miscegenation, and Race in *The Prairies*," *American Literary History* 22.4 (2010): 724–51.

17 Edmond Halley, "An Account of the Cause of the Change of the Variation of the Magnetical Needle. With an Hypothesis of the Structure of the Internal Parts of the Earth: As It Was Proposed to the Royal Society in One of Their Late Meetings," *Philosophical Transactions* 17 (October 1692): 563–78, 564.

18 I discuss the role of the "accident" in scientific and theological discourse of this period in chapter 3 of this book.

19 Peter Sinnema, "'We Have Adventured to Make the Earth Hollow': Edmond Halley's Extravagant Hypothesis," *Perspectives on Science* 22.4 (2014): 423–48, 423.

20 Sinnema, "'We Have Adventured to Make the Earth Hollow,'" 423–25.

21 David Standish, *Hollow Earth: The Long and Curious History of Imagining Strange Lands, Fantastical Creatures, Advanced Civilizations, and Marvelous Machines below the Earth's Surface* (Cambridge, MA: Da Capo Press, 2007), 32.

22 Cotton Mather, *The Christian Philosopher*, ed. Winton U. Solberg (Chicago: University of Illinois Press, 2000), 116.

23 Qtd. in Hester Blum, "John Cleves Symmes and the Planetary Reach of Polar Exploration," *American Literature* 84.2 (June 2012): 243–71, 249.

24 Blum, "John Cleves Symmes," 246.

25 James McBride, *Symmes's Theory of Concentric Spheres; Demonstration That the Earth Is Hollow, Habitable Within, and Widely Open about the Poles* (Cincinnati, OH: Morgan, Lodge, and Fisher, 1826), 35.

26 This article, written by Floyd Hamblin, originally appeared in the Utica *Observer*, but it was reprinted several times, and so Chipman could have read it in any number of newspapers.

27 Victoria Nelson, *The Secret Life of Puppets* (Cambridge, MA: Harvard University Press, 2001), 6.

28 Nelson, *The Secret Life of Puppets*, 6.

29 Elizabeth Hope Chang, "Hollow Earth Fiction and Environmental Form in the Late Nineteenth Century," *Nineteenth-Century Contexts* 38.5 (2016): 387–97, 388.

30 Jules Verne, *A Journey to the Centre of the Earth*, trans. William Butcher (Oxford: Oxford World Classics, 1992), 138.

31 Rosalie Colie was the first to note the biblical and typological significance of Marvell's fruits and trees in "Marvell's 'Bermudas' and the Puritan Paradise,'" *Renaissance News* 10.2 (Summer 1957): 75–79. There is, however, a longstanding debate among Marvell scholars about whether the "apples" in question are actual apples or pineapples. (See David McInnis's "The Apples in Marvell's 'Bermudas,'" *Notes and Queries* 54.4 (2007): 418–19. For my purposes, the species of the fruit is not as significant as its abundance.

CODA

1 For a comprehensive overview of the history of DNA sequencing, see James M. Heather and Benjamin Chan, "Sequencing the Sequencers: The History of Sequencing DNA," *Genomics* 107.1 (2016): 1–8.

2 Spencer Wells, *The Journey of Man: A Genetic Odyssey* (Princeton, NJ: Princeton University Press, 2017), xiv.

3 Wells, *The Journey of Man*, xiv.

4 For more on the prevalence of such genetic testing, and its potentially far-reaching consequences, see Yaniv Erlich, Tas Shor, Itsik Pe'er, and Shai Carmi, "Identity Inference of Genomic Data Using Long-range Familial Searches," *Science* 362 (November 9, 2018): 690–94.

5 Priscilla Wald, "Blood and Stories: How Genomics Is Rewriting Race, Medicine, and Human History," *Patterns of Prejudice* 40.4–5 (2006): 303–33, 318.

6 Kim TallBear, *Native American DNA* (Minneapolis: University of Minnesota Press, 2013), 5.

7 TallBear, *Native American DNA*, 5.

8 This study is described in detail in Tudor Parfitt, *Journey to the Vanished City*, 2nd edition (New York: Vintage Departures, 2000).

9 Parfitt, *Black Jews in Africa and the Americas* (Cambridge, MA: Harvard University Press, 2013), 163.

10 Nicholas Wade, "DNA Backs a Tribe's Tradition of Early Descent from the Jews," *New York Times* online, May 9, 1999, https://www.nytimes.com. Wade's own book, *A Troublesome Inheritance: Genes, Race, and Human History* (New York: Penguin, 2014) claims that natural selection occurring in recent human history has resulted in differential IQs among different world populations, along with differences in political and economic development. On August 8, 2014, a letter signed by over one hundred faculty members in population science and evolutionary biology from many research institutions was published in the *New York*

Times Book Review. It asserts that Wade's book "juxtaposes an incomplete and inaccurate account of our research on human genetic differences with speculation." The scientists further state, "We reject Wade's implication that our findings substantiate his guesswork. They do not" (Graham Coop et al., "Letter: A Troublesome Inheritance," Stanford Center for Computational, Evolutionary, and Human Genomics, available at https://cehg.stanford.edu).

11 Thomas W. Murphy, "Lamanite Genesis, Genealogy, and Genetics," in *American Apocrypha: Essays on the Book of Mormon*, ed. Dan Vogel and Brent Metcalfe (Salt Lake City, UT: Signature Books, 2002), 48. Murphy expanded on this argument and responded to critics in a later piece: "Simply Implausible: DNA and a Mesoamerican Setting for the Book of Mormon," *Dialogue: A Journal of Mormon Thought* 36.4 (2003): 109–32. He also coauthored a brief piece with Simon Southerton on this topic: "Genetic Research a 'Galileo Event' for Mormons," *Anthropology News* 44.2 (2003): 20.

12 Simon Southerton, *Losing a Lost Tribe: Native Americans, DNA, and the Mormon Church* (Salt Lake City, UT: Signature Books, 2004), viii.

13 Southerton, *Losing a Lost Tribe*, 99. It is worth noting that the term "Mongoloid" is itself outdated and no longer in general use. Indeed, Southerton's use of this term illustrates the potential slippage between the discourse of genetics and that of outmoded racial science.

14 Wald, "Blood and Stories," 332.

15 Wald, "Blood and Stories," 333.

16 Southerton, *Losing a Lost Tribe*, 206.

17 David G. Stewart, "DNA and the Book of Mormon," *FARMS Review* 18.1 (2006): 109–38, 110.

18 Stewart, "DNA and the Book of Mormon," 111.

19 Stewart, "DNA and the Book of Mormon," 112–13.

20 "Book of Mormon and DNA Studies," Church of Jesus Christ of Latter-day Saints, January 2014, https://www.churchofjesuschrist.org/manual/gospel-topics/book-of-mormon-and-dna-studies.

21 "The FIRM Foundation Mission Statement and Goals," FIRM Foundation Online, http://firmlds.org/about.

22 *Annotated Edition of the Book of Mormon: Another Testament of Jesus Christ*, trans. Joseph Smith Jr., ed. David R. Hocking and Rod L. Meldrum (Salt Lake City, UT: Digital Legend Press, 2018), 554.

23 Wells, *The Journey of Man*, 1.

24 Wells, *The Journey of Man*, 40.

25 Wells, *The Journey of Man*, 54.

26 Wells, *The Journey of Man*, 196.

27 Wells, *The Journey of Man*, 196.

28 NOVA, "Great Human Odyssey," NOVA website, https://www.pbs.org (accessed May 15, 2019).

INDEX

ABOUT THE AUTHOR

Elizabeth Fenton is Professor in the Department of English at the University of Vermont and author of *Religious Liberties: Anti-Catholicism and Liberal Democracy in Nineteenth-Century U.S. Literature and Culture* and coeditor of *Americanist Approaches to The Book of Mormon*.